Open Minds and
Everyday Reasoning

Open Minds and Everyday Reasoning

Zachary Seech
Palomar College

Wadsworth Publishing Company
Belmont, California
A division of Wadsworth, Inc.

Philosophy Editor: *Kenneth King*

Editorial Assistant: *Gay Meixel*

Production: *Ruth Cottrell*

Print Buyers: *Diana Spence, Karen Hunt*

Designer: *Donna Davis*

Copy Editor: *Sheryl Rose*

Cover Design: *Paula Goldstein*

Cover Photo: *The Stock Market/© 1989 Masahiro Sano*

Signing Representative: *Sue Lasbury*

Compositor: *TypeLink, Inc.*

Printer: *The Maple-Vail Book Manufacturing Group*

7 8 9 10 11 12 02 01 00 99 98

Library of Congress Cataloging in Publication Data
Seech, Zachary,
    Open minds and everyday reasoning / Zachary Seech.
      p. cm.
    Includes bibliographical references and index.

    1. Reasoning. 2. Disposition (Philosophy) I. Title.
BC177.S387   1992
160--dc20   92-19528
                                                                CIP

To Valerie
And to Kyle, Trevor, and Todd

Preface

Certainly you know what it's like to argue for a view long past the point where you know you're wrong. You must also know what it's like to tune out while someone is talking, as you grope for a counterargument that will devastate this defender of a distasteful perspective. These things happen when we become more interested in winning an argument than in learning something from the other person. Your students know these experiences. That's why it's important to teach not only technical skills of analysis — which can be used in the service of a person's prior bias — but also the attitudinal skills of open-mindedness and honest inquiry. With clear, unprejudiced thinking as a goal, students can size up others' arguments more fairly, as well as their own.

Exciting things have happened in the area of teaching thinking skills since my earlier book, *Logic in Everyday Life*, was published in 1987. Among the most exciting is the increasing interest in dispositions — the frames of mind that incline a person to approach a problem or issue in a certain way. The success of *Logic in Everyday Life* was accompanied by requests from students and professors to extend the early emphasis on attitudes and fairness (Chapter 1, "Being Reasonable," in that edition). This has been done in *Open Minds and Everyday Reasoning*. The first two chapters develop that theme, which is then continued throughout the book in conjunction with instruction in clarity and analysis.

The focus on open-mindedness fits the practical approach of *Open Minds and Everyday Reasoning* well. The emphasis, as in *Logic in Everyday Life*, is on skill acquisition, which is now highlighted by descriptive section titles rather than skill boxes. The student does not learn *about* how to reason effectively; the student learns to *do* it. Accordingly, the everyday, informal aspects of reasoning receive more attention than traditional logic in its formal garb. Still, this textbook can be useful both to teachers who offer a completely nontechnical critical thinking course and to teachers who teach a more traditional logic course. I will preview the book's structure, then suggest how it can be used in either of the just-mentioned courses.

Open Minds and Everyday Reasoning is divided into four parts. Part One invites students to ask the question, "Do I Have an Open Mind?" Part Two: "Am I Being Clear?" Part Three: "Is My Reasoning Good?" Part Four, a three-chapter guide to writing, assessing statistics, and making decisions, is titled "Reason in Action."

Part One, "Do I Have an Open Mind?," begins the book with chapters on "Being Unreasonable" and "Opening Closed Minds." In this introduction, readers explore the need for open-mindedness by reflecting on their own discussions with others on hot topics. Starting with Chapter 2, I title the main sections of each chapter with imperative verbs to describe what the student will learn to do (e.g., "Start with Yourself," "Use Language Fairly"), and continue this practice throughout the book. Part Two, "Am I Being Clear?," binds together Chapters 3 through 5: "Saying What You Mean," "Presenting Orderly Thoughts," and "Basic Mapping." Here students learn to express themselves clearly — or at least carefully — and to follow a line of reasoning while recognizing sidetracks. Part Three, "Is My Reasoning Good?," includes Chapters 6 through 9: "Constructing Good Reasoning," "Recognizing Fallacies," "Recognizing Other Kinds of Faulty Reasoning," and "Evaluative Mapping." Now the students learn to distinguish between good reasons for believing something and reasons that are not so good. Part Four, "Reason in Action," closes the book with three especially practical chapters: "Writing to Make a Point," "Working with Hypotheses and Statistics," and "Making Difficult Decisions."

If you want to downplay technical terminology and formal or structural analysis of arguments for a critical thinking course or a practical logic course, consider the following suggestions for using the text. The section on deductive validity and inductive strength in Chapter 6 (in the section "Don't Overstate the Strength of Your Inference") can be omitted. Then, in Chapter 8, everything can be deleted except, perhaps, for the section "Understand When and Why Analogies Fail" and the subsection "When and How to Point Out Errors." Chapters 5 and 9 teach how to map arguments. Here you can (1) exclude both chapters entirely, (2) include Chapter 5 on how to follow a line of reasoning (Basic Mapping) but exclude Chapter 9 on how to include an analysis of that argument as part of the map (Evaluative Mapping), (3) include both chapters, but exclude the use of formal terms on the map as this option is described in Chapter 9, or (4) include both chapters, along with the use of traditional terms in Chapter 9. If this fourth plan is adopted, however, the Chapter 6 discussion of deductive validity and inductive strength also should be included.

I want to draw the professor's attention to three features of this book. *First*, the chapter on writing focuses on thesis defense, the sort of writing in which the author makes a claim and supports it with evidence. Some of the pointers in that chapter also apply to other kinds of writing. You can assign this chapter early to guide students' first writing projects in the course, but you will have to delete some of the material for them at that stage, depending on how much, if any, argument mapping they have learned. *Second*, the inductive/deductive distinction in *Open Minds and Everyday Reasoning* follows Brian Skyrms' excellent work in *Choice & Chance* (Wadsworth, 1986) and avoids the difficulties of making the distinction on the basis of the intention of the arguer or on the basis of a contrast between generality and specificity. I concede that there are advantages to basing the distinction on the intention of the arguer. These are preserved in Chapter 6 by teaching the student not to overstate the strength of the conclusion, i.e., not to ruin good inductive reasoning by suggesting you have established the conclusion with an undemonstrated and perhaps impractical certainty. *Third*, the concept of a fallacy look-alike enables us to teach students not to charge someone with fallacy when the similarity between the suspect reasoning and the fallacy's definition is incidental or partial. Fallacies have always been difficult to teach when a careful distinction between fallacies and their counterfeits has not been made. In the practice activities that close Chapter 7, students are taught to see this important difference.

I thank Sue Lasbury, who encouraged me to write the original book and was so helpful in my efforts to revise it. She is always supportive. Debbie Sherrill, philosophy research assistant at Palomar College, spent many hours, days, and months helping me review and reconstruct the textbook to ensure that it would be straightforwardly written and helpful to students. The dozens of staff members and many hundreds of students at Lincoln Middle School in Vista have clarified my vision of how critical thinking skills should be taught. These insights invariably contributed to my ability to teach college-level courses as well as noncredit programs. For the enthusiastic administrative support that enabled us to make the project a success, I thank George Boggs, President of Palomar College; Patricia Campbell, Principal of Lincoln Middle School; and Rene Townsend, Superintendent of the Vista Unified School District. For giving the program its initial impetus, I thank Donna Hamilton and Nancy Cavanaugh. I also thank my wife, children, and parents for their consistently enthusiastic support.

At Wadsworth Publishing Company, philosophy editor Ken King has from the beginning in 1984 shown interest in this project and given it his careful attention. He is a very skillful editor, and the success of the textbook owes much to him.

I thank several others as well: at Wadsworth, Cynthia Campbell, Pamela Grand, Hal Humphrey, Bob Kauser, Gay Meixel, and Joy Westberg; Ruth Cottrell, production editor and Sheryl Rose, copy editor; dozens of supportive colleagues at Palomar College, including each member of the Behavioral Sciences Department; and the staff and conferees at the annual Conference on Critical Thinking & Educational Reform at Sonoma State University.

Course instructors across the country commented in detail on the manuscript and helped shape the book into its final form. Among those were

Douglas P. Davis, Saint Bonaventure University; Michael DiMaio, Salve Regina College; Steve Giambrone, University of Southwestern Louisiana; Katherine Ramsland, Rutgers University; Major Kenneth D. Shive, U.S. Military Academy; and Thomas T. Tominaga, University of Nevada.

Z. S.

Contents

PART

THREE
Is My Reasoning Good? 95

ONE
Do I Have an
Open Mind?

■

C H A P T E R

ONE

Being Unreasonable

Dozens of times in almost every day—hundreds of times on some days—we need to reason something out. We take information that is available to us and draw conclusions. Often we act on these conclusions, and how well our lives go depends, in part, on how well we have reasoned.

Generally speaking, we are quite good at our task. We are good thinkers and the conclusions we draw are correct. Whether we are concluding that the interstate highway route will get us to grandma's house more quickly than the old river road or that the quiet and apparently shy sales clerk really *was* stealing money from the cash register, we normally know what counts as good evidence and what doesn't, and we generally know when we have enough evidence and when we don't. At times, however, we don't reason as well as we should. This is often because we've already made up our minds. When we start with an emotional commitment to one conclusion, or a prejudice against another conclusion, the chances are good that we will have a hard time being reasonably objective and thinking clearly.

POINTS OF LOGICAL VULNERABILITY

For virtually everyone, there are topics about which that person, we say, "just cannot be rational." This may be overstatement. However, what we mean is that this person has great difficulty in being objective on these topics. He or she finds it difficult, in some cases, to consider the evidence impartially and draw a sensible, justified conclusion. These topics are the **points of logical vulnerability** for that person.

Points of logical vulnerability vary from one person to another. Although it is often recommended that we avoid the topics of religion and politics in order to keep out of nasty arguments, many other topics can bring out the fight in at least someone. In these instances, a psychological commitment to a certain belief or against another belief keeps the person from weighing fairly the evidence for each side of the question. For one person, nothing that the Democratic nominee for president could do or say would show him to be an honorable or intelligent person. For another person, nothing that the Republican nominee for president could do or say would show her to be an honorable or intelligent person. Some people would be unable to accept any significant criticism of a particular political or economic system, regardless of the merit of the criticism. Others can see nothing that is right about that same system. Sometimes the touchy topic *is* a political or a religious one, but the problem can be even closer to home. It may be that nothing can be said on behalf of my new brother-in-law to convince me that he has my sister's best interests at heart. On this point, I am probably not being rational.

What are *your* points of logical vulnerability? It is worthwhile to reflect in order to identify them. An awareness of your points of logical vulnerability can prevent you from becoming unjustifiably self-righteous and can further prevent you from managing to believe that some quite nonsensical reasoning makes sense. Such arrogance and irrationality serve only to put a person in a foolish position.

Often, when you desperately want a particular belief to be true, then almost any reasoning offered in support of that conclusion looks like good reasoning, and when you desperately want a particular belief to be false, then the reasoning that appears perfect for your neighbor may seem obviously inadequate to you. Ironically, the very same kind of reasoning may appear good to you in one context and bad in another. If you are aware of your points of logical vulnerability, you will be more likely to notice when you are inclined to shortchange yourself logically.

WINNING AND LOSING

Sometimes we have a hard time keeping an open mind simply because losing face is considered a fate worse than being wrong. In debatelike conversations with other people, we may find ourselves defending views that are not supported by the evidence, either because we simply want those views to be correct or because we started the conversation with this position (or are known for previously holding this position) and we don't want to lose the argument. We assume that it's always good to win an argument and that it's always bad to lose one. So we first choose a position, sometimes with good grounds and sometimes without, and then proceed to look for evidence to support that position, discounting or minimizing the value of evidence that opposes the position. At times we even fool ourselves into thinking that we are being objective in our assessment.

A "win, don't lose—whatever the cost" attitude is often obvious in conversation. Two minutes' worth of listening to a conversation is sometimes enough to identify those speakers who have such an approach. But a similar attitude can color a person's reading and listening as well as his or her speaking. When our mind is already made up, or we are at least inclined toward a certain position, we may take in information selectively. Listening to a political speech or reading a campaign pamphlet, listening to someone arguing that the city needs a new library or reading a letter to the editor in the local newspaper, being told why you shouldn't buy that new car or reading about the virtues of thrift—in all of these situations, we can easily dismiss or overassess the merits of the reasoning with which we are presented.

Most people will find that their tendency toward a combative stance in conversation—or in reacting to what they read or hear—is more extreme with some persons than with others. Your reaction to a particular point— even with the same wording—may vary, depending on whether it has been presented by Mom, Aunt Darcy, or that surly looking mail carrier. As with points of logical vulnerability, it is worthwhile to reflect on this with the intention of gaining insight into yourself and your habits of argumentation. Habits of this kind are not easy to break.

WORD WARS

Winning and losing, victory and defeat, are concepts that we use in reference to personal quests for achievement, in sports, and in military operations. The military metaphors are the ones that dominate the way we talk about dispute on hot issues. We hear talk of *attacking* another's position, with the hope that the other person will have to *retreat* from that position. This is the way we would talk about a military offensive against an enemy post. We even hear people say they need to *combat* a certain dangerous view. People say they are going to *aim at* the view that an *opponent* has presented. Political campaigners have been known to think and talk like this, but they're certainly not the only ones. Some people say that they *shot down* or *blew away* another's ideas. We also hear of *standing one's ground* and *going on the offensive*, and we hear of *arsenals* of logical skills and *assaults* on other positions. Indeed, it's a war in the streets, the workplaces, and the homes. Perhaps we can actually enhance good thinking by lessening hostilities.

BIAS AND PREJUDICE

Martin is biased on some issues. School busing, prayer in the schools, and affirmative action are three of those issues. He has plenty more. Lena has a bias on some other issues. For example, she is consistently and therefore predictably biased on some environmental issues and on AIDS care and AIDS research funding. Martin and Lena both display a bias on gun control and on U.S. relations with Iraq. However, on the gun control issue they are both biased toward the same — or at least similar — views, but on the Iraqi issue their favored perspectives are quite different or, as we sometimes say, worlds apart.

Our biases create points of logical vulnerability. In other words, we can be blind and thus vulnerable to errors in reasoning because we favor one way of looking at an issue. The English word *bias* evolved from an Old French word, *biais*, meaning "slant." We often speak of having a certain slant or angle to our views when we want to suggest that we *lean toward* one way of seeing things. Bias develops in different ways, and some bias is more dangerous to our reasoning than others.

We say that someone "is biased" or "has a bias" on an issue if that person favors one perspective on that issue. Benino may be biased toward a positive view of the newly elected president. (We would usually say simply that he is biased toward the president.) He may wish for the president's success and prefer to see the president in a positive light. Rene may be biased against the new president. She may be irked that this president was elected and expect that this presidency will constitute a pathetic chapter in her nation's history.

From the preceding description of Benino and Rene, you can't really determine whether either bias was formed (1) before much relevant knowledge about the president was collected, (2) in spite of a preponderance of opposing evidence, or (3) after careful and consistent observation and with well-reasoned judgment. Let's discuss each of these three possibilities.

Forming an Opinion Too Soon

When your mind is made up before you have examined and reflected on the information that could help you come to a rational understanding, you have a *prejudice*. You have "prejudged" (as the word *prejudice* suggests) the issue, person, group, or idea. In social relations, this can result in unfair attitudes or actions toward individuals or groups. If Mom or Dad prejudges the moral character of young Devon's friends on the basis of their clothing and hair-cuts alone, their conclusions may be faulty and their decisions about or assessments of those friends may be unfair and even demeaning. *Stereotypes* are caricatures — simplistic and usually extreme ideas — of groups or situations. They sometimes lead to patterned expectations; individuals of a group are expected to vary little, if at all, from a preconceived idea of what individuals in that group are like. Stereotypes nourish prejudice. I may think I know my new acquaintance's basic political views simply because I know she is in the military service. I may think I can trust you just because you dress and talk as I do. In each case, my prejudgment may bias me toward a false perspective. It may even prevent me from recognizing, or lead me to dismiss, evidence to the contrary when I encounter it.

Forming an Opinion That's Contradicted by the Evidence

Perhaps you sometimes maintain a particular view in spite of the accumulation of considerable evidence against that view. Even though George doesn't actually disbelieve what he reads about the slippage of the United States' international economic power, he manages to continue to think of his nation in a role that may now be less justified. He likes thinking about it in this way, and resists any revision of his comfortable and traditionalist model. Even as he invests his money, he thinks of the sound investments of ten years ago as if they were the sound investments of today. Kenna's most obvious bias concerns the public schools in her district. She has been convinced since her own troubled high school years that the quality of education available here is uniformly pitiful. She has failed to appreciate the phenomenal increase in effectiveness that the schools accomplished over the last several years under the new superintendent. The district has received nationwide recognition and the state Secretary of Education has termed the turnaround "astounding." Scores on standardized, nationally normed tests have attested to the shift, as has student retention and community reaction overall. Kenna, however, waves off all this and recounts yet again her litany of old complaints.

Forming a Well-Reasoned Opinion

Not all biases are unreasonable, like prejudging or beliefs that contradict our observations. Sometimes our tendency to hold on to a certain view is based on evidence that supports such a bias. Now, while it's true that some people prefer to use the word "bias" only to describe unjustified perspectives, if it refers to any leaning toward a certain view as more evidence is anticipated, some biases would not be so bad. For example, I may disbelieve a disparaging story about you because the reported behavior seems unbelievable based on the counterevidence of the personal character I've seen you display over the years. What I know about you (not just how much I like you) has produced a bias toward you on this issue. This is not irrational. Of course, if I continue to disbelieve the report after the addition of overwhelming evidence, then my bias may reflect a blinding and irrational commitment to one perspective.

Emotions are not to be avoided; they need not be enemies of insight and clear thinking. I should not try to rid myself of my enthusiastic allegiance to my school, my friends, my family, or even my moral and political views. These contribute to a richly meaningful life. My biases become dangerous when I allow them to cloud evidence and suggest unwarranted conclusions.

SIGNS OF DEFENSIVENESS

When someone says you have been *defensive* on an issue, we might think that you have been evasive and unwilling to talk about the issue at length. However, this is not the only way to show defensiveness. Actually, your frame of mind is a defensive one whenever you concentrate more on defending one view than on openly evaluating a new view. You may, in fact, appear to be quite "on the offense," to the point of being "offensive" and overbearing.

Not all views are correct, but virtually all deserve our honest appraisal. (Being honest with yourself may be more difficult than being honest with other people.) Consider one helpful test for detecting defensiveness: When the other person is speaking, are you listening in order to find strong points in the reasoning, or are you trying to think of a "comeback" response that would devastate the other position and demonstrate clearly that you were correct all along? If you are only seeking victory over an opponent, your defensive posture will prevent you from gaining new insight or understanding.

Usually others notice our defensiveness and unwillingness to listen before we notice it in ourselves. We give both verbal and nonverbal signs that we are closed to new ideas—or at least some particular new ideas. Since we do notice them more readily in others, consider which of these you have observed in others. Later you will be asked to assess yourself in the same way.

Among the verbal and other voice-related signs of a closed mind, we find the following. Many people raise their voices as they become impatient or upset with someone's ideas. So much can be communicated by the tone of a voice: irritation, condescension, resentfulness. Ridicule, mockery, and disgust can be communicated by the tone and the rhythm of a person's voice. A well-placed, overdone sigh can suggest that the poor listener has just had to put up with so much foolishness! The knowing laugh of someone who wants to make you think of your last comment as pitiful can be especially irksome. (Ridicule is usually hard to take gracefully.) More explicitly verbal is the insult that attacks a person or a person's ideas. Continual interruptions or responses coming so quickly that the person could hardly have pondered your comments give the distinct impression that the respondent thinks it's much more important for you to hear what he's about to say than for him to consider your comments.

Some people say there are subtle nonverbal signs that suggest that you do not welcome the other's comments. Crossed arms, for example, are said to reflect this. There are, of course, more brazen nonverbal messages. These include the condescending sideways shake of the head that seems to say "no, no, no, a thousand times, no!"; various facial expressions, including rolling the eyes upward; ignoring comments; yawning dramatically or waving off remarks; folding arms and staring blankly; or even the symbolic turning away or closing up the ears with the hands so the listener doesn't have to hear such miserable stuff!

RESULTS OF DEFENSIVENESS

What do *you* think of a person who acts defensively when you are making a point? Have you ever admired someone for being defensive and closed-minded about your views or views about which you were personally neutral? You probably think of the person as rather weak of character and unable to honestly handle the mental and emotional challenge. You may think of that person as a "sad case" who just can't deal with some ideas that are seen as threatening. You may shake your head, literally or metaphorically.

Undoubtedly, *you* appear like this to others when you respond defensively. It's ironic that just when we may be feeling most noble and righteous, in defense of a view we hold dear, others see us as pitiful creatures. The person who walks by you on the street as you stand there arguing in a desperate or demeaning tone will probably think well of you *only if* your views are overheard and are similar to those of the passer-by.

The person with whom you are arguing—on the street, over the phone, in an office, or wherever—may judge you harshly. This, however, is not the only damage that can be done by your defensiveness. A person's immediate reaction to a closed mind may be to close his or her own — or at least to become so defensive that the mind begins to close. You've certainly seen this. Two closed minds fending off the other's views without ever really considering them — disputing, but not really opening themselves up to any reasoning.

Besides looking foolish to others and making it more difficult for someone you're addressing to be open-minded, there is a more obvious problem with defensiveness: By expending so much attention and energy on putting down another view or fending off other reasoning, you end up missing insights from that other perspective. (Even if the other view is not completely correct there is probably something to be learned by listening closely and openly as you think through and discuss the issue.) Finally, if you become defensive often, it may develop into a habit, so that you are habitually and typically defensive. That is not an admirable trait of character.

■

PRACTICE ACTIVITIES

Set I.I *The following six tasks are intended as projects to help you apply the topics discussed in Chapter 1 to your own life.*

1. Your points of logical vulnerability are those topics about which you find it difficult to weigh fairly evidence on each side of an issue. This is usually due to a bias, which is sometimes a prejudice, toward one side of the issue. Help yourself understand one of your own points of logical vulnerability by writing a Point of Logical Vulnerability Paper. In this paper you should do the following five things:

   a. Name one of your points of logical vulnerability. Choose one which you think you should try to improve on.

   b. Indicate which side of the issue your bias inclines you toward.

   c. Without saying why your perspective is justified, describe any psychological roots of your bias.

   d. Give two specific examples of your own behavior showing how you have demonstrated an unwillingness to even consider views on another side of the issue. If you don't have examples of this, use another point of logical vulnerability.

  e. Describe how a less closed-minded approach would benefit you.

2. Give yourself some time to reflect on your points of logical vulnerability by going somewhere where it's quiet when you have at least a half-hour to yourself. On a sheet of paper, list your own points of logical vulnerability in a column down the left-hand side. This may take some thought and time. Then on the right-hand side of the same paper list the points of logical vulnerability that you see in someone whom you spend time with and know well. This might be a family member, close friend, or workmate.

   Now draw a connecting line between the same issue in each of the two columns. These are topics to be especially wary of. If both of you have similar views on the same issue, the danger is that each of you will reinforce your own biases, feeling as if, throughout a conversation, you examined each perspective reasonably, when you might not have. If the two of you have different perspectives on the same issue, the chances increase that you will fall into a win-lose mentality and that these volatile issues will be ones on which the other's strong evidence appears weak or you contrive your own weak evidence to appear strong to you. In either case, your points of logical vulnerability will set you both up for antagonism or defensiveness. Be careful on these topics.

3. How often do you take on a win-lose attitude, avoiding the other's points and overstating your own? For one week, keep a close record of when, with whom, and under which circumstances you start thinking like this. Then review your record to find patterns.

4. List additional expressions of war or violence that people use when they talk about verbal disputes.

5. List verbal and nonverbal signs of defensiveness that you have observed in others. Try to create a longer list than was presented in Chapter 1.

6. Which signs of defensiveness do you sometimes display? List them. Then try to recognize these behaviors as they begin to surface in future conversation (or even as you react to something you have read).

7. What can be done to defuse or soften the aggressiveness or defensiveness of another person who is conversing with you? Chapter 2 will include some suggestions, but it would be worthwhile for you to see what you come up with first on your own.

For Further Reading

St. Aubyn, Giles, *The Art of Argument*. Buchanan, NY: Emerson Books, 1962.

A short book on reasoning in practical settings. Irrationality and prejudice are discussed in Chapters 1 and 2.

Tannen, Deborah. *That's Not What I Meant!: How Conversational Style Makes or Breaks Relationships*. New York: Ballantine Books, 1986.

A nonacademic book by an academic author, dealing with styles of self-presentation and how these relate to disagreements and misunderstandings.

■

C H A P T E R

TWO

Opening Closed Minds

D o you have a closed mind? Or are you open-minded? Certainly this is an important question that calls for some introspection and reflection. It's also a misleading one. If you ask a roomful of people to tell you whether they are closed-minded, some will probably confess that they are. When you then ask who is open-minded, others will claim that label. Soon, if not immediately, some of the people will display a tentative facial expression, as if the question were confusing. They either will have found themselves about to admit to closed-mindedness *and* to claim open-mindedness, or they just will not have been able to decide on a category for themselves. This is probably because the question suggests a false dilemma (a reasoning error that we'll consider in Chapter 7).

It's a false dilemma because the two alternatives — being simply an open-minded person or a closed-minded person — are not the only possibilities. Most of us find that we are more open-minded at some times than at others, more open-minded with some people than with others, and more open-minded on some topics than on others. So open-mindedness can be a matter of degree and can vary for the same person, depending on the circumstances. There aren't many people who are always open-minded and there aren't many people who are always closed-minded. Furthermore, other people's open minds can be nudged to a more closed position by what we say and do. That's the "bad news," and it demands some vigilance of us. However, there is also "good news": Other people's closed minds can open a bit, or even a lot, because of what we say and do. Chapter 2 focuses on how to open those wholly or partially closed minds. Good reasoning is sometimes rendered ineffective because of antagonism or other defensive attitudes, but these factors can sometimes be overcome.

First, let's say a word about our definitions: Although it may seem that we don't need to explain so common an expression as "open-minded" or "closed-minded," not everyone understands these expressions the same. Let's settle on one way of understanding them.

A person who is being very open-minded welcomes opportunities to think about things in a different way, even if the new way provides a less comfortable or convenient perspective. When we are completely open-minded, we are just as willing to see weaknesses in our own reasoning as we are to see weaknesses in the other person's. Also, we are just as willing to see strengths in the other person's reasoning as in our own. A closed-minded person resists such changes of view. Often, when we are very closed-minded, virtually any reasoning offered in support of a statement we want to be true strikes us as good reasoning, and almost any reasoning offered in support of a statement that we want to be false strikes us as bad reasoning. Thus, we may contrive and overstate our own reasonings, while failing to notice any merit at all in the points made by the person who is seen as an opponent.

Doesn't it really seem, now, that people are seldom completely one way or the other and that we can often be influenced to be more open or closed by how we are approached and by other circumstances as well?

START WITH YOURSELF

One very good way to contribute to open-mindedness in the people whom you deal with frequently is to start with yourself. Try to make yourself more open-minded, and you will often find that others will be more (though perhaps not completely) open-minded with you.

You can begin by becoming more sensitively aware of your own points of logical vulnerability and by monitoring yourself for defensive reactions on these as well as other topics. In your mind, separate the person offering an idea from the idea itself. Neither condemn the person because of the idea nor reject or ridicule an idea simply because of who offered it. Use language that makes it easier for you and others to see each other's point, rather than language that biases unfairly or builds hostility. Listen openly even to ideas that irk you. It may not be likely or desirable that you change your basic personality. Still, it is possible to make positive changes in your own thinking and behavior.

Chapter 2 is designed to help you think about and begin that process. Good luck. Work hard. Virtually all of us need to pay attention to our thinking skills.

USE LANGUAGE FAIRLY

Some people frequently try to use language "to their advantage" in efforts to intimidate someone with another view by belittling that person. As you know, these people can be tedious, upsetting, and hard to deal with. Many of us who seldom stoop to personal attacks still cloud an issue by describing favored or unfavored views with emotionally charged language that downplays or overplays one perspective.

How carefully do you think about the words you choose to express yourself? Undoubtedly you're more careful at some times than at other times. That's natural, but on some occasions where word choice is important, we use words that not only miss the mark, but even undermine our actual intentions. Your words can endear or offend, describe fairly or misrepresent, convince or be ineffective. The not always simple task of "saying what you mean"—precision in language—will be explored in Chapter 3. For now, let's just consider the issue of *fair* language, the language of the open mind.

Don't Get Personal

Sometimes, when one person should be directing criticism to the reasoning or the position that another person has presented, he or she instead directs the attack toward the *person* who has presented the reasoning or position. This tactic is sometimes used when the person can think of no better criticism of the point being discussed. Here is an example.

EXAMPLE

David is discussing with his neighbor, Gary, the need for a tax cut. David says to Gary, "Taxes are much too high. I just can't believe how much is taken out of my paycheck for taxes. There's no doubt that we need a tax cut." Gary responds, "Well, I pay a lot in taxes, too. But if we're going to maintain vital services as well as reduce the national debt, a tax cut is just not possible."

The conversation continues, with each man giving reasons why his own position is the correct one. Finally, David strikes a confident pose, waving a finger at Gary and riveting his eyes on his opponent. "Okay, listen to this," he says. "On the basis of even *your own* assumptions, I can show you that, to be consistent, you must agree that I'm right. Now, follow my reasoning. . . ." David presents his reasoning carefully, ending with a challenge to "show me where I'm wrong."

Gary doesn't say anything for a moment. He looks down at his shoes and tightens his lips. Then he darts a look at David, raising his eyebrows. "You really *like* to argue, don't you?" he asks pointedly. "You don't really care about the topic when we've having a conversation like this. You're just arguing for argument's sake. I never did like that about you. Can't you ever just ease up a little?" ∎

■
Getting Personal?

In an article published in the *Washington Post* (National Weekly Edition) on November 10, 1986, "The Nobel Prize for the Obvious," James M. Buchanan is said to have won the Nobel Prize in economics for very ordinary, unremarkable opinions. The following paragraph is taken from that article.

> Buchanan opposes pork-barrel politics. Who doesn't? He's cynical about politicians afraid to raise taxes. Who isn't? Among his long-held remedies for curing deficits, Buchanan joins the flat-earthers and full-mooners in calling for "the constitutional restraint" of a balanced-budget amendment. The professor, whose salary of $114,100 is $39,000 higher than that of the members of Congress whose big-spending ways he deplores, argues that we should have deficits only in times of depression or major wars.*

*The Washington Post, *November 10, 1986. ©1986 Washington Post Writers Group. Reprinted with permission of the Washington Post Writers Group.*

In this conversation, Gary has resorted to **getting personal** with David. Instead of attacking David's reasoning or the position that he is taking, Gary has shifted to a personal attack on David.

What are the results of such an attack? Certainly, different people will react differently to a particular kind of comment. In this case, the response is crucial to the direction of the whole conversation. When we are attacked personally, we commonly reach right down to that same level and respond either with a defensive and hostile justification of ourselves or by attacking the other person in a similar way. David might, for example, respond by saying, "I'm no more argumentative than you are, you hypocrite. Do you remember the time . . . ?" Here David counterattacks by getting equally personal and stinging. This is most often the very worst kind of response.

First, whoever responds like this is cooperating in setting up an adversary relationship that promises more emotion than reason, more contention than insight. Second, both people are now off the topic. Furthermore, since attacks on the person are common when the speaker simply has nothing better to offer, by coming down to the attacker's level and responding defensively or aggressively, the second person allows the shift just when his or her point may be on the verge of being established. If, instead, he or she can maintain a balanced perspective on the conversation as a whole, holding personal emotions in check, a response that gets the conversation back on track can be offered. For example, in the situation previously presented, David could respond by saying, "Perhaps I do get argumentative. But the topic we've been discussing up to now isn't my character, it's the issue of taxes. Now, think about the point I just made about a tax cut. Did you think there were any mistakes in my reasoning?" With such a response, David keeps himself from a demeaning emotional display and, at the same time, does what he can to revive their comparatively rational discussion — to get the conversation back on track.

Be Aware of Emotionally Charged Language

You can learn by seeing the merit of other people's arguments — arguments that you would never have thought of on your own. You can learn by seeing how your own arguments fall short when measured against another person's insightful criticism. This is the profit in the exchange of ideas. At times, nevertheless, people make this kind of learning difficult for themselves. They think out their positions and word their arguments in ways that polarize, minimizing the chance that each person will learn from the other.

A confrontational "win-lose" attitude (see Chapter 1) is encouraged when you characterize the other's view with expressions that presume its inadequacy. By describing the other's view as "outdated" or "archaic," for example, you suggest that, however well the position may be presented and whatever its merits might be, you are not going to give it serious consideration. This invites an aggressive, confrontational response from the other person because people are often embarrassed or angered by the suggestion that their whole perspective is off-base.

The same effect is commonly produced by characterizing the person's entire view or approach with negatively charged expressions such as *foolish, extreme, outrageous, shallow, superficial, partisan,* and *irresponsible.* Although it is no shame to be a sophomore or an adolescent, the expressions *sophomoric* and *adolescent* also have strong negative charges in some contexts.

Rhetoric, in one sense, may be defined as "the use of language to persuade and/or to affect emotionally." At times you may choose to craft your language *only* rhetorically, in order to deliver your point as powerfully as possible. At other times (often, one would hope), when you want to be very fair and avoid prejudice and closed-mindedness, you will need to avoid language that is unfair because it biases the discussion of a specific issue. In a discussion of abortion, for example, if you refer to abortion as "murder," you discourage mutual learning for the reason expressed previously: The implication that you will not give serious consideration to a view easily gives rise to a combative frame of mind. Such language not only affects the other person but can psychologically commit you, in the continuing discussion, to the blind defense of such an impassioned stance. Similarly, referring to a social-welfare program as a "giveaway," a seriously religious person as a "Holy Roller," or the change of a hard-line position as "selling out" may contribute rhetorical punch to your argument, but it will

---

■
Defector or Traitor?

"It's impossible for someone to defect from the United States. [Former CIA agent] Edward Lee Howard is not a defector. He's a traitor." — Michael Armacost, under secretary of state for political affairs (reported in *Newsweek*, November 17, 1986).

---

probably do so at the price of an opportunity to expand the insights of each thinker who is participating in or observing the discussion.

The language we use to express ourselves varies from the neutral to the very emotionally charged. Humans are emotional beings. Emotions are a part of life both when we are at our best and when we are at our worst. They constitute a grand and pervasive aspect of humanity, and life without them is close to inconceivable. Your emotions should often enter into your communications with other people, but not in a way that unfairly biases your reasoning or its presentation.

Some expressions — words or phrases — generally have an emotional charge that is "positive." If we accept the statement that includes such an expression, we are more inclined to think well of whatever or whomever that expression characterizes. Some other expressions generally have a "negative" emotional charge. If we accept the statement that includes such an expression, we are more inclined to think poorly of whatever or whomever that expression characterizes. Certainly, if we use the terms *generous* or *thoughtful* to describe a person, we expect her to receive our comment as a compliment and not with indignation. Furthermore, we expect that people who hear our description will be at least somewhat well disposed toward her, unless they have a reason to reject that description. If, however, we use negatively charged terms like *selfish* or *rude*, we can expect that she and those who sympathize with her will be indignant or at least hurt because of the comment. We also expect that people who hear our description will think less of her unless they reject the description.

Adjectives are not the only words that can be emotionally charged. Nouns (*saint* and *sinner*, *gift* and *bribe*), verbs (*share* and *hoard*), and adverbs (*efficiently* and *wastefully*) can all be emotionally charged.

Two facts should be noted: (1) the emotional charge of an expression can vary, and (2) not every word has an emotional charge.

1. The emotional charge of an expression can vary with different contexts and with different hearers or readers. For an example of variation with context, consider the implications of "getting together with the old college *gang*" and "getting involved with a violent street *gang*." For an

example of variation with different hearers or readers, consider the person for whom the normally positively charged word *immaculate* has a negative emotional charge because of his father's insistence, years ago, that his room be kept in "immaculate" condition. Other expressions, such as *conservative* or *work*, may as readily be positively *or* negatively charged; they may vary from person to person, with no exceptional circumstances necessary to account for the difference.

2. Not every word has an emotional charge. Normally, we do not anticipate that a person will react emotionally to words such as *plate*, *group*, *fabric*, *hear*, or *bring*; nor do we anticipate an emotional reaction to most pronouns or prepositions.

People sometimes communicate impressions that they do not intend. The reason for this miscommunication can be a failure to distinguish between the emotional charge of two expressions that seem synonymous to the communicator. To one person, the difference between an "assertive" person or program and an "aggressive" one may be inconsequential. To another person, the difference may be great. If the first person is the communicator and the second is the intended recipient of the message, an unintended but strong impression may result.

Depending on the choice of words in the description, an incident or a person can actually appear to have either of opposite general characteristics. Consider the following sequence of occurrences.

EXAMPLE

Four of the five members of the city council were at their seats at the main table when the weekly council meeting began at the usual 7 P.M. time on Tuesday. The nameplate at the vacant seat had SUE LASBURY embossed on it. At 7:10, the door opened suddenly. Ms. Lasbury moved across the room with long strides and dropped quickly into her chair. She looked at the current speaker and nodded in silent agreement a few times. Soon the interruption was forgotten by almost everyone. ∎

Think of how this incident might be perceived or described by, first, someone who is sympathetic to the council member and, second, someone who is hostile to her.

B.C.   **BY JOHNNY HART**

Reprinted with permission of Johnny Hart and Creators Syndicate Inc.

If the late entrance were reported (in an article, to a friend, or however) from a sympathetic perspective, the description of the incident might run thus: "Several minutes into the meeting, missing only some preliminaries, Lasbury entered swiftly, strode confidently to her seat, and promptly sat down." From a hostile perspective, it might run like this: "A full ten minutes into this important meeting, Lasbury barged in, audaciously strode to her seat, and plopped herself down."

Which account is correct? To a significant extent, both accounts are correct. Each describes the same incident. Neither "makes up" occurrences that did not take place. If it is true that this was an important meeting and that only preliminaries were missed, the introductory phrase of each statement is correct. Choosing to stress the length of tardiness and the importance of the meeting certainly leaves a different impression than choosing to stress the inconsequential nature of the meeting time missed, but each statement is nevertheless correct. Now, should we describe dropping "quickly into her chair" as "promptly sitting down" or as "plopping herself down"? Each way of putting it conveys a different impression about Ms. Lasbury's attitude, but neither is easily proven nor obviously false. Finally, was her stride "confident" or "audacious"? Again, neither is easily proven. Perhaps facial expression or body carriage would best reveal the truth of the matter, but the assessment may still remain very subjective.

To a significant extent, then, both accounts are correct and, beyond that, each is interpretive but not easily shown to be false. Furthermore, there might be *no intention to mislead* with either account! Because people can be naturally biased, or just lazy about observations and conclusions, either view might seem to its proponent to be "just the facts." To the hearer or reader, moreover, the account offered might seem to be "just the facts," true or easily shown to be false. ("Then she *didn't* really sit right down?") The problem is that some inferences (about character and attitude, in this case) that might be drawn from the particular account are not presented in a clear premise-and-conclusion form. Because of this, erroneous inferences may be

---

■
Euphemisms

A euphemism is an expression that is used in order to avoid a common but negatively charged expression. The euphemism usually has no notable emotional charge.

In an effort to avoid the harsher expression, *lady of the evening* may be substituted for *prostitute*, *passed away* may be substituted for *died*, and *underprivileged* may be substituted for *poor*. Consider the shift from the term *pro-abortion*, which has taken on a negative emotional charge generally, to the term *pro-choice*. (In this case, the two components of the new expression — *pro* and *choice* — have a positive emotional charge rather than no emotional charge.) Consider the shift from the term *crippled* to the more general term *handicapped* or *physically challenged*. In education, the stigma of having "flunked" a grade in school led to the use of the now common expression *retained in the same grade*. (Of course, the result is the same: the student repeats the grade.)

---

harder to spot. *It probably won't occur to the hearer or reader that different word choice could, within the range of "the facts," present a different view.*

The vividness of emotionally charged language is usually unobjectionable and is an essential ingredient in pleasurable conversation or colorful description. When the choice of expressions blinds us to a clear analysis of evidence, however, our reasoning suffers.

LISTEN!

Someone might say that you "listened" to another person's point of view if you sat quietly while that person spoke, especially if you looked as if you were paying attention and you could afterwards repeat the main ideas that were presented. This is indeed part — but only part — of the active listening that is an important aspect of open-minded conversation.

Many of us have learned how to appear as if we are giving full consideration to another point of view while we are actually devising a plan of attack (there's that combative language again). Linda, for example, nods her head up and down slowly as she listens to Sandy describe her views on abortion. "I understand your point of view," Linda says, but she hasn't tried at all to see that opposing perspective. She has been thinking about what she would say when Sandy stops talking, but she has been nodding and muttering the "uh-huh" of agreement all the while. Although Linda now launches into a defense of her own ideas, she doesn't appear to be as closed-minded as she really is. She has mastered the art of deception in masking her win-lose approach to the topic. William is not subtle, however. His interruptions of Sandy and his rising, choppy, accusing voice reveal his inability to listen openly. Still, the result is the same. No one is benefiting from an exchange of ideas.

Is this a troublesome habit for you? Is it a problem only on your points of logical vulnerability, with certain people, in certain moods, or when you're tired? Try the following four steps.

1. Give your attention. Forget about formulating a response or a next point. Don't interrupt in order to fit in comments of your own. If you're afraid you'll lose track of a certain idea, write a reminder word on an available slip of paper or ask the other person to remind you later to mention something about X (use a key "reminder" word here). Yes, you might lose track of a certain formulation of the idea, but it's better than losing the whole exchange and lapsing into a one-sided conversation. Temporarily suspend commitment to your own views as you listen. If your commitment to your own view is well based, the old position will reassert itself. If your previous view is enriched and modified, all the better. The open-mindedness that allows you to change or modify your ideas is a virtue, not a vice.

2. Understand before responding. Key terms may be vague or new to you. You may suspect that terms that are familiar to you are being used in a different sense. Ask for clarification. This is when interruption may be worthwhile. Even incidental words sometimes are worth an inquiry. (The definition of terms will be discussed in Chapter 3.)

   If you start missing each other's points, start rewording the other person's previous point before going on to comment. You can ask, "Now, is this what you're saying?" and follow up with a brief summary. In conversations where misrepresentation (referred to as *setting up a straw man* in Chapter 4) or poor listening is a constant problem, you can even agree to reword the previous comment *each time* before continuing.

3. Reflect before responding. "Let me think about that for a minute." The request is a reasonable one. If you start talking the very second another person responds, you may not be giving the other ideas enough thought. It will certainly *appear*, at least, that you are more interested in your own remarks than in anyone else's. Even the comments that seem off-base, requiring a firm response from you, may have bits of insight if you just stop to find them.

4. Acknowledge good points. As you begin your response, draw attention to anything, basic or incidental, on which each of you agrees. In other

words, stress the common points shared by each perspective. This keeps the other person from thinking that you don't respect his or her intuitions and reasoning at all. If, after listening, you have any concessions to make — any points on which you have changed your mind — offer these first.

When you are reading a newspaper editorial or article, or a pamphlet that endorses a divergent view from yours, or when you are listening to television news or commentary, you won't have the opportunity to make an immediate response that will generate an on-the-spot interchange with the people who hold the other view. Still, the discipline of good listening skills can allow you to broaden your perspective.

SEE ANOTHER SIDE

Most of us would like to be certain about more things than we can justifiably claim certainty about. There's so often more to be considered, including evidence that conflicts with what we *want* to believe. The problems we typically deal with in our daily lives as consumers, workers, family members, and citizens call for an ongoing assessment of the strength of our evidence and reasoning. It is important for us to continue to be open to — and to actively seek — the additional information that can either secure or challenge our present opinions and beliefs. Sometimes there is a high price for being wrong.

As careful as we may be to consider fairly each aspect of certain issues, we sometimes get lazy or fall victim to one of our points of logical vulnerability on *other* issues.

A person needs to see more than one side of an issue in order to weigh the evidence in any meaningful sense and to arrive at fair conclusions. If a person, after noting which evidence he or she judges to be relevant and important, finds that it all supports the same position, the chances are good that there is counterevidence (evidence against that position) that has not been considered seriously enough. This is especially true on social issues, which are so often complex and elusive. You probably know people who believe that there is basically "nothing to be said for" an opposing view on abortion, labor-management disputes, the national defense budget, or price supports for farmers. Check your own points of logical vulnerability. Admitting that there is *some* relevant support for a conflicting claim does not require you to remain skeptically indecisive. You can judge what it is reasonable to believe while acknowledging that the issue has other sides that you honestly and carefully (that's the trick!) judge to be less compelling.

(At this point, it may be helpful to reread the sections on points of logical vulnerability and winning and losing in Chapter 1.)

Psychological research confirms a blindness to the power of evidence that supports personally distasteful conclusions. The phenomenon of being more alert to evidence that supports a welcomed conclusion and less receptive to the presence and power of counterevidence has been described by psychologists as "the fallacy of positive instances." Indeed, sometimes the very existence of counterevidence never comes to mind. When it does, psychologists agree, it may not be well received. In a study performed in 1979,* three psychologists presented Stanford University students with two supposed research studies on whether capital punishment deterred crime.

The two studies had opposing conclusions. After students read both studies, there was stronger disagreement than ever between those students who had favored capital punishment on grounds of crime-deterrence and those who opposed capital punishment. The people on each side readily accepted the study that confirmed their preconceptions and were very critical of the evidence that supposedly counted against them.

These findings are neither exceptional nor surprising. We have all seen how people weigh evidence when a point of logical vulnerability is involved. Besides, there is resistance to the simple acknowledgment that "the view I've been holding until now is wrong."

Two problems exist, then. First, when analyzing an issue on our own, we need to be able to think of evidence that does not readily occur to us — evidence on different sides of the issue. Second, when evaluating arguments produced by us or another in support of conclusions we resist, we need to be receptive to the actual force of the evidence.

Although there is no simple and sure way to acquire either of these skills, consider two suggestions. First, when trying to think of evidence that is relevant to the issue, you can start by asking the general question "What *kinds of evidence* could bear on this issue?" Essentially, the same search is initiated by asking "Which *sources of information* could help to build insight in this matter?" Just list the kinds/sources. Don't concern yourself with the question of whether any evidence is available from each category. After making the list (more items for the list may occur throughout the process), enumerate the evidence that *is* available from each category. The disciplined use of this method lessens the chance of overlooking (1) entire types of evidence, as well as (2) unfavorable evidence within categories. It is simply a more deliberate, less haphazard search for evidence.

Thomas, for example, has wanted for years to attend Whitson College, from which his mother had graduated in 1969. He has managed to convince himself that they have the best business department of any college in the

*C. G. Lord, L. Ross, and M. Lepper, "Biased Assimilation and Attitude Polarization: The Effects of Prior Theories on Subsequently Considered Evidence," Journal of Personality and Social Psychology 37 (1979): 2098–2109.

Northeast. He dismisses claims about weaknesses in Whitson's program as easily as claims about strengths in other colleges' programs. Although there may be other reasons for attending Mom's college, Thomas should be wary of the possibility that his bias is blinding him on the issue of which school has the best business program. He may force himself into a fairer analysis if, before drawing his conclusion, he asks *what kinds of evidence would help to determine which school offers the best education in business?* He might then decide to see if he can find out (1) how many graduating seniors have received job offers, (2) how many graduates continued to be successful in their enterprises, (3) the seniors' average score (or the distribution of their various scores) on the Graduate Record Examination, (4) the credentials of the faculty in the business department, and so on. He can do this for each of the schools he is seriously considering. Probably, in some of these categories information will be partially or completely unavailable to him. Nevertheless, he will not so easily skew the evidence if he decides where to look for it before he searches out the information itself.

The second suggestion is this. When trying to consider fairly the weight of "unfriendly" evidence, you can make a serious effort to "put yourself in the other's shoes" or in the other's *position*. To take on the other person's perspective, you might start by focusing on the other's feelings as if they were yours. Each of us knows the feelings of pride, resentment, concern for the plight of others, and, generally, all the feelings that are common to human beings. If you then associate the other's feelings with the same objects and beliefs as that other person does, you may be in a position to produce respectable arguments for this view that might have previously eluded you.

The person who opposes all social welfare programs might temporarily put aside her own perspective in favor of a focus on the other person's feeling of sadness for those who have been "caught in the system" despite an industrious nature. Sadness and concern for the undeserved misfortune of others are familiar feelings. The situation of Pennsylvania steelworkers who have worked hard to support families and who are suddenly "unemployable" at age fifty or fifty-five because of the closing of the steel mills provides a focus for those feelings. Now, if such a change of perspective is genuinely accomplished, the result is likely to be a greater appreciation for the other's arguments. A further possible result is the capacity to generate additional evidence and argument on this "other side" of the issue. Similarly, another person, someone with sympathy for the less fortunate, may view *any* attack on welfare programs as a reflection of lack of concern, or even meanness. This person might temporarily put aside his perspective in favor of a focus on the other person's feelings of anger about widespread abuses of welfare programs or fear for the nation's financial solvency in consideration of the great expense of the programs. In either case, allowing oneself to feel the emotion(s) the other person experiences, and tying this emotion to specific instances that seem to justify such emotion, should bring about appreciation of that other perspective and perhaps the discovery of yet new evidence to consider on "that side" of the issue.

COMMENT AND RESPOND CONSTRUCTIVELY

It's true that you cannot control other people's tongues (and pens) enough to ensure that they will always be open-minded or even polite. Still, you can influence others by how you conduct yourself. You are responsible only for your own comments and actions and you will sometimes have to be content that at least you have been reasonable. Sometimes we are tempted to justify our own stridency, hostility, or closed-mindedness by simply pointing out that the other person is no better. This fallacy in reasoning, called Two Wrongs Make a Right, will be explored in Chapter 7. The best any of us can do is to start with ourselves.

One basic rule of civilized discourse is that we should routinely allow the other person to save face. This means that we don't belittle someone else, although we may openly disagree with that person's ideas. It is possible to think through ideas together and even to be sharply divided on an issue without being nasty. We sometimes don't stop to think about what our tone of voice and body language are communicating. Instead, we can emphasize points of agreement, offer concerns and be honest about what divides us on the issue, but be able to walk away knowing that beliefs rather than people have been victims.

■

PRACTICE ACTIVITIES

Set 2.1

1. Describe in writing the next two or three occasions on which someone else gets personal with you, demeaning you rather than discussing an idea or behavior. Describe the range of feelings you experience on each occasion.

   The next two or three times you find that you get a bit personal yourself, watch for any signs that the other person has reacted as you did. Describe what you find.

2. Write two accounts of the same series of events. In one account, employ positively charged expressions to reflect favorably on a

certain person, group, or process. In the other account, use negatively charged expressions to reflect unfavorably on that same
person, group, or process. Do not change any factual claims in the
second account. By changing the emotional charge, however, you
will change the implied conclusions.

3. Write a pair of accounts as in the preceding assignment. This
time, include within each account both a favorably described and
an unfavorably described person, group, or process. The one
receiving a favorable treatment in the first account should receive
an unfavorable treatment in the second account, and the one
receiving an unfavorable treatment in the first account should
receive a favorable treatment in the second.

4. In each of the following examples, replace the positively or negatively charged expression with wording that is neutral or less
charged.

   a. From a letter to the editor of *Philip Morris Magazine*, Summer
   1991:

   > I'm a voter who is fed up with the government sucking
   > "blood-taxes" from smokers like vampires, and then hav-
   > ing the gall to put us outside to smoke. If we can send
   > shuttles to space, we can ventilate buildings and airplanes.

   b. From an article in that same issue of *Philip Morris Magazine*:

   > When excise taxes are earmarked, the revenue raised by
   > the tax is used to support a particular program or public
   > project. Earmarking [of tobacco products] is just another
   > cloaking device used by anti-tobacco activists and tax pro-
   > ponents to make excise tax hikes more palatable. Anti-
   > smokers claim that the earmarked excise tax is really chari-
   > table—a few pennies donated by everyone. Only it's not
   > from everyone and it's not donated. Smokers alone have
   > their pockets picked.

   c. From "Government Is Strangling Transit" in *The Freeman*, July
   1991, written by an economist for the Laissez Faire Institute in
   Tempe, Arizona:

   > Publicly owned and operated transit has been a colossal
   > failure. Billions of taxpayer dollars have been frittered
   > away with little or nothing to show for it.

   d. From "Church and State" by Edd Doerr, *The Humanist*,
   July/August 1991:

   > George Bush, who likes to call himself the "education
   > president," has proposed that Congress approve his plan

to spend $230 million per year (for openers) to induce local public school districts to include sectarian private schools in so-called school choice plans. The tax support is presumably to be provided through tuition vouchers. The Bush plan would deny federal funds to districts which refuse to include religious schools in their choice plans — a not-very-pretty form of blackmail.

e. From "Freedom and the Future" by Margaret Thatcher, *Daughters of the American Revolution Magazine*, May 1991:

The task of reforming and liberalizing the Soviet Union is a far more dificult one than any of us had supposed a few years ago. How do you persuade people brainwashed by egalitarian propaganda that inequalities are the side-effect of rising prosperity for all? How do you tell them that higher living standards can only be attained at the short-term price of higher unemployment? And how do you do any of this while the demoted bureaucrats, the discredited politicians and all those who flourished under totalitarian mediocrity are out to undermine everything you do?

f. From "Our Liberty Is Our Life" by Franjo Tudjman, President of Croatia, *Manchester Guardian Weekly*, May 1991:

When the Founding Fathers of the United States decided that colonialism was a dead concept, they revolted. They broke the chains of England and fought to be free. The global community was split on the effect such an "independence" movement would have on others' colonial holdings. But the leaders of the American Revolution would not be deterred, and in the end freedom prevailed. Colonialism died, a new world order appeared. Today, Communism is dead, and a new world order is evolving.

g. From "Life Terms" by Michael Kinsley, published under "TRB from Washington" in *The New Republic*, July 15 and 22, 1991:

. . . during the 1988 presidential debates . . . Michael Dukakis accused George Bush of wanting to brand women who seek abortions as criminals. Bush burbled that while he opposes abortion, "I haven't sorted out the penalties." The next morning campaign manager James Baker declared, "Frankly, he [Bush] thinks that a woman in a situation like that would be more properly considered an additional victim." That sounds compassionate, but it is nonsense. If every fetus is a fully human being, a woman *neg.* who procures an abortion is exactly like someone who hires a gunman to murder her child.

h. From a letter to the editor, *Rutgers University Alumni Magazine*, September 1985:

neg. Being a graduate of the University of California which comprises nine campuses, I cannot understand the stone-age mentality of the author who had trouble dealing with a system on only three campuses.

i. From *Newsweek*, November 24, 1986:

neg. The Iranian dealings once again showed the president carrying on his own seat-of-the-pants diplomacy, this time with most of his experienced advisers sidelined in dissent and only the gung-ho staffers of the National Security Council on board to give dubious advice.

j. Written by a columnist for the *San Marcos Courier*, August 15, 1985:

neg. Let's deprive the pro-Soviet U.N. of our headquarters in New York and let them go to Russia or wherever they desire. One U.N. big-shot said if that happened they'd be glad to go to Geneva, Switzerland—I say, let 'em go.

k. From a column in the *San Marcos Courier*, August 8, 1985:

neg. Obviously, [Assemblyman] Bradley is quite willing and even anxious to spill blood for the political advantage of the coming Republican campaign. If he and his gang prevail in the next election, you can be sure that abortion, school prayers and the death sentence will be the main issues in the decade to come.

l. From the opening paragraph of an editorial entitled "Spy Panic," in the *Los Angeles Times*, July 28, 1985:

neg. The news is full of spy cases, creating considerable worry about the nation's legitimate secrets and how to protect them. Unfortunately, Congress is reacting hysterically with quick-fix solutions that do not promise to stop the spying but do pose a serious threat to basic civil liberties.

5. Practice careful listening with at least one acquaintance. Choose a topic that is reasonably interesting to each of you, but on which you do not have identical points of view. Before either may respond to the other's comment, that comment must be reworded and summarized to the satisfaction of the person who originally made it.

Set 2.2 *For each of the following claims, think up as much relevant evidence for differing perspectives as you can. First list the kinds of evidence that would be relevant; then see if you can offer specific evidence that you know to be true. In other words, first ask, "What kinds of evidence would we need" to support or reject this claim? Then ask, "What evidence do I have?"*

1. Harvard University offers the best general education in the United States.

2. Chrysler makes the best-built American cars.

3. Republicans are more inclined toward military solutions to international political problems than are Democrats.

4. All college students should have a course in logic or critical thinking.

5. The United States uses military force too often to resolve international problems.

6. Men are more aggressive by nature than women are.

7. There have been actual instances of ESP (extrasensory perception).

8. People who have played team sports are more successful in their careers than are those who haven't.

9. Children at age fourteen generally would not make decisions as well as adults would if they were allowed to vote in national elections.

10. A person's character is determined more by environmental than by biological — including genetic — factors.

11. People's actions are basically self-serving.

12. The Soviet economy will improve over the next two years.

Set 2.3 *Identify typical emotions of people on different sides of the issue. Attempt to feel these emotions and associate them with specific objects and beliefs. Write down the additional evidence that comes to mind in each case.**

1. Capitalistic economic systems contribute to the development of intelligence in people more than communistic economic systems do. (Note: If you don't know the difference between a capitalistic and a communistic economic system, look up the information or skip to the next statement.)

2. Given time for development, computers will be able to perform every kind of thinking function that humans can perform.

You don't have to work at these exercises in the order presented here.

3. Prayer should be required in public schools.

4. A period for silent meditation should be required in public schools.

5. Religion is a subject that should be taught in high school.

6. The quality of American cars has been decreasing in recent years.

7. Sex education in the schools leads to increased promiscuity.

8. Local politicians (for example, mayors) should make a complete public disclosure of their personal finances.

9. Females and males should be permitted to compete on the same interscholastic sports teams.

10. Parents should be trained and licensed for parenthood.

11. Handgun ownership should be restricted.

12. Early termination of pregnancy should be permitted by law.

For Further Reading

Adler, Mortimer. *How to Speak, How to Listen*. New York: Macmillan, 1983.
A popular book that has several good chapters on reasonable conversation.

Bramson, Robert M. *Coping with Difficult People*. New York: Dell, 1988.
Reflections of types of arguers and how to deal with them productively.

Chaffee, John. *Thinking Critically*. Boston: Houghton Mifflin, 1985.
A textbook organized in a workbook format. Chapter 3, "Thinking Critically," offers exercises for analyzing "points of logical vulnerability" and "fairmindedness," although these expressions are not used.

Creighton, James L. *Don't Go Away Mad: How to Make Peace with Your Partner*. New York, Doubleday, 1990.
A recent book with ideas on how to keep emotions from clouding the issue.

Keyes, Ken, Jr. *Taming Your Mind*. Living Love Center, 1975.
A simple, readable nonacademic guide to patterns of thinking that affect our perspective on everyday events. (This book was originally published by McGraw-Hill under the title *How to Develop Your Thinking Ability*.)

Murphy, Kevin J. *Effective Listening: Your Key to Career Success*. New York: Bantam Books, 1987.
The best book on open-minded listening.

Skwire, David. *Writing with a Thesis*. New York: Holt, Rinehart and Winston, 1985.
A handbook of advice and examples focusing on logical and persuasive writing. Skwire's book touches on many of the skills discussed in this text.

P A R T
TWO
Am I
Being Clear?

■

C H A P T E R

THREE

Saying What You Mean

"It's not what you say, it's how you say it." This common expression reflects, among other things, the importance of carefully choosing your words when you are expressing a point.

We all learned the basics of verbal communication in our first several years of life and continued to perfect these articulation skills as we forged toward adulthood. Talking and writing are basic skills that serve as a foundation for both simple and sophisticated feats of reasoning. We often take these skills for granted.

When we want to express a thought, we sometimes quickly reach down into our metaphorical bag of words and come up with ones that are similar to the words that would communicate most clearly and precisely, but are not quite right. Sometimes this sloppiness in language poses no problem at all. At other times, it leaves unintended impressions that undermine the speaker's or writer's intentions. Occasionally, it just leaves things unclear, and that, depending on the situation, can create problems.

When we don't manage to say exactly what we mean, we have to deal with the resulting need for apologies, re-explanations, and repetitions of incorrectly done work. Worst of all, sometimes the misunderstandings caused by misstatement are never brought to light for correction. On points of logical vulnerability and other important matters, then, it's generally best to be precise the first time around.

RECOGNIZE VAGUENESS

An expression is **vague** when it is not specific enough to meet the needs or desires of the hearer or reader. In other words, when the speaker or writer is *too general* in presenting a point, we say that the point is vague. We also sometimes say that the person who originated the expression was "vague on that point."

32

When the teenager, on her way out the door, is asked by her parent, "Where are you going?" her answer may simply be, "Out." This is a vague answer, since the parent clearly knew that the teenager was going "out." The parent asked the question in order to get more specific — less general — information than that.

Here is another example of vagueness.

EXAMPLE

A student has asked his teacher to explain her reason for assigning an F to his report. The teacher answers: "I have assigned that particular grade because, on a careful examination of the report, no other grade is warranted. Applying the rule of determining the grade on the basis of the quality of the work, this is a justified grade." ∎

The professor's answer is vague. Notice that her explanation is so general that it could be offered to *any student* who was inquiring about an F that was given for *any assignment*. Clearly, the student in the preceding example wants the professor to discuss deficiencies that are specific to his report. The problem is not that the professor's response was false, but that it was not helpful because of its generality.

Is vagueness, then, always an error? Can we assume, for example, that any speaker or writer would avoid vagueness whenever he or she realized that the statement offered could be replaced by one that was more specific? For the answer to this question, think about the following exchange.

EXAMPLE

At a press conference, the president of the United States recognizes the news correspondent from a major television network and receives this question: "Mr. President, U.S. Marines who are armed for combat, although technically a foreign peace-keeping force, are presently in a tense situation as they hold their positions only two miles from a large contingent of hostile militia. I'm sure, Mr. President, that the American people would like to know what your response, as commander in chief of American armed forces, would be if these hostile troops advanced on the U.S. positions."

The president pauses, smiles, and responds. "I'm glad you asked that question, Mr. Bonno. I believe that the American people *are* concerned about this, and I believe that they deserve an answer. To every American who is concerned about how American strength will be wielded, I want to make it perfectly clear that if U.S. positions are advanced on, I will swiftly and without hesitation take every military or nonmilitary measure that is appropriate to the situation." ∎

Certainly the president's answer is vague. We know no more now concerning the U.S. response to the hypothetical militia advance than we did before his answer. The answer was simply too general to distinguish between alternative courses of action that are either under consideration or are being ruled out. Still, it is important to notice that the president undoubtedly *wanted* to be vague. Politically, a specific answer to such a question can be undesirable. Not wanting to call attention to the vagueness of his answer, however, the president speaks as if he were presenting a reasonably substantive reply.

Sometimes, indeed, we are vague on purpose. When asked about the host's strange-tasting wine or that atrocious dress someone has chosen, we may respond, "It sure is different." We are being vague to evade specifics. When someone asks our assessment of her unorthodox political or religious perspective, we may evasively respond, "It's a really interesting view." While it may be true that we've found the view "interesting," it would also have been possible, but perhaps not desirable, to say specifically how we felt. We employ vagueness in this case—again—to avoid a more specific answer.

We should recognize vagueness and, when appropriate, revise our own comments. It is at times also necessary to request clarification from another speaker or to recognize that the written passage you are examining is simply too vague for your thorough assessment of that point of view. Some casual comments will be vague but will not warrant a follow-up demand for specifics. In other cases, the omitted specifics will be necessary for a fruitful interaction.

BE PRECISE

Often, the reason for vague communication is that even the communicator has only a vague sense of the point being communicated. The problem here is not that the person is failing to say what he or she means; the problem is that the person simply isn't clear on the point in more specific terms. He or she must first think and observe more attentively, then choose the words that communicate the special character of the experience or concept under consideration.

Almost all of us are occasionally weighed down by a mental drowsiness that yields vague, minimally informative communications in place of precise and vivid ones. Consider our everyday conversations.

EXAMPLE

"How was the film?" you ask before Mom has even closed the front door behind her.

"It was great," Mom says. "It was just one of those very enjoyable shows. You know."

"What did you like about it?" you ask.

"Just everything," Mom responds with enthusiasm. "I don't know *when* I've ever seen such a good movie." ∎

With a bit of thought, Mom could probably enrich her own reflections on the experience as well as tell you what set it apart from others. Perhaps there were unique camera shots that constantly invited the viewer to change the perspective in which a person or object was viewed. Perhaps the plot involved an elusive puzzle that called for a certain sort of playful creativity. Perhaps the characters were portrayed with interesting contradictions in their personalities.

If Brent gave "the best" speech of any sophomore in the competition, it is probably worth considering the way in which he excelled. Was the speech forceful, well organized, humorous, emotionally moving, or insightful? Did Brent place his pauses so well that his main points were consistently underscored? Exactly what was so good about the speech?

If you're proud that your local high school is an "excellent" school, it is certainly worth considering the ways in which it may be distinguished from others. Is the faculty especially well informed or caring? Are effective teaching techniques used widely in the school? Do students learn research techniques especially well? Is there good school spirit? (How is this spirit displayed?) Exactly what is so good about the school?

If the book your friend had recommended so highly was "disappointing," it is probably worth considering the contrast between what you expected and what you feel the book offered. By taking the time to think, you can be specific in choosing your description. You can best communicate the greatness of your soccer coach or a certain disc jockey by reflecting, then being specific when choosing your description.

Efforts at precision in thought and self-expression yield a personal benefit: alertness to the rich variety of one's own experiences. When you are offering evidence and drawing conclusions, another benefit of precision is that you are more specific and informative, and thus your reasoning is less

---

■

Watch Your Language

Sloppy self-expression can certainly result in misunderstanding and foster yet more unclear thinking. It has another drawback, too. It can leave others with a poor impression of your mental sensitivity so they don't expect the very best thinking from you. They might even fail to see the strength of some of your good reasoning because of these lowered expectations.

In conversation, do you produce lots of uncompleted sentences because you haven't anticipated what you were going to say? One sentence dies partway through, and you start another, then perhaps another. Try to complete your sentences. If you do find that you are at a loss to finish your sentence (and it happens to almost everyone), acknowledge the shift by saying, for example, "Let me start over." You don't want to give the impression that your mind is a chaotic home for a disorderly family of ideas.

Second, avoid habitual filler expressions that add little but sound to your discussions. Some people use these in almost every sentence.

1. "Um" is one that seems to function only to keep another person from interrupting. It suggests that "I'm still thinking and I'll have something to say in a moment."
2. "Like" is a useful word but it can also function as a filler expression. In the sentence "He was like right there when I said it," the word "like" can be eliminated.
3. "You know" and "I mean" are useful phrases, but they can be stuck into sentences that don't need them.
4. "And stuff" as well as "and everything" are sometimes used to mean "etcetera," and are sometimes just inserted into sentences at hardly predictable places.
5. "Kinda" (kind of) and "sorta" (sort of) are abused and overused qualifiers.

These and excessive use of trendy colloquial expressions can foster a mental laziness in speaker and hearer that works against specificity and precision in thought and words.

---

subject to misunderstanding, such as in the *straw man* misrepresentation discussed in Chapter 4.

Think about how you can make helpful distinctions and qualify claims so that what you say is more often accurate, informative, and interesting. Instead of saying (falsely) that "Everyone in the state knows the senator is a crook," just say that "The senator's reputation as a crook is widespread." Actually, while you're at it, it wouldn't hurt to be more specific than "crook," since a person might be called this because of felonies or misdemeanors, thievery or confidence games, and even (sometimes) legal or illegal activities, as well as vicious and damaging misdeeds or relatively harmless ones. I might be branded a crook whether I steal an apple or a fortune, whether I avoid a tax or ruin ten careers for personal gain.

Sometimes what we say is just confusing or inconsistent. Upon hearing that the National Football League planned to begin scrambling telecasts of its games, the owner of a Pacific Beach (Calif.) sports bar that gets lots of Sunday football game business said, "Without the NFL, there's no way around it, we may have to close." What did he mean? "There's no way around it" suggests they will *have to* close, but then what do we make of the word *may*? Undoubtedly the owner could clarify if we asked him. His misstatement is probably just a result of speaking spontaneously and emphatically to a reporter from the *Los Angeles Times*. Still, the point is that for more effective communication of your views or your reasoning, mental alertness — paying attention to what you say — will often enable you to recognize that you have misstated so you can clarify or restate, and will often add a tone of intelligent discourse to your comments.

Sometimes distinctions and qualifications are needed on claims like these:

"Killing is wrong."

"Small cities don't have the money to support a major city library or museum."

"The communities with the highest per-capita income have the best school systems."

Killing is wrong under which circumstances? Under all circumstances? Does that mean the killing of humans? Do you include capital punishment? Don't *any* small cities have the money to support a major library or museum? Are there no good schools in less affluent communities? A careful rewording of the statements will make each more precise and less subject to misunderstanding. In each case, the basic clarifying question is: Are there exceptions? How inclusive is the claim intended to be? The problem of generalizations is considered in the next section.

CLARIFY GENERALIZATIONS

We often generalize. Much of the reasoning that produces generalizations is strong and compels us to consider seriously, and sometimes act on, the general conclusion. We have learned, however, that we are supposed to be very cautious when accepting generalizations. What is the basis for such a special caution? The answer is that, while generalizations are not objectionable in themselves, problems arise when we fail to distinguish between generalizations and universal statements.

"Don't generalize!" Most of us have given, received, or heard this warning. Most often the warning is meant to discourage stereotyping and similar grouping of all people of a certain sort. Generalizing, it would seem, is one of the greatest sins a thinker can commit. **Generalization** is not, however, primarily an enemy of rational thought. It is an ability without which there would be no rational thought. We generalize each time we make observations of a particular kind, then expect that such observations could readily be applied to wider experience. The ability to categorize on the basis of similarities is part of what makes us intelligent beings. How is it, then, that the words *generalize* and *generalization* have taken on such negative connotations?

Statements that we call generalizations present claims that are intended to be *generally* true. That is, the claim is expected to be true in most cases of that kind. These generalizations are usually based on experience. "Summer is warmer than winter" is a generalization that holds true on most days. "Behaviors that are rewarded get repeated," psychologists tell us. Does this mean that there are no exceptions to this claim? No. The claim is intended only as a *general* claim. If you were to approach a psychologist who had made such a remark, deriding her because you knew of a case in which a rewarded behavior was not repeated, she would tell you that there was no intention to suggest that the generalization held in all cases. You simply misunderstood, you would be told.

Universal statements are statements that are general in the sense that they refer to many individual cases. However, universal statements are *intended* to apply in all cases. "Three-month-old babies cannot walk." There are no exceptions to this general claim, and this was recognized when the claim was made. It is a universal statement. A practical difficulty arises because the grammar of generalizations and of universal statements is often identical. You can't always tell the difference between them merely by hearing or reading them. Thus, when we say, "Rewarded behavior gets repeated," the generalization can be mistaken for a universal statement.

Generalizations are so often perceived as dangerous because they are easily mistaken for universal statements. In fact, when we condemn "generalizations," we are usually rejecting unwarranted universal statements. We actually find ourselves calling universal statements generalizations. Hence we warn people not to generalize. After all, one simple counterexample (a case in which the general claim is not true) is sufficient to disprove the claim. It is *overgeneralization* that we have been warned about. If our generalization has been mistaken for a universal statement, we say, "It's *only* a generalization!"

Sometimes, indeed, we really can't tell whether a particular statement was intended as a generalization that allows for exceptions or as a universal statement that doesn't. Think about the following statement. "Social revolutions — uprisings of the people against their rulers — do not come when conditions of oppression are actually at their worst; they come after conditions have begun to improve. It is then that the people finally see the possibility of something better." Upon hearing or reading that claim, having in mind a historical instance in which this was not true, you may be tempted to disagree with the statement. Whether you have grounds for objection will depend, for one thing, on the statement's intended function as either a generalization or a universal statement. The same wording can be used in both cases.

Dicto simpliciter is a Latin name (meaning "simple saying") for the mistake we make when we apply a true generalization inappropriately in a particular case. In other words, we treat the generalization as if it were a universal statement (or at least as if it were intended to have too extensive a range of application). If, despite Uncle Harry's serious heart condition and the physician's warning to engage in no strenuous exercise, we insist that Uncle Harry should jog "because jogging is good, healthy exercise," our error is that of *dicto simpliciter*. The true generalization is here applied to an exception, an instance in which it does not hold true. Similarly, if five-year-old Andrea says, when asked by her aunt what she will do this weekend, "I'm going to the surprise birthday party for you," her confusion between a generalization and a universal statement may explain why she gave away the secret. "Children are supposed to tell the truth when their aunt asks something, aren't they, Mom?"

Universal statements or generalizations that can be mistaken for universal statements must be used with caution. Remember that universal statements can be disproven with a single counterexample. If a statement is intended as a generalization but might be mistaken for a universal statement, unnecessary and distracting attention to that statement is invited. Evidence that *should* be accepted might not be. Even if you settle the issue after some discussion, getting back on track with the entire original argument may be difficult. On the other hand, if a statement is intended as a universal statement but might be mistaken for a generalization, it is possible for it to be accepted when it should be challenged. Further, this confusion could weaken the overall strength of the reasoning, because the generalization would probably not offer as much evidence for the conclusions.

In conversation, ask for clarification when you don't know whether a generalization or a universal statement was intended. In your reading, at least recognize those statements that might have been intended differently than you were inclined to read them at first sight.

DEFINE TERMS

"Define your terms." This is the traditional wording of the demand that a person announce the way in which certain important words or phrases are being used. This demand, or a less abrupt and more specific version of it, is issued less frequently than it should be. People have argued for hours without realizing that each of them was using one or more key expressions differently. With attention to the need for definition, they might have saved both time and temper and made more progress in reasoning together. The task of formulating that definition, of course, is not always easy, but it will save you frustration in the long run.

First, it is necessary to identify vague expressions and to agree on one definition. Next, it is sometimes necessary to assess the adequacy of the definition.

Identifying Terms to Be Defined

In an exchange of reasoning, precision and effective communication may require more than careful word choice by each person. Even when a person has been reasonably attentive to the wording of his or her comments, misunderstanding can arise. Words or phrases that are central to the discussion may be used in different ways by different people. In such cases, those terms must be defined in order for everyone to be on "the same track."

In a discussion of communism, for example, one person may be arguing *against* a communism that would be defined as "any totalitarian political system in which Karl Marx is cited as a founder of the political philosophy." Another person may be arguing *for* a communism that would be defined as "any political system in which wealth and privilege are generally evenly distributed." Since these are different issues each of which is worthy of our attention, evidence to support one view may not be relevant to the issue on the other person's mind. If these people do not notice that the term is being used differently — and this happens often — they may spend unnecessary time and experience unnecessary frustration trying to make their points and come to an agreement. This will hamper their communication until someone feels the need to ask, "What do *you* mean by 'communism'?"

Only in rare conversations does each person know the other's mind so well that there is no need to come to an explicit agreement on the meaning of a term like *communism*. Discussions of the existence of God also may suffer from a failure to recognize the need for definition. Topics like "just" wars, spying, and education may produce confused exchanges because of a failure to ask, "What do *you* mean by . . . ?"

The need to agree on a definition is usually not limited to the term that identifies the central issue, however. A discussion of any of the topics mentioned in the last paragraph could easily involve the use of other expressions for which a person might not think to ask for clarification.

Central Issue	Related Terms That May Require Definition
Communism	Freedom
	Labor
	Workers
God	Faith
	Destiny
	Evil
	Love
"Just" wars	Aggression
	Self-defense
	Peace
	Security
Spying	National security
	The national interest
	Loyalty
Education	Good teacher
	The student's full potential
	Well-rounded person
	Basic skills

This is only a sampling of terms that might be used differently by different people. These terms are not usually multiple-meaning (ambiguous) expressions with specific but very different meanings. They are simply so general that the variation in their use may easily affect the strength of an argument.

When you are presenting your own reasoning, you should do your best to recognize terms that require definition and to specify your meaning before misunderstanding arises. When you are following someone else's reasoning, you should do your best to recognize such terms, and you should not hesitate to seek clarification when this is desirable.

Assessing the Definitions

The need for each person to use the same definition is clear. However, a "correct" definition is not always crucial to the argument. Consider, for example, the two conceptions of communism that were presented in the preceding section of the text. It is worth discussing the merits and shortcomings of "totalitarian political systems in which Karl Marx is cited as a founder of the political philosophy." It is also worth discussing the merits and shortcomings of "political systems in which wealth and privilege are generally evenly distributed." Here, it is more important that we carry on a clear and reasonable discussion than that we are "right."

In other cases, certainly, the accuracy of the definition we agree on is very important. If, for example, we are discussing "whether it is possible that the free press in the United States has, in any sense, undermined the democratic principles of the nation," we must be careful to define *free press* in a way that accurately describes the status of the press in this country.

An accurate definition is neither too broad nor too narrow. A definition is too broad when it includes items to which the term being defined does not apply — it includes too much. Consider an attempt to define the term *professor*: "A professor is a teacher." This definition is too broad. It includes kindergarten instructors and high-school teachers. Here is another definition: "A professor is a person who has acquired extensive knowledge in at least one area." This definition is too broad also. It includes physicians, architects, horse trainers, and watchmakers. Even if we combine those two definitions ("A professor is a teacher who has acquired extensive knowledge in at least one area"), the resulting definition remains too broad. Many precollege teachers have in fact acquired extensive knowledge in at least one area.

A definition is too narrow when it excludes items to which the term being defined does really apply — it includes too little. The following definition is too narrow: "A professor is a person who has an advanced degree and teaches at a college or university." It excludes those people who have been honored with professorships on the basis of nonacademic expertise; although most professors have advanced degrees, not all do. An accurate definition is neither too broad nor too narrow. It neither includes nor excludes too much.

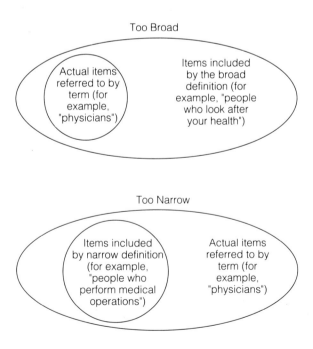

Too Broad

Actual items referred to by term (for example, "physicians")

Items included by the broad definition (for example, "people who look after your health")

Too Narrow

Items included by narrow definition (for example, "people who perform medical operations")

Actual items referred to by term (for example, "physicians")

Some definitions are *both* too broad and too narrow. These definitions include items that should not be included and exclude items that should not be excluded. If we were to hastily define *dictator* as "a cruel political leader,"

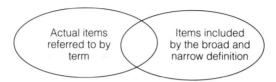

our definition would be both too broad and too narrow. It would incorrectly exclude benevolent dictators who may not be cruel, and it would incorrectly include political leaders who are cruel but who are not dictators.

Accurate definitions are often difficult to produce. In some cases, they may be *impossible* to produce because of the variety of items to which the term may apply and because of irregularities in the common usage of the term.

PRACTICE ACTIVITIES

Set 3.1 *Rewrite these sentences, making them more precise. Create the specifics from your imagination. Then rewrite the sentences in another way, again making them more precise than the text's original sentences. This time, however, make them suggest something different from what you did in your first rewrite.*

1. It was such a nice wedding.

2. He's a good storyteller.

3. She's in poor health.

4. This newspaper is not worth the paper it's printed on.

5. I like the way the bartender handled himself when the customer threw her drink in his face.

6. A good time was had by all.

7. She has just the right qualities to be a good salesperson.

8. I'll tell you, as a realtor, that this is the best deal on a house purchase that you'll find.

9. Jimmy Carter was the best president we ever had.

10. Jimmy Carter was the worst president we ever had.

11. Clergymen just don't make good politicians.

12. We appreciate your applying for the job, but you're just not the right person for the job.

13. Money isn't everything.

14. That's not the way to talk to someone who is just trying to help you.

15. In some ways he's a good teacher and in some ways he's a poor teacher.

16. That was a boring baseball game.

17. That painting is beautiful.

18. I'm a reasonably good tennis player.

19. Professional sports in this country are a national embarrassment.

20. It's not possible to be honest and to be a successful politician.

21. From the Associated Press, in a report on the Mexican earthquake of 1985:

    Every increase of one number on the [Richter] scale means that ground motion is 10 times greater. A magnitude of 8 indicates a great earthquake.

Set 3.2 *Write a one-page defense of any point of view on an issue of your choice. Be precise and specific. Read it to someone else, then answer three questions of clarification or information that the hearer asks you. Take your time as you answer, avoiding sentence fragments, vague expressions, and filler words. Ask the hearer to assess your answers according to those criteria.*

Set 3.3

1. Write eight statements, four of which should be clearly recognizable as universal statements and four of which should be clearly recognizable as generalizations that allow for exception.

2. For each of the following claims, say whether it seems to have been intended as a generalization or as a universal statement, or whether it might reasonably be understood in either way.

   a. For many scholars, pronounced differences in language represent significant cultural differences.
      —Patrick R. McNaughton, "Is There History in Horizontal Masks?" *African Arts*, April 1991.

individ.

universal

Some =
generalization

b. Like all products of a committee, the recent report presented to New York's commissioner of education, Thomas Sobol, is for the most part banal, bland, and leadenly written.

—"Mr. Sobol's Planet," *The New Republic*, July 15 & 22, 1991.

generalization
(= some)

c. To <u>many</u> investors, Japan's economy looks as solid as a rock, and American investment money has been pouring into Japan.

—Neland D. Nobel, "Japanese Economy Teetering," *The New American*, July 16, 1991.

not all
generalization

d. Americans believe that government is too big, too wasteful, and has too much power.

—James Q. Wilson, author of *Bureaucracy* (Basic Books), quoted in *UCLA Management*, Fall 1990.

gener.

e. When observers seek a prognosis on the future of African politics, they take Kenya's pulse.

—Patricia Stamp, "The Politics of Dissent in Kenya," *Current History*, May 1991.

generalization
(did everyone really?)

f. Everyone wanted autographs and the players were resigned to the ritual.

—Trent Frayne, "Summer Magic," *Macleans*, July 8, 1991, describing the scene in the crowded lobby of the Bonaventure Hilton Hotel before the 53rd Major League All-Star game in Montreal.

general'z.

g. In recent months, conservatives have been celebrating the feats of computer technology in war.

—Irwin M. Stelzer, "The Shape of Things to Come," *National Review*, July 8, 1991.

h. Stockbrokers are notorious for using everything from tide tables to football games to make market prognostications.

—Trent Frayne, "Summer Magic," *Macleans*, July 8, 1991.

universal

i. Every great advance, every profound insight in the sciences and other intellectual disciplines, has torn down barriers and distinctions between those disciplines.

—Frederick Turner, "Design for a New Academy," *Harper's*, September 1986.

j. . . . it is precisely *values* that our education system lacks.

—Frederick Turner, "Design for a New Academy," *Harper's*, September 1986.

generalization

k. Modern life is so complex that politicians must often feel like generalists in a specialists' world.

—John Cole, "Pay's Role," *New Statesman & Society*, June 14, 1991.

general.

l. Nations, no less than individuals, are often negligent of their blessings.
—Pico Iyer, "An American Optimist," *Time*, July 22, 1991.

general?.

m. Generally speaking, all breeds and varieties of poultry that are raised as a hobby, wholly for their ornamental or aesthetic value, fall into this ["Fancy"] group.
—John Taylor, *Backyard Poultry Keeping*, 1976.

general.

n. Normal science . . . often suppresses fundamental novelties because they are necessarily subversive of its basic commitments.
—Thomas S. Kuhn, *The Structure of Scientific Revolutions*, 1962.

universal

o. No nation's security has ever been guaranteed or even significantly enhanced by arms control.
—George F. Will, *Newsweek*, August 16, 1986.

gener.

p. Barring exceptions, temples are chiefly distinguished by "order," Doric or Ionic.
—M. I. Finley, *The Ancient Greeks*, 1964.

universal

q. The history of all hitherto existing society is the history of class struggles.
—Karl Marx and Friedrich Engels, *Manifesto of the Communist Party*, January 1848.

r. It is impossible to escape the impression that people commonly use false standards of measurement—that they seek power, success and wealth for themselves and admire them in others, and that they underestimate what is of true value in life.
—Sigmund Freud, *Civilization and Its Discontents*, 1930.

3. Find in print (newspapers, magazines, books, or pamphlets, for example) four examples of statements that were clearly intended as universal statements, four that were clearly intended as generalizations, and some that are difficult to determine.

Set 3.4

1. Is the proposed definition too broad or too narrow? Why?

B
a. Terrorist: A person who engages in acts of aggression.

N
b. Journalist: A person who writes articles for magazines.

B
c. Anger: A very strong emotion.

N
d. Government official: An advisor to the president of the United States.

N **e.** U.S. senator: A member of Congress.

N **f.** Science: The study of biology, chemistry, or physics.

N **g.** Illegal aliens: Noncitizens who are living in the United States.

N̶ **h.** Drugs: Illegal substances that chemically affect the body.

N **i.** Bribery: An attempt to obtain money or other gain illegally.

  j. Blackmail: An attempt to obtain money from someone by threat.

N **k.** Priest: A clergyman of the Roman Catholic church.

N B̶ **l.** Saint: Someone who does good deeds.

N **m.** Exports: Manufactured items that are sent out of the country for sale.

N **n.** Civil war: An armed struggle between factions within one nation, (with neither group having a legitimate claim to authority.)

B **o.** King: The supreme ruler of a nation.

B **p.** Computer: An electronic device for manipulating information.

B **q.** Mayor: An important person in a city.

  r. Republican (politician): A conservative politician who favors increased defense budgets and decreased federal welfare budgets.

B̶ **s.** Famine: Food shortage.

B N̶ **t.** Prison: A place to incarcerate those who are charged with or convicted of crimes.

2. Find in a full-size dictionary some definitions that seem to you to be too broad or too narrow. Explain in each case why the definition is too broad or too narrow by identifying what has been inappropriately included or excluded. (Be rigorous in your thought but not picky.)

3. For each of the following expressions, construct the most accurate definition you can.
   a. spy
   b. traitor
   c. terrorist
   d. patriot
   e. genius

f. war

g. saint

h. homosexual

i. family

j. democracy

k. immigration

l. executive

m. religion

n. citizen

o. private enterprise

p. remedial education

q. illiteracy

r. wisdom

s. progress

t. the military

For Further Reading

Fogelin, Robert J., and Walter Sinnott-Armstrong. *Understanding Arguments*. New York: Harcourt Brace Jovanovich, 1990.

A textbook that begins with a distinctive focus on rhetoric.

Moore, Brooke Noel, and Richard Parker. *Critical Thinking*. 3rd ed. Mountain View, CA: Mayfield, 1992.

A textbook with a good section (Chapter 2) on clarity.

FOUR

Presenting Orderly Thoughts

It's the old story of the drunken monkey. All of his attention is wrapped around the little object in front of him. He picks it up and turns it over. He looks and looks with wide eyes. For him nothing else exists in the world. Then, all of a sudden, a bright light shines at him. The monkey looks up. Even as he drops the object in his hand, he has forgotten it. His attention is captivated by the light. It's all that exists in the world for him. He steps toward it, shielding his eyes, and vaguely but intensely wonders what that brightness is all about. The little object of such recent interest is history. Then a bell rings loudly from behind him. The monkey turns and can think only of the bell. Light and object are history, perhaps never to be recalled.

Is your mind sometimes like this drunken monkey? You focus on what's being said, you follow the line of reasoning, until you are imposed on by a loosely associated idea, or until the conversation or written material you're following shifts subtly but abruptly. You don't notice (or hardly notice) the shift, and now you are "following" attentively, but you couldn't retrace those steps and recall how one point related to the other.

If you don't often host that drunken monkey, you're exceptional. Most of us need to recognize sidetracks in our thinking and keep track of the sequence of our main ideas when we try to think an idea through and communicate it. In addition to that, we often need to keep an eye on other people's monkeys!

AVOID SIDETRACKS

Like the "side track" that runs alongside the main track at a railroad station, sidetracks in thinking may lead to destinations different from the originally intended ones. Sometimes we purposefully lead someone off track. Sometimes we are purposely led off track. Often, however, the shift is only a result of sloppy thinking; no one has actually intended to mislead the process of clear reasoning. The result, however, is the same. We are not resolving the issue *because someone has simply lost track of the issue.*

When you get personal (see Chapter 2), the whole topic shifts from the issue to the person. When you go off on a sidetrack, you are still dealing with the same overall issue, but a shift of focus has confused the issue.

Setting Up a Straw Man

"That's not what I said!" he scolds. He is frustrated that you have distorted his message. You may be embarrassed. You may be angry. You may be defensive. It is, however, quite a common fact of discourse. Sometimes our messages get twisted.

When people are taking sides in conversational debate, misrepresentation of another person's position or reasoning is not uncommon. Sometimes this is done purposely. Another cause is careless listening. Someone responds not to the actual position or reasoning of the other person but to a different, though similar, position or sequence of reasoning. That is what happens in the following example.

EXAMPLE

Dr. Turanos, noted child psychologist, is appearing as a guest on a television talk show that is hosted by a flashy but grating interviewer. Dr. Turanos opens by commenting that "children in our society should be allowed significantly greater latitude in evaluating alternatives and making their own decisions, at least in many areas." The talk show host narrows his eyes, smiling slightly as he looks at Dr. Turanos. Then he turns to the camera and studio audience, shaking his head from side to side. "I thought I had heard it all. Today's guest offers the outlandish suggestion that children be deprived of parental guidance and be allowed to make all of their own decisions. This 'expert opinion' certainly defies the common sense of most of us." ∎

The position that is under attack by the sarcastic talk show host—that children be given neither guidance nor limits in making decisions—is not the position of Dr. Turanos, who has suggested only that children be given somewhat more say in matters that concern them. How much more? He is not precise. But he has claimed neither that children should be wholly without controls nor that this freedom should extend to all decisions that a child might want to make. Presumably, Dr. Turanos will correct his host if given a chance.

In the preceding example, if some viewers in the television and studio audiences were not sufficiently attentive, they might indeed mistake the host's **straw man** position for the one actually presented in the first place. They would then be mistaking a counterfeit for the real thing, just as a scarecrow—a "straw man"—is a counterfeit that is sometimes mistaken for the real thing—a person—by hungry crows in the field.

Sometimes, surprisingly, such a misrepresentation can fool someone concerning his or her own stand! Consider whether this has ever happened to you. You are defending one view on an issue, but your friend has a different view. You discuss the issue, exchanging defenses of the favored view and attacks on the opposed view. At some point, you realize that the discussion has shifted. The view your friend is now attacking is not the view that you had been supporting at the beginning of the discussion. It seems, however, that, not having noticed the subtle shift yourself, you have been actually defending this manufactured view in which you do not really believe. You are arguing for a position you would normally reject, simply because the "straw man" version of your own view took you in. In your determination to outargue the friend, your thinking became muddled. When the friend made the shift, you should have said, "But that isn't what I've said." Instead, this shift slid right by you. Most of us can reluctantly remember occasions when we have, in this way, been victims of our own carelessness or argumentative natures.

Notice that the "straw man," whether presented intentionally or not, misleads us when the counterfeit view is similar to the original, though different in some significant way. If the two were not somewhat similar, we would not mistake one for the other. Usually, however, the counterfeit is more vulnerable to a logical or factual attack than the original.

Pursuing a Tangent

Sometimes we get off the track of the conversation by shifting the focus to a topic that is not directly related to the discussion. This is known as **pursuing a tangent**. When someone notices such a shift in focus, this comment is often made: "He's gone off on a tangent." This means that, although the person who has made the shift is neither attacking the person nor misrepresenting what the person has said, he has shifted his comments to a different topic. Like the setting up of a straw man, this shift may go unnoticed by the listener or even the speaker. In writing, it may go unnoticed by the reader or even the writer. Here is an example:

EXAMPLE

Tracy and her mother are discussing whether it would be reasonable for the sixteen-year-old to spend all of her savings on a car. If she had a car, she wouldn't have to take the bus to work after school. This would, in the end, save time so she could get her homework done and get into bed at a more reasonable time than she does now.

Tracy and her mother stay on the topic for about twenty minutes. In that time, they discuss insurance rates, maintenance costs, and the problem of where the car could be parked safely at night. (They live in a dangerous neighborhood.)

Then, with a reflective gaze and a half-smile, Tracy's mother muses, "You know, your Dad used to park his old Chevy in a different place each night when we lived at South Side. I used to ask him why he did that, but I never could get a straight answer."

Tracy then says, "Dad is generally pretty secretive, isn't he — even with you? He hardly ever explains how he feels or why he does things."

"Yes, he is. But I never realized that you noticed. Actually, you notice a lot about the way Dad and I interact, don't you?"

And the conversation continues, winding along its unpredictable way. ∎

It's fine that Tracy and her mother are getting a chance to talk about the family. Sometimes a rambling conversation is very pleasurable, and even productive. If it is not necessary for Tracy and her mother to settle the car issue right now, there is no harm in the shift. Only if, for some reason, it were important that they come to a decision without delay would their lack of focus pose a problem. That kind of situation is found in the following example.

EXAMPLE

Mark hadn't wanted to take the statistics course in the first place. Now it seems to him that his concerns had been justified. Although he was good at math and had no problems with the statistics course until the past few weeks, his concern is increasing day by day. He can correctly perform any of the five "t-tests," but he is very often unable to determine which "t-test" to use for a particular statistics problem. Hypothesis testing also frustrates him. Tomorrow is the last day he can drop out of the course and he is tempted to do it.

Eric is visiting Mark tonight. Although he doesn't expect to teach Mark both skills in this one evening, he is hoping to convince him that there is a very good chance that he can master these skills in time for the test next week. Mark would certainly like to be convinced.

Mark and Eric have been looking at statistics problems for only a half hour when Eric comments that Mark should use the library's computer program that was designed to teach these skills.

"Is the software for IBM or Apple computers?" Mark asks.

"IBM."

"That's convenient for me," Mark responds. "By the way, have you read about the new IBM machine that's coming out?"

"Yes, I just found out about it today. It's supposed to be able to . . ."

The conversation goes on until Eric notices the time and apologetically insists that he must leave.   ■

Pursuing a tangent *has* posed a problem in this case. Mark needs to determine whether it is likely that he would be able to pass next week's test. Tomorrow is the last day to drop the course. The half hour spent before

---

The activity of "going on a tangent" can be conceived in a visual way by thinking about the meaning of *tangent* in geometry. In this sense, the straight line in the following figure is considered a tangent to (touching at one point) the circle.

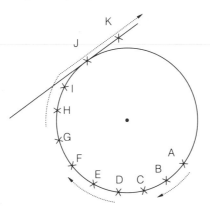

Now, if we think of the center of the circle as the topic under discussion, then points A through J can be viewed as the comments that, in the course of the discussion, relate to (or "center on") the topic. At a certain point, however (in this figure it is at point J), a comment that *does* relate to the topic is pursued in a way that is now irrelevant to that original topic. Someone has gone off (or "flown off") on a tangent.

Mark's ominous phrase, "by the way," was insufficient. He regrets having pursued that tangent for so long.

Pursuing a tangent also generates problems in the following two situations. First, it can create a problem when the person who is pursuing the tangent is supposed to be presenting essential information. Consider, for example, the math teacher who, instead of explaining that confusing point of calculus, tells how he is "reminded of the time when . . ." and proceeds to relate a long personal anecdote. Second, pursuing a tangent presents a problem when, in a dispute, someone evades the issue by changing the subject subtly. When this happens, the other person may feel frustrated in his or her attempt to develop a continuous line of reasoning or may even fail to notice the shift (as with the straw man), unwittingly getting wrapped up in the discussion of the tangential point.

Shifting Ground

Try to catch a grasshopper. It's not easy because the grasshopper won't stay in one place and because it jumps so quickly from one position to another.

Sometimes we get off track "by shifting ground." Like the grasshopper, we won't stay in one position. The sidetrack of **shifting ground** appears when the reasoner changes her or his own position without acknowledging that any shift whatsoever has taken place.

When we shift ground, we do something similar to the setting up of a straw man. However, rather than misrepresenting another person's view or failing to notice that this person has misinterpreted our own view, we initiate a misinterpretation of what we have already said (or written).

Very often such a shift takes place when the reasoner recognizes a weakness in the position or reasoning that she or he has already presented. Still, as with setting up a straw man, this can be the result of mere inattention. Here is an example of the sidetrack of shifting ground.

EXAMPLE

Upset by the grade report he has just received, showing his marks for the previous semester, Samuel complains about grading in general.

"There shouldn't be any grades," he laments. "If learning is our purpose here, and grades — which don't always show how much you learned — are so overemphasized that they become almost our sole focus, what's the point?"

Although Leila understands Samuel's frustration, she is not one to stifle her own comment when she sees another side to the issue.

"Well, it's true," concedes Leila. "Grades are overemphasized. Many students are more concerned with their grades than with what they learn in a class. Many *teachers*, knowing that grades are important to students, stick tightly to a schedule so that all the intended material can be covered. They pass up those opportunities to pursue a topic in depth if the digression is not scheduled and won't be 'testable.' Still, it wouldn't be such a good idea to eliminate grades altogether. Students *need* feedback. It's useful to know how well you have mastered the material. Sometimes you don't know it as well as you think you do. It would be foolish not to have a way to communicate the student's degree of success."

Leila's comments seem reasonable to Samuel. "Well, of course you need to be able to do that. I'm not saying that all grading should be abolished. My point is that a different system of grading should be used—one that avoids the problems of the system we use now. That's all I'm saying!" ∎

It seems that Samuel's game is "catch me if you can." His stated position—"there shouldn't be any grades"—is criticized, and he shifts ground to a different position—"a different system of grading should be used"—as if this were nothing more than the point he had originally intended. Perhaps Leila's criticism of this position will occasion another shift. How frustrating this must be for Leila! There is nothing wrong with changing your mind. The admirable characteristic of open-mindedness often dictates such a move. The *unacknowledged* shifts are the ones that threaten—and sometimes kill—progress in evaluating the subject under consideration. We must be willing, when appropriate, to concede that our own previous position was too extreme and that it must be modified or that we were simply wrong.

RECOGNIZE ARGUMENTS

Almost all of us are good thinkers most of the time. The conclusions we draw need not be constantly revised. Still, we occasionally offer or accept reasoning that should not convince. We sense, on some of these occasions, that the reasoning is somehow faulty. However, if we do not feel confidence in our own abilities to scrutinize the reasoning and locate the step that causes the feeling of uneasiness, we are left with impressions and emotions, rather than a reliable pattern of thinking. To help you organize your thoughts so they can be easily understood and evaluated, you might find it helpful to distinguish between persuasive or argumentative discourse and other kinds of discourse — between "evidence-giving" and other uses of language.

Persuading versus Informing and Explaining

Sometimes we use language, as we speak or write, to convey information. At other times we use language to persuade. Certainly the task of informing is often an important part of the task of persuading. Still, we can distinguish between these two general functions. We most often wonder about questionable "reasoning" when the attempt is to persuade.

The press secretary to the president of the United States, as he describes to the press corps a typical day for the president, may begin by saying "The president awakens at 5:30 A.M. and, during a brief 6:00 meeting, is updated on crucial national and international affairs by his top aides. At 6:20 he breakfasts with . . ." If the press secretary continues in this manner, we can see that he is informing rather than attempting to persuade. Now, it is certainly possible that under the guise of informing, he is hoping also to persuade us of something — perhaps that the president is a conscientious, hard-working person. However, the secretary's task can still be identified as primarily, or at least formally, one of informing.

When someone gives *reasons* for believing something, apparently hoping that another person will come to the same conclusion by considering those reasons, the discourse is geared toward persuasion. When the political campaign manager says, "You should vote for my candidate because he has experience and is the only honest person who is running for this office," he or she is involved in an attempt to *persuade* the listeners.

A third function of language is explanation.* We can also wonder about questionable reasoning when a person is *explaining why or how* something occurred as it did. For example, your neighbor may explain to you why his day has gone poorly by giving the reason that his horoscope — and thus "the stars" — had determined that things would not go his way today. Consider two more examples. First, your neighbor may explain his failure to land a certain job by offering the reason that his extraordinary qualifications (knowing these qualifications, you find this hard to believe) intimidated the supervisors who were conducting the job interview. Second, your neighbor

---

These three functions often overlap. In addition, other functions of language can be identified. J. L. Austin, for example (in How to Do Things with Words, Harvard University Press, 1962, and elsewhere), describes the "performative" use of language. He observes that when we verbally make a bet or when we pronounce marriage vows we thereby perform an act. Language in such cases is not primarily informative, persuasive, or explanatory.

may explain that his car didn't start because its battery was disconnected. Notice that the neighbor's reasons in these explanations were not offered in order to convince you that he had a bad day, that he didn't get the job, or that the car wouldn't start. The "reasons" were suggested as, in a sense, the cause of those events. We might doubt that these are the actual causes, but he is not offering them as reasons for believing that the events occurred. He expects you to believe that they occurred; he is explaining why they occurred.

In this book we will focus primarily on the "persuasive" kind of reasoning illustrated in the earlier example of the political campaign manager's *reasons for believing* you should vote for that candidate. To convince you that a particular "conclusion" is true (or ought to be accepted and acted on), an "argument" is constructed. These terms will be further explained in the next section.

When we try to be persuasive, we should do our best to be both rational and fair. It's what we would hope for from others, and it's what we owe them as well.

Unfortunately, people are sometimes convinced with poor reasoning. Sometimes this is because they are not listening carefully. Sometimes it is because they are mystified by the reasoning but are embarrassed to admit it because they fear that the reasoning is good and they don't want to appear stupid. Often it is because one of their points of logical vulnerability is being addressed.

We can sometimes be persuasive without good reasoning. We can also have good reasoning without successfully persuading! We will have to consider, then, not only how to reason well but also how to present our position in a fair but effective way. We need to strive for correct *and* persuasive reasoning.

A basic skill, necessary for a fair evaluation of the merit of any persuasive reasoning, is that of identifying the point to be proven and the evidence offered in support of it. This important skill is discussed next.

Conclusions and Premises

You have been giving evidence and drawing conclusions ever since you were a child. Reasoning, silently or aloud, is such a common and defining human activity that we may take it for granted, not working at it hard enough at some times because it comes so easy at other times.

One basic skill of reasoning is the ability to distinguish between the point to be proven—the conclusion—and the evidence that supports it—the premises. When you present your thinking to others, you should clearly identify the premises and the conclusion. When you try to figure out someone else's line of reasoning, a first step is to distinguish between the point to be proven and the evidence offered as support for that point. If this is not done correctly, you will be evaluating a straw man counterfeit of the intended line of reasoning. If you lose sight of this distinction between the point to be proven and the supporting evidence in reasoning that you have constructed on your own, then the danger is that you may be unable to clarify or defend the reasoning adequately.

Before thinking about how to emphasize the main points of your argument by clarifying the connections between your evidence and the points you intend to support, let's consider how evidence and conclusions have to be found *in other people's reasoning*.

The **conclusion**, in someone's attempt to persuade, is the statement that presents the point to be proven. Whether we are reading written material or listening to a friend talk, if the purpose of the communication is persuasion, then we should quickly scan, visually or mentally, for the conclusion. In fact, *we cannot hope to analyze the reasoning unless we can first identify the conclusion*.

If someone stopped you by the side of the road and asked, "Is this the best route to get there?" you would probably respond, "To get *where*?" Similarly, we certainly can't tell if a person's reasoning leads correctly to its destination — the point to be proven — unless we know what the destination is.

Before discussing how to identify the conclusion, we should define two words: **argument** and **premise**. When we consider reasoning, the word *argument* is used to refer to the conclusion and to the statements that present the evidence — the reasons for believing the conclusion. (In this sense of the word, *argument* does not suggest the red faces and white knuckles of dispute, as it does when we speak of "having an argument with Dad.") A statement that presents a reason for believing the conclusion is called a *premise*.

By its name, it would seem that a conclusion should *conclude* an argument — that it should come at the end. Sometimes the conclusion does appear at the end of the argument. Consider, for example, the following reasoning, which ends with the conclusion that "Castro must be a ruthless leader."

> Stalin was a dictator and he was ruthless. Hitler was a dictator and he was ruthless. Castro is a dictator. So he must be a ruthless leader too.

The conclusion is presented after the evidence. There are three premises; they are the first three sentences. The final sentence states the conclusion that the speaker or writer wants you to accept on the basis of the evidence offered. (Notice, however, that the argument is not a good one. Even if the premises are true — and even if the conclusion is true — the truth of the premises is insufficient, taken alone, to *prove* that the conclusion is true.)

This reasoning could, however, be presented differently. For example, the conclusion could be stated before the premises. Consider the following presentation of the same reasoning.

> Castro must be a ruthless leader because he's a dictator. Think about other dictators: Stalin was a dictator and he was ruthless. Hitler was a dictator and *he* was ruthless. Don't you see a connection here?

Here we have the same three premises and the same conclusion. Besides the slightly different wording, the only difference is that the conclusion is presented before the premises.

Another alternative is to offer a conclusion after the beginning but before the end of the argument. Reasons for believing it are now presented both before and after the conclusion. The argument about Castro can now be seen with yet another construction.

> Castro is a dictator, so he must be a ruthless leader. Hitler was a dictator and he was ruthless. Stalin, another dictator, was ruthless as well. It's all so obvious!

Here the conclusion is presented after one premise but before the others. The conclusion, in fact, can appear almost anywhere. This is so in the short argument we have been examining, and it is so in nearly any argument you can imagine. Now, if the conclusion can appear almost anywhere in the argument, and if we cannot analyze the reasoning unless we first locate the conclusion, it is reasonable to ask "How do I find the conclusion in someone's reasoning?"

First, notice that you normally have no trouble determining what someone's point is in everyday conversation. In the process of learning the English language, you have become adept at identifying the main points and — at least generally — following the reasoning. Don't be confused by the use of the special term *conclusion*. You have been identifying conclusions virtually all your life.

Second, you can watch for **conclusion indicators** and **premise indicators**. Although we normally follow arguments easily, on some occasions the flow of the reasoning may not be obvious. Perhaps an unfamiliar and technical topic is being discussed. Perhaps the argument is unusually detailed and complex. Perhaps our emotions are clouding our thoughts. In such circumstances, we may need to think through an argument carefully in order to follow it.

We can often locate a conclusion by finding a conclusion indicator in the argument. A conclusion indicator is a word or phrase that commonly precedes a conclusion. Go back to the three versions of the argument about Castro. In two of them the same word introduces the conclusion that

"Castro must be a ruthless leader." (The exception, notably, is the version in which the conclusion appears first.) The word is *so*. This word is perhaps the most frequently used conclusion indicator in everyday conversation. You should be able to think of other conclusion indicators. Among the most familiar are *therefore, thus,* and *consequently.*

These, however, are not the only conclusion indicators. Other words, such as the seldom used *hence,* also serve as conclusion indicators. There are also phrases that perform this same task of introducing a conclusion. Some examples are *it follows that . . . , we can conclude that . . . ,* and *this proves that . . . .* You may be able to think of many other ways of introducing a conclusion. So do not merely learn the words and phrases mentioned here. Listen carefully to persuasive reasoning when it is presented by people around you. Develop a sense of the variety of ways to signal the arrival of a conclusion.

Premise indicators are also helpful when you are trying to follow someone's reasoning. A premise indicator is a word or phrase that commonly precedes a premise. Most common are the words *because* and *since.* Again, various phrases will also perform the same task. Examples are *due to the fact that . . . , in light of the fact that . . . ,* and *for the following reasons . . . .* Again, you may be able to think of many more.

Now, premise and conclusion indicators can be very helpful when you are trying to follow a line of argumentation. Do not, however, rely mindlessly on them. The English language does not function strictly mechanically, so that a particular word or phrase always has the same meaning or purpose wherever it occurs. As we know, the context of the expression — where it occurs in a sentence or a paragraph, the words around it, and even the occasion and circumstances of the communication — helps us to understand how the expression is being used in each case. This insight applies to premise and conclusion indicators in that many expressions that commonly introduce premises and conclusions sometimes serve other purposes.

Consider, for example, the word *so*. In the sentence "I was so angry," the word indicates intensity, and in the sentence "So far from home was the pup that he had to run for two hours before seeing the familiar front gate of the farm," the word indicates extent. In neither case does the word *so* serve as a conclusion indicator. Similarly, in the sentence "Thus far we have encountered no difficulty," the word *thus* does not function as a conclusion indicator. In the sentence "I've been lonely since you've been gone," the word *since* does not function as a premise indicator.

You must ultimately rely on your own good sense of the intention of the reasoner when you listen or read. Premise and conclusion indicators are a great help, but you must still be able to think through the reasoning. Finally, be aware that sometimes the line of reasoning cannot be clearly detected simply because it was not clear in the mind of the reasoner in the first place.

Now, how difficult is it for other people to clearly identify your conclusions—your points to be proven—and your premises—your evidence? What you have learned about how to follow someone else's reasoning can help you construct clearer arguments of your own. This will be discussed in the next section.

EMPHASIZE YOUR MAIN POINTS

You can help your listener (or readers) follow your reasoning. Be conscious of your shifts between conclusions and their premises. Also be conscious of your shifts between premises that lead to the same conclusion and between different conclusions that you draw as you pursue a continuing line of reasoning. Often the sentences just flow from our mouths in such a cascade of enthusiasm, indignation, or impatience that we hardly keep track of our previous remarks and we hardly anticipate where we will end up. If we don't pay close attention to our own line of argument, we cannot easily help anyone else keep track of it.

For each argument, consider where to place the conclusion. If you want your own argument to be understood easily, consider stating your conclusion at the beginning of your argument. By stating the conclusion at the beginning, you allow the listener or reader to evaluate the relevance and strength of each premise as it is presented. If a person knows the point the premise is intended to support while that premise is being presented, then evaluating the argument may not require a mental *re*construction of the argument. By stating the conclusion late in the argument, you do require the other person to think back through each premise after the point the premises are meant to prove is revealed. (Would you want to bet on the accuracy of the reconstruction?) There will, of course, be exceptions to this general advice.

Actually, you may find that you often help someone keep track of your reasoning best by first stating the conclusion, then offering the premises, and then *restating* the conclusion to avoid the interference of straw men.

Use conclusion indicators and premise indicators to organize your line of reasoning for others. Freely and emphatically employ these indicators to make your ideas as clear as possible.

As we ramble on, presenting our views on abortion, gun control, Middle East politics, or raunchy music, a number of different points might be made and argued for. A person who has kept track of his or her own lines of reasoning can help organize those thoughts by concluding with a brief review of the main points, both premises and conclusions, that highlight that series of remarks. Such a simple restatement of views, or "re-view," should abbreviate the longer discourse that preceded by (1) shortening the sentences as much as possible, and (2) omitting minor points as well as parenthetical comments and tangents. This sort of restatement is called a *paraphrase*.

What are parenthetical comments? Not every statement offered as part of an argument has a role as conclusion or premise. Some of the statements offered might actually be not at all essential to the success of the argument. In looking for the conclusion, we need to recognize such nonessential statements so we can more easily follow the reasoning.

Sometimes statements within an argument are made only parenthetically. In written material, parenthetical remarks may be marked off with parentheses — ( ). The sign (marks the beginning of the statement and the sign) marks the end of the statement. In a spoken argument, we do not have the visual help of these signs. Sometimes in written material, a statement may function parenthetically but still not be signalled by parentheses. We must recognize that such statements are neither conclusions nor premises. The following short argument includes such a statement.

> There's no reason to worry about the party. John has taken care of the refreshments. Ann will have the whole house decorated and ready. And Phil will have party games arranged. Uncle Ed did that last year. Do you remember?

The conclusion is that there is no need to worry about the party. The reasons for believing this rest on the arrangements being made by John, Ann, and Phil. The statement "Uncle Ed did that last year" is only a parenthetical remark. Likewise, the "Do you remember?" is not an essential part of the argument.

When we follow up a parenthetical remark with continued discussion of that or another insufficiently relevant point, we find ourselves pursuing a tangent. In this case, the entire topic of discussion shifts, at least for a while. In the example above, the speaker may go on to talk about Uncle Ed. Such remarks would be neither premises nor conclusions. Similarly, in an effort to prove that American military strength should be increased, the arguer may condemn a lack of moral fiber in the country. A single remark or two of this sort, if insufficiently relevant to the conclusion, may be considered parenthetical. If the remarks continue so that the focus of discussion shifts, then we would consider the speaker to have embarked on the pursuit of a tangent. In either case, such irrelevant remarks should not be considered as part of the argument unless they are really intended as evidence for the conclusion. In that case, the statements would simply fail to present adequate support for the conclusion, thus detracting from the strength of the overall argument.

The concepts of parentheticals and paraphrases will be pursued in Chapter 5's explanation of how to map out your reasoning graphically.

BE AWARE OF UNSTATED CONCLUSIONS AND PREMISES

Sometimes, even when the point of an argument is obvious, no sentence that has been uttered — or written — actually states this conclusion. You may listen or look as carefully as you can, but the statement that presents the conclusion is nowhere to be found.

An unstated conclusion may still be implied or suggested by the premises. In the following example, the conclusion is implied but not actually presented in words.

The murder weapon was found in Cain's possession, and only his fingerprints were on it. He had one of the strongest of motives — revenge. Finally, only he had an opportunity to be alone with the victim. Need I say more?

The conclusion that a listener is intended to draw from these observations is obviously that Cain is guilty of murder. The unstated conclusion is signalled by the statement "Need I say more?" This tells us that there *is* something more that has not been said and suggests that the listener should easily identify the unstated conclusion. Various other phrases might be used to signal the unstated conclusion in this way. For example, consider that the statement "The conclusion, my friend, is obvious" also suggests both that there is an unstated conclusion and that it is obvious.

Often, although the conclusion is unstated, no signalling phrase is offered.

Only three people knew where the map was hidden — Varley, Garth, and Smythe. Now the map is gone, but it had been hidden so well that no one could have found it by mistake. And two of the men — Varley and Garth — have perfect alibis.

If this were from the dialogue of a movie script, we could imagine the speaker and his listener exchanging knowing looks at this point, both having drawn the same conclusion. What clearly follows from these statements, which serve as premises, is that *Smythe took the map*. Although there is no signalling phrase to suggest that we identify the missing conclusion, the point of the speaker's observation is nevertheless obvious.

Premises, as well as conclusions, are sometimes unstated but implied. The unstated premise can be considered to be an *assumption* — it is taken to be true but is not actually offered as part of the argument.

In some cases, the premise is left unstated simply because it is too obvious to mention. This is the case in the following example.

> *Of course* the United States is larger than England. Why, Oklahoma itself is larger than England!

The conclusion is that the United States is larger than England. The single premise states that Oklahoma is larger than England. That premise alone, however, does not establish the conclusion that the United States is larger than England unless we also recognize that Oklahoma is not as large as the United States. The speaker has not, however, offered this as a premise. Should she have done so? Certainly there is no need if she knows that the listener is aware of the fact already. Almost without exception, we can consider this premise to be known if the listener is an American.

One advantage of discourse between persons who have a common culture is that many things go unsaid. We can assume, in most cases, that a fellow American will know that Oklahoma is one of the fifty states in the Union. This is only one example of the information-sharing characteristic of a culture that allows people to reasonably make certain assumptions. We can usually assume also that when we refer to the Super Bowl, most Americans will know already that this is a football game and that football games are played with a somewhat oblong ball. We do not need to supply this information in the form of premises. (The likelihood that this information can be safely assumed goes up or down depending, of course, on which Americans we are addressing.) We can also generally assume that when we refer to the president of the United States, Americans will know that the office of the president is an elective one.

A culture, however, need not be a national group. As the word is being used here, any grouping of people who share significant similarities and information comprises a culture. When one physician, for example, addresses another, certain assumptions about the other's knowledge of technical terms are normally made. The physician need not explain such terms to another physician, although the absence of such an explanation might be foolish when addressing most nonphysicians. If the physician is arguing for a certain stand on a health care issue, certain premises that would be presented in the argument to the nonphysician could be omitted in the argument to the physician.

Of course, there are many such subcultures — information-sharing, often value-sharing communities within a larger culture. They are based on professional groupings, youth movements, and many other commonalities.

Missing premises are notably important when they are contentious — possibly but not obviously true, and thus subject to contention. Such premises are often value judgments or questionable generalizations. It is especially important that we recognize these unstated but essential premises in our own or in another's reasoning. The questionable assumption may be that your own nation must be in the right in a particular international conflict, or that members of a certain minority group or social group will hold a particular position on a certain issue. With unstated assumptions like this, it is necessary to be very aware of our points of logical vulnerability.

When you present your thoughts for another's evaluation, you may certainly omit the quite obvious conclusions and the simply uncontentious premises. Fairness usually demands an explicit statement of the contentious premises. However, sometimes the contentious premise that might be overlooked if left unstated is a spicy one that will draw attention from the rest of the argument. In these cases, you might defer mention of that premise until other aspects of the argument are resolved.

■

PRACTICE ACTIVITIES

Set 4.1 *In each of the following cases, a "sidetrack" occurs. Decide where the shift takes place and determine whether it is a sidetrack that involves setting up a straw man, shifting ground, or pursuing a tangent.*

[handwritten: 2 misrepresent what someone said]

1. Senator Bonds made these remarks on the floor of the U.S. Senate on September 1, 1990, as he decried a proposed tax increase on beer:

   The average price of a six-pack already costs more in taxes than in raw material and labor combined, and state beer tax collections have risen nearly 650 percent since 1950. To me it seems that this screwball proposal will single out one class of Americans who drink beer and say, "You are more responsible for the deficit than anyone else. Therefore, we are going to single you out to lay the tax burden on you."

2. *Rubens:* All successful politicians — in whatever official position — are corrupt. You need to be willing to make moral compromises to get ahead in politics.

   Larkin: What about Mayor Atwood? When you supported him in that letter to the editor last year, you wrote that he had never been involved in dirty dealings and that, as far as you're concerned, he was entirely trustworthy.

Shifting ground (margin note)

Rubens: That may be possible in local politics. In fact, I'm sure that the mayor is a good man. I only said that in big-time national politics, you've got to be corrupt to get ahead.

3. The manager of the college baseball team pulled aside the second baseman. "David, we have just a few minutes before the game. I want to explain what I think you can do to improve your batting and lift you from the slump you're in." David listened.

pursuing a tangent (margin note)

"You have an unusual stance at the plate. I think that if you adjust your stance as I'll suggest, you'll have more success. You know, a lot of professional baseball players have actually done quite well with peculiar batting stances. Smokey Burgess was one. Smokey used to . . ." The tales of stars of the past go on until the manager is interrupted by his coach, who says it's game time.

4. *Steve:* The ancient Greeks made great strides in scientific thinking.

Strawman (margin note)

Lisa: Oh, come on. Just think of the staggering multitude of advances made in the past hundred years: the harnessing of electricity and Einsteinian physics, for example. Don't these sorts of examples prove to you that the Greeks weren't the smartest people in history?

5. During a study break at the college library, Kent mentions his new history course to Paige. "My history course is really going to be difficult. In the first two weeks, we've covered three long chapters in the textbook. There are weekly assignments in addition to four major papers that we'll have to write."

straw man (margin note)

Paige is puzzled. "You told me before that this course was not required for graduation. I don't understand. If you don't like the course, why don't you just drop it?"

6. Professor Scolis says, "Education in the United States is sorely in need of reform. Memorization of facts is still emphasized more than creative and critical thinking skills." Professor Libris responds, "The view you advance with that comment is no better. After all, if the schools required no memorization of facts, students would not be adequately prepared in subjects like math and history."

straw man (margin note)

7. Dear George,

I'm writing to explain more clearly why I felt I had to fire you from your job here at Phantos Corporation last week.

Although no one could seriously fault you for failing to anticipate that the machines would not support the heavier metal casings, our concerns focus on your handling of the immediate results of that mismatch. We on the Executive Review Committee considered three specific courses of action that you might have taken. First, you might have informed Ed Hollings, who, as second vice-president, oversees the acquisition of new materials and the adoption of new processes. He then could have taken the responsibility for continuing the manufacture or he could have informed Andy Levine. I'm sure you haven't heard, as a matter of fact, that Andy went into the hospital for emergency surgery just two days ago. He is in serious condition and perhaps, since you were one of the people he liked best, you could send him a card or call his wife to express your concern. I'm sure that would be greatly appreciated.

It looks like Andy will be off the job for at least two months. We all wish him a speedy and complete recovery. He's a very good man.

Andy's address is Room 306B, Weinraub Memorial Hospital, in Kinsey City.

I'm sorry to send the bad news.

> Regards,
> Jim Leben
> President

8. *Carolyn:* There aren't any places to get a decent education in this part of the state. You have to go outside the area to get quality schooling.

   Sarah: The state university has a very good reputation scholastically.

   Carolyn: Oh, I don't mean State. I mean the smaller local schools.

   Sarah: Well, you know that Patterson College has some excellent programs. They have an archeology program that is better than most at big universities. And their art department is supposed to be excellent.

   Carolyn: I don't mean that every single program is bad. It's just that these schools have a lot of weaker areas, too.

9. After a taste of LaMarr's morning coffee, Jess asks, "Did you do something different when you were making the coffee this morning? It tastes just a bit different."

   "Look," snaps LaMarr, "if you don't like the taste of the coffee, you can just make up a pot for yourself!"

10. Lieutenant Wren, ending a few minutes of quiet reflection, comments earnestly to her husband, "You know, I'm finding that I really respect Major Zeleny." Her husband responds, "I'm glad to hear that. It's certainly important to like the people you work with."

11. Here is an excerpt from a *U.S. News & World Report* interview (September 29, 1986 issue) with Scott Helband, a college admissions officer at Yale from 1982 to 1984.

    Q: Is the essay the most important part of the application?

    A: Because each piece really weaves an application together to portray the fabric of a human being, there isn't one document that is all important.

Set 4.2

1. Which of the following are arguments, and which are not? Any argument here will have a conclusion and at least one premise. Remember that premises are reasons for believing the conclusion. Also remember that not all arguments are good ones. Do not consider any unstated premises or conclusions to be part of an argument in this exercise, and remember the distinction between reasons in an argument and reasons in an explanation.

   a. George F. Will wrote *Men at Work*. Macmillan Publishing Company in New York published the book in 1990.

   b. From the *San Francisco Examiner*, August 8, 1990:

      Recent events in Iraq, Kuwait and Saudi Arabia seem once again to point out how fragile our world really is. And one man . . . has made life truly miserable for tens of thousands of people. Billions of dollars have been lost in the stock market in the past four trading sessions. It's been a truly unreal pounding.

   c. From *The Press Democrat*, Santa Rosa, August 7, 1990:

      The financial leader of a Miami group of investors says he considers his $135 million offer serious even though he has never spoken with the team's principal owner.

   d. From *Improving Writing* by Alan Casty:

      All words are abstractions; that is, all words are mental tools. [Therefore,] They are not the real thing, the item in life itself.

   e. Paraphrase from *Siddhartha* by Hermann Hesse:

      Since all stones are divine and everything divine is worthy of worship, any stone is worthy of worship.

   f. He moved to Detroit because his mother lives there and she needs daily care in her condition.

g. *Conclusion:* You will enjoy this movie. It's a well-done horror story and you love those.

h. *Conclusion* Westminster College is the best small liberal arts college in the state. Their faculty is well prepared and professionally active. Also, the students come in with high scores on college aptitude tests, and most of them are successful in their professions after they graduate.

i. I have three reasons to dislike him: (1) he damaged my reputation unjustly, (2) he was unnecessarily rude to my family, and (3) he refused to repay the money I had lent him.

j. *Conclusion:* He is an inconsiderate person. I have three reasons for believing this: (1) he damaged my reputation unjustly, (2) he was unnecessarily rude to my family, and (3) he refused to repay the money I had lent him.

k. From "Biblical Roots of American Liberty" by Edmund A. Opitz, *The Freeman*, July 1991:

> Religion, at its fundamental level, offers a set of postulates about the universe and [humanity's] place therein, including a theory of human nature, its origin, its potentials, and its destination. Religion deals with the meaning and purpose of life, with man's chief good, and the meaning of right and wrong. Thus, religious axioms and premises provide the basic materials political philosophy works with. The political theorist must assume that men and women are thus and so, before he can figure out what sort of social and legal arrangements provide the fittest habitat for such creatures as we humans are. So, some religion lies at the base of every social order. *indicator*

l. From the same article by Mr. Opitz:

> The central doctrine of the American political system is our belief in the inviolability of the individual man or woman. This is one of the self-evident truths enunciated in the Declaration of Independence: "We hold these Truths to be self-evident, that all Men are created equal, that they are endowed by their Creator with certain unalienable Rights, that among these are Life, Liberty, and the Pursuit of Happiness." The "equality" which is the key idea of the Declaration means "equal justice," the Rule of Law, the same rules for everybody because we are one in our essential humanity. *premise indicator*

m. From "Women in the 1920s Ku Klux Klan Movement" by Kathleen M. Blee, *Feminist Studies*, Spring 1991:

In 1920, women won the right to vote, culminating a sev-
enty-two year struggle for greater access to the political
sphere. Yet, women's politics changed in another way in
the 1920s. When women gained the franchise, the issue
that had united women with different backgrounds and
politics disappeared. Women's political goals and ideo-
logies had grown more diverse even before the ratification
of the Nineteenth Amendment as the separate gender
spheres of the nineteenth century dissolved. The extent of
this diversity became even more clear without the unifying
cause of suffrage. Cleavages of class, race, ethnicity, and
region, constant features of women's politics in the United
States, now increasingly eroded gender unity in political
goals.

n. Part of an address by George Washington to the Continental
Army:

The time is now near at hand which must probably determine whether Americans are to be freemen or slaves;
whether they are to have any property they can call their
own; whether their houses and farms are to be pillaged
and destroyed, and themselves consigned to a state of
wretchedness from which no human efforts will deliver
them. The fate of unborn millions will now depend, under
God, on the courage and conduct of this army. Our cruel
and unrelenting enemy leaves us only the choice of brave
resistance, or the most abject submission. We have, therefore, to resolve to conquer or die. Conclusion *indicator*

o. Attributed to Daniel Webster:

A sense of duty pursues us ever. It is omnipresent, like the
Deity. If we take to ourselves the wings of the morning,
and dwell in the uttermost parts of the sea, duty performed
or duty violated is still with us, for our happiness or our
misery. If we say the darkness shall cover us, in the darkness as in the light our obligations are yet with us.

p. From an article entitled "A Return to the Spirit of '76," *The New
American,* July 2, 1991:

Over the past 50 or 60 years, one of the prime objectives of
liberalism in the U.S. has been systematically to reduce the
majority of citizens to the intellectual level of dependent
children, thus assuring that politicians can play the role of
"Papa" and the welfare state that of "Mama." Liberalism
strives to stultify those under its sway, for only the most

abject ignorance can assure the continued performance of the liberal mode of thought. This is the essence of liberalism.

q. From an article entitled "Are Some Topics Unworthy of Serious Debate Because 'Everybody Knows' What Is True?" *Liberty*, May/June 1991:

Had the German people felt safe to challenge the virulent anti-Semitism of the Third Reich—the prevailing orthodoxy that the Jews were responsible for Germany's problems—it is almost certain that the persecution of the Jews would not have occurred. But the German people were afraid to question what "everybody knew."

conclusion indicator

r. From an article entitled "Religious Freedom Versus Landmark Preservation," *Liberty*, May/June 1991:

Should religious buildings be exempt from historic landmark preservation laws? When property is designated a historic landmark, the owner's right to alter or demolish that property may be severely restricted. Although minor structural changes may be permitted, large-scale renovation projects that transform the building's original character generally are not.

not an argument

Some of the most important architectural treasures in America's cities are houses of worship—churches and synagogues. The limiting of a congregation's right to do as it may wish with such property has led many religious leaders to claim that mandatory landmarking of religious property is a clear interference with the free exercise of religion, and hence a violation of the First Amendment.

argument

2. Return to the passages that you decided were arguments rather than nonarguments in the preceding exercise. Now identify any unstated premises or conclusions you think are implied in these passages.

Set 4.3

In each of the following arguments, find the conclusion. There are no unstated conclusions or premises to watch for. Each of the first ten arguments has at least one premise or conclusion indicator that can help as you try to find the conclusion.

1. That house is too expensive for you, because once you paid the loan you'd have only $250 a month to live on. You have at least that much in monthly bills now. On top of this, your job is not very secure.

2. No one can predict political events with consistent reliability because there are simply too many situational variables. Besides, although statistics can help us to generalize, humans are notoriously unpredictable as individuals.

3. The other contending teams in the American League West will not be much improved next year, so the Oakland A's are likely to win the division again, since they are likely to be even stronger than they were this year. And this year they won the division easily.

4. I don't like math, so I'm sure there's no way I could pass that math course even if I did register for it. It's supposed to be a very difficult course, and from what I hear, the instructor is just about no help at all!

5. My roommate is moving out. Consequently, I will have to move out as well. I can barely pay my present portion of the rent.

6. No priests are dishonest, but many of them are intelligent. Therefore, there are at least some intelligent people who aren't dishonest.

7. Mr. Allison must be in charge today because whenever Ms. Wilkinson is out of the office, Mr. Allison is in charge. And she *is* out of the office today.

8. Mike has to take either algebra or statistics next year. Since Mike always takes the course with the shortest textbook and the algebra textbook is shorter, it's clear that he'll be taking the algebra course when next year rolls around.

9. If I pass at least one of my two math courses, Math 12 or Math 15, I will be able to graduate this year. It is certain that I will at least pass Math 12. Thus I will undoubtedly be graduating this year.

10. That bird has a swooping flight pattern so it couldn't be a finch, because finches don't have flight patterns like that.

11. Your talent at commercial art is among the best in the country. The company knows that. Everyone involved in making the hiring decision already likes you. Of course you'll get the job. No one else who is remotely qualified has even applied for it.

12. This will be a good Christmas. Aunt Ann will be visiting us this year, and she's always fun. Betty will be home for Christmas this year. And for once we have enough money to buy everyone a decent present. Besides, the first Christmas in a new house is always exciting.

13. I need a computer. My business accounts are now too complicated to keep organized without a computer. It would help with

the kids' homework. And Susan could use it for word processing in her college classwork.

14. Anger is not productive. Neither are the other hostile emotions such as jealousy and envy. Any nonproductive emotion is to be avoided. Clearly, then, we should try to maintain a sense of serenity and emotional balance in our lives.

15. The YMCA deserves the support of our community. It offers programs for senior citizens. Most of the inexpensive physical education and crafts classes for children are available through the YMCA. It continually offers quality programs on a nonprofit basis.

Set 4.4

1. During a conversation in which you are presenting your own point of view, try paraphrasing for the other person(s) any lengthy reasoning you have offered. Give the paraphrase at the end of your comments. You can introduce the paraphrase by saying, "In other words," "To summarize," "To put it briefly," or by using a similar verbal cue to indicate that you are going to "sum up."

2. During a conversation with divergent points of view, try paraphrasing someone else's reasoning before you respond with your own point of view. You can introduce the paraphrase by saying, for example, "Now, as I understand it, what you're saying is this . . . ."

For Further Reading

Cederblom, Jerry, and David W. Paulson. *Critical Reasoning*. Belmont, CA: Wadsworth, 1991.

A textbook in which chapters 2 and 3 give a good, easy-to-read introduction to premises, conclusions, and argument structure.

Churchill, Robert Paul. *Becoming Logical*. New York: St. Martin's Press, 1990.

Another textbook with a good introduction to premises and conclusions.

C H A P T E R

FIVE

Basic Mapping

When someone asks, "Did you follow my reasoning?" do you often say, "No, I didn't"? If you do, you are an uncommonly honest person regarding this matter. People are often too embarrassed to make such an admission, thinking that this would reveal a lack of intelligence. Most of us know what it is like to nod our heads knowingly while we are sadly lost in tangles of language that sometimes even the speaker isn't really following.

Keeping track of other people's lines of reasoning is sometimes difficult. What's the relation between those last two points? we may wonder. What point is he trying to make now? Which evidence is supposed to support which conclusion? Let me see, what was the point he made a minute ago? And, again, what's the relation between those last several comments?

Often when we *think* we are following the reasoning, we aren't. We may believe ourselves to have followed the reasoning if we have noticed no outrageous claims or sudden shifts of focus. However, to have followed an argument is to have understood the relations between premises and the relations between those premises and their conclusions. If you cannot reconstruct the argument within a premise-and-conclusion structure, then you need to ask for repetition or clarification. Like other skills, your ability to reconstruct or "map" arguments improves with practice.

We are impressed by the person who accurately repeats the reasoning offered by the president of the United States in a televised news conference at which twenty minutes were spent justifying a new policy or recent action. That ability to follow and retain the line of reasoning is perhaps more impressive than the ability to critically evaluate the reasoning. "That's amazing! How do you do that?" we might respond, as if it were an exceptional circus trick.

We are impressed by the person who pursues a detail of the political topic that is under casual discussion at a party, then relates it back to the very point at which the conversation had diverged—after we had entirely forgotten that there was a connection to be made! That person was aware all along of the relation of the side issue to the previous points in the discussion.

Both of these impressive characters have kept track of a long line of reasoning so well that they understood and retained at least the major connections within that line of reasoning. How have they accomplished this? They may hardly be able to explain how they do it because people who are good at this often operate intuitively instead of consciously following fixed rules. They do not have to piece together an argument or explanation in a mechanical way. However, almost anyone can learn to follow someone's reasoning in a self-aware way. This is done by learning how to recognize which statements are intended as *leading to* which other statements, and by learning ways to remember at least the main points in a long line of reasoning.

MAP YOUR OWN REASONING

Very often we don't follow *our own* reasoning. Although that may sound silly, it's true. Occasionally, the series of conclusions and evidence that we have just finished presenting is a maze from which our own memory can't retrieve even the main points and their relations to each other.

You can help yourself keep track of your own reasoning by graphically mapping out that reasoning. One simple way of mapping your reasoning is to draw downward arrows from abbreviations of your premises toward abbreviations of your conclusions.

Although some sorts of reasoning are more easily and productively mapped than others, it's worth learning how to map your reasoning because these maps often help you think through or keep track of an argument. Depending on the situation, you may find it useful to map out some lines of reasoning *before* you present that reasoning to someone else, *after* you have presented it, or even (though this would be rare) *during* your presentation.

By mapping an argument *ahead of time*, you can organize your thoughts for an oral or written presentation that is easy to follow and well thought out. Whether you are addressing the city council, talking to your supervisor at work, writing an editorial for the newspaper, or preparing a college essay, your ideas will be better organized if you have mapped them out ahead of time. Your responses to inquiries will also be less likely to reveal confusion in your own mind, and you may even have been able to predict and "prethink" various criticisms.

By mapping an argument that *you have already presented*, you can review your line of reasoning to determine if it should be changed and you can add other points for the next time you air your thoughts on that subject. Occasionally, you will even be able to scratch out a rough map *as you talk* in an informal setting, helping you to think ahead and structure your argument intelligently.

Each of these tasks can be accomplished at the level of "basic mapping" (examined in this chapter) that charts only the premises and conclusions themselves, or at the level of "evaluative mapping" (covered in Chapter 9) that goes beyond the basic structure of an argument to include an assessment of the reliability of the basic premises and the inferences or "moves" from premise to conclusion. In basic mapping, you display evidence and conclusions; the task is to plan or understand the argument. In evaluative mapping, you also evaluate the reasoning; the task is to decide how much of the reasoning you should accept.

In order to learn the fundamentals of mapping, consider a simple example of how someone might put together a particular line of reasoning. Suppose that one of the very good teachers at your college is in danger of losing her job because of the institution's financial distress, and a committee that is charged with making a recommendation on this issue has agreed to hear some student testimony. You want to convince this committee that this professor is an excellent teacher and should definitely be retained on the teaching staff. You collect your thoughts ahead of time. *Let's see. I know that she received an award for teaching excellence at the college where she previously taught.* You scratch out an abbreviation of this point on a sheet of paper and draw a downward line (on an angle since you expect more ideas to come your way) to the conclusion you intend to establish.

Now you don't have to worry about forgetting that point while you put your mental effort into coming up with some more ideas. *Many of her students go out of their way to take every single course she teaches, and that's only true of the most exceptionally talented teachers in the whole school.* You add these points about her campus "following" by using a plus sign to join their abbreviations and a bracket to further emphasize that these two premises work together.

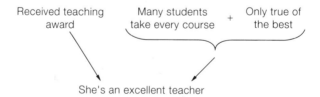

As you speak to the review committee on the teacher's retention, you can use your map for notes or you can recall the map from memory. In either case, the plus and brackets show that this pair of premises constitutes a single point or subargument. You don't want to make a mistake, nervously listing your points by saying, "First, she received a teaching award; second, many students take all her classes; and third, that's true of only a few teachers." This awkwardly suggests that the second and third premises are separate points, when actually the second premise is a persuasive one only when it's considered in light of the third. The two premises thus make up a single reason (related to but separate from the receipt of the teaching award) for believing that she's a good teacher. The plus and brackets remind you not to present the second and third premises as separable.

Now that these points are committed to paper, you can search your mind (or, through conversation or research, others' minds) for additional evidence for your conclusion. Let's say you ask a colleague in that teacher's academic department for ideas, and discover another point you would like to mention. *Over the past eight years, this teacher's students have taken nationally standardized tests in her field, and have an average score that is at the ninety-first percentile. That is, her students consistently score higher than nine out of ten who take the test.* You add this to your map.

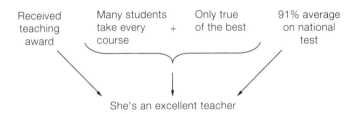

You could continue to build premises onto your map. Some maps are extensive; this one is so short that it may hardly be worth the trouble of constructing it. However, let's stop here for now in order to think about how maps can be useful. You can use the map we've been constructing — or a more extensive version of it — to prethink what you will say at the meeting. "Off-the-top," unprepared presentations, or only vaguely preconsidered ones, often leave the speaker wishing for another chance. You can also use the map to consider ways of recording the points you will present to make the presentation more effective. Is it better to begin by referring to the teaching award or the test results or her popularity with students? Which should you end with? It can help your planning if you have the alternatives actually mapped out on paper, especially if the map is an extensive one. The map can also help you memorize the points you want to make. For many people, a visual element aids learning. If you're not going to try to memorize the points, the map can serve as your notes for the presentation.

A map of your reasoning can also help you organize your thoughts before writing them in a letter to the editor, a school paper, or a memo or other proposal that you prepare at your place of employment. Most newspapers print letters to the editor that are convoluted and confusing, providing us evidence that mapping is a desirable preparation for writing.

As noted earlier, mapping can also help you to evaluate reasoning you have already presented, and it can provide a quick way to keep track of your own points and think ahead as you present impromptu remarks.

Before going on to discuss the mapping of other people's reasoning, let's look again at the plus and brackets that signal a set of premises that function together.

In the map that we created to help our fictional professor, the two premises that were tied together with a plus and brackets were these: (1) Many of her students go out of their way to take every single course she teaches, and (2) That's only true of the most exceptionally talented teachers in the whole school. Notice that the first of these premises creates a strong case for the conclusion only because of the second premise. These two are not separate points, each of which—apart from the other—supports the conclusion. The remaining premises (that she received a teaching award and that her students test well) can be considered relevant and persuasive without references to each other or to the two bracketed premises. Thus, they earn separate arrows showing that they are separable ways to support the conclusion.

Consider a different example. If I were arguing that "you won't get that job" (conclusion) by telling you that, according to the advertisement, "applicants must have their own transportation for making deliveries" (premise) and "you don't have your own transportation" (premise), a map of this reasoning would have to display the plus and brackets indicating that the premises work together. It would look like this.

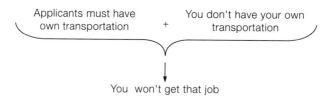

The premises must be joined together on the map because neither premise supports the conclusion unless you consider the other premise. Even if applicants must have their own transportation, that doesn't show that you won't get the job *unless* we also consider the fact that you don't have your own transportation. Now, if we add the premise, "Besides, the boss refuses to hire people as young as you are," the map will look like this.

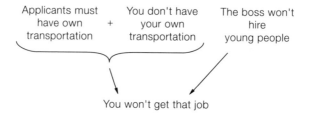

The additional premise would not be connected to the first two by a plus and brackets, although three, four, or more premises are sometimes joined in this way. Here, the additional premise has its own arrow because this reason for believing the conclusion can be assessed without referring to the other two premises. This premise doesn't depend on the other two. The two joined premises require each other in order to make any case at all for the conclusion. Later, in Chapter 9 on evaluative mapping, each arrow will represent another inference to be assessed for logical strength. The strength of one of these arrow-lines of reasoning doesn't depend on the other. That's why they are separate. One might be better support for the conclusion than the other.

Usually you will be able to tell whether premises should share a single arrow and be connected on your map by a plus and brackets. Sometimes it's less clear. For example, if I map out the points I want to make in my job interview, I might support the conclusion "You should hire me" (though I will word it more subtly at the interview) with four reasons: I have experience at a similar job, I have a good educational background for this job, I am young enough to serve your company for many years, and I have leadership skills and potential. Should each premise have its own arrow pointing downward to the conclusion? After all, these reasons are not (at least directly) dependent on each other. You could evaluate one reason without knowing about the others. On the other hand, should all the premises be joined by pluses and one big bracket, since none of these alone would constitute a strong reason for hiring me, but all considered together make the case for hiring me? With several "component" premises that add up to a single line of reasoning, perhaps either map could be correct. The correct mapping depends on whether the arguer *intends* the premises to stand alone or be considered together as one line of reasoning, although in this case the plus-and-bracket option yields a stronger inference than any of the separated inferences would.

MAP OTHER PEOPLE'S REASONING

When you map your own reasoning, you're usually trying to come up with the best reasoning you can. If a premise that you have mapped seems to be a weak one, you can erase it or scratch it out and replace it with a better one. If you are mapping out reasoning that you have already presented, you are just recalling your own points. When you map someone else's reasoning, however, a new problem arises: You sometimes find yourself trying to figure out what that other person intended. Sometimes the conclusion is hard to identify simply because the wording of the argument is unclear. Sometimes you have little idea whether certain premises are to be joined by a plus and bracket, or whether they are meant to stand alone. Sometimes there are unstated but seemingly implied conclusions or premises. Neither mapping nor any other way of following that line of reasoning will clarify all the elements in a confusing line of reasoning.

Nevertheless, it is often worth the effort to map other people's reasoning. You can anticipate someone's remarks to you by mapping out what you expect them to offer you in support of their conclusion. You can map out someone's written or oral comments after they have been presented, so you can consider the ideas and perhaps prepare a written or oral response. Occasionally it will be helpful to map while you hear a formal presentation delivered.

Remember that in mapping reasoning that someone else has offered, you are trying to retrieve *their* patterns of reasoning. You are not mapping in order to show what they could have or should have said. So don't worry if the reasons don't support the conclusion as well as they should. You are mapping their argument, not yours.

In mapping other people's reasoning, you will sometimes find that an important element in the argument, a premise or a conclusion, has been left unstated but is clearly implied. (You may refer back to Chapter 4 to refresh your memory on unstated premises and conclusions.) Be cautious that you don't read into the argument something that wasn't intended. The unstated element can be drawn right on the map, at either end of an arrow of inference, or beside another premise and joined to it by a plus and bracket. However, in order to remember that this was unstated and that *you believe* it is suggested by the speaker or author, indicate on the map its status as an unstated element by placing the unstated element in parentheses.

Since most reasoning that is worth mapping has several steps of reasoning involved, with conclusions being used in turn as premises to establish additional points, let' go on to discuss and map arguments with multiple conclusions.

MAP REASONING THAT HAS MULTIPLE CONCLUSIONS

Is it possible for an argument to have more than one conclusion? Yes. As you know, a person sometimes has more than one point to make about a topic that is under discussion. If, in the course of a discussion, evidence is offered for more than one point then we have multiple conclusions. The person is arguing for more than one point.

There are two kinds of arguments in which we might find multiple conclusions. First, we have the arguments in which more than one conclusion is presented as following from the same premises. Here is an example.

The defendant can be shown to have been out of the state at the time. Thus, he could not have been the man who robbed the bank. Nor could he have been the driver of the getaway vehicle.

In this argument, there is only one premise. From that premise we draw two conclusions: the defendant could not have robbed the bank and he could not have driven the getaway vehicle. It is also possible, of course, to draw multiple conclusions from a *set* of premises.

The preceding argument would be mapped like this.

The reason for believing that he was not the robber is also given as the reason for believing that he was not the driver of the getaway vehicle. Each of the two conclusions is supported by the same premise.

Second, we have the "stepladder" arguments in which a conclusion is offered as a premise in support of a further conclusion. Consider the following conversational passage.

> You ask if I'm *certain* that the younger Harrell boy is too young to be served alcohol legally? I surely am. I remember that two years ago he was still too young to vote. The voting age is eighteen. Now, that means that he can't be more than nineteen years old. And the drinking age is twenty-one. Obviously, then, the boy is too young to be served alcohol — at least legally.

In this passage, the **ultimate conclusion**, stated both at the beginning and at the end, is that the Harrell boy is too young to be served alcohol legally. But the statement "he can't be more than nineteen years old" can also be called a conclusion because evidence is offered to support this claim. It is not, however, the ultimate conclusion to be drawn. It is, instead, a **transitional conclusion** that, once supported, is presented as a premise in another phase of the reasoning.

The argument can now be reconstructed and understood like this:

Premise: He could not vote legally two years ago.

Premise: The voting age is eighteen.

Conclusion: He can't be more than nineteen.

Premise: He can't be more than nineteen.

Premise: The drinking age is twenty-one.

Conclusion: He cannot be served alcohol legally.

It's as if there were two arguments, with the conclusion of one being identical with a premise in the other. Be aware, however, that the ultimate conclusion need not be presented last. It can be presented at the beginning or elsewhere. An ultimate conclusion, then, is a statement that in a particular argument serves only as a conclusion; it is not a premise in support of any further point. A transitional conclusion is a statement that serves as both a premise and a conclusion in the same argument. In other words, the transitional conclusion is a statement that is offered as evidence for another statement *and* has one or more statements offered as evidence for *it*. Statements that serve as premises but not as conclusions of either type may simply be called **basic premises**.

To save ourselves the repetitious writing of *premise* and *conclusion* when we reconstruct arguments, we can write out the premises without the label, then draw a line under them as if we were going to see "what they add up to," and write the conclusion under that line. A "therefore" sign (∴) may precede the conclusion.

Now, if we write out the transitional conclusion only once, the preceding argument can be sketched like this:

He could not legally vote two years ago.

The voting age is eighteen.
_____
∴ He can't be more than nineteen.

The drinking age is twenty-one.
_____
∴ He cannot be served alcohol legally.

The braces that frame the two subarguments may be omitted.

A map of the argument would look like this.

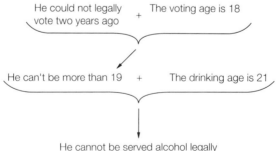

Starting from the ultimate conclusion this time — the bottom of the map — review the reasoning. What reasons are given for believing that he can't be served legally? The two premises combine to make a single point, so they are joined with a plus and bracket: he can't be more than nineteen and the drinking age is twenty-one. Now, what reason is given for believing that the drinking age is twenty-one? None. So no arrow points to that statement. (It's a basic premise.) Finally, are any reasons given for believing that he can't be more than nineteen? Yes. (A conclusion that's also a premise is a transitional conclusion.) He wasn't old enough to vote two years ago and the voting age is eighteen. Again, these two premises must be joined since neither supports the conclusion without the other.

Now, look over one more argument with an accompanying map and consider an explanation of why it would be mapped that way. Then you will be given three other arguments so you can try out your own mapping skills.

Suppose you had read the recent article "Filling the Leadership Vacuum: The Need for a National Education Plan," written by Dennis M. Adams and Mary Hamm and published in *Educational Record*. You want to be sure you know what the authors say, because you have been asked to discuss their ideas. First, you reread the article. Then you map out the authors' reasoning. For our present purposes, let's just map the introduction to the article. Here it is.

We've heard plenty of rhetoric recently urging the restoration of America's competitive position in the world economy by improving the knowledge, spirit, and overall educational quality of our youth. However, the whole debate is pointless if we have no national educational policy for pulling top talent into the teaching profession, training them, and providing ongoing professional development. Recognizing that American education is urgently in need of renewal is one thing, comprehensive strategic planning is quite another. It is time for the United States to formulate a deliberate national education policy.

We are the only technologically advanced country on the planet without effective educational leadership on a national level. A decentralized approach to the prime national educational objectives of training highly qualified teachers results in a dissolution of the issues. This does not mean that we can't extol the virtues of diversity and pluralism, yet we need a coordinated approach to defining our problems and resolving them.

Mapped, the argument looks like this.

The map shows two separable avenues for arguing that the United States needs a national education policy. On one avenue, it's suggested that educational renewal is necessary and that this requres strategic planning. Why is renewal necessary? Look at the first sentence. Although that opening sentence simply says that *we've heard* "plenty of rhetoric urging the restoration of America's competitive position in the world economy" through education, as you read on, you see that the authors accept this as a reason for renewal. Since this need for a competitive position is clearly implied but not directly stated, you can put that premise in parentheses on the map. (It's so nearly explicit that, in this case, the parentheses are optional.) A second avenue to support the conclusion is provided with the premise from the second paragraph: A decentralized approach to national educational objectives results in a dissolution of issues.

When you map (or "diagram," as some people say) an argument, sometimes you will have to leave out certain statements to get at the heart of the reasoning; sometimes you will have to reword statements; sometimes you will have to combine or even separate statements. Just be careful not to misrepresent when you map reasoning that is not your own. Not all that is said in a paragraph or conversation belongs on your map, but all of the premises and conclusions *do* belong on your map.

Now, make a map of the reasoning in each of the following conversational arguments. Then see the following pages for an accurate map and a short discussion of each.

1. I'm sure that Wes would be able to explain the major philosophies of history because any competent historian would be able to explain the major philosophies of history and there is really no doubt that Wes is a competent historian. After all, his Ph.D. in history is from a university with quite a good history department, and he recently received an award for distinguished service from the American Historical Association.

2. The practice of grading students' school assignments should be abolished. In the first place, it's unfair. Second, besides being unfair, there are practical disadvantages in focusing on grades. Both students and teachers can be distracted from the actual learning process with excessive concern for measurement, recording, and justification of the quality of performance in the course. This distraction seriously impairs the educational process. Now, back to the point of the unfairness. Some students have much more time available to study than others. Often, the difference in grades reflects just this. And, speaking of fairness, no one is really qualified to judge the work of another person, and this is exactly what grading amounts to.

3. Despite his experience and education, which qualify him formally for the position, the job candidate we interviewed last kept apologizing for

personal inadequacies and he told us that he *hoped* he could learn the job. We can conclude from this display of insecurity that he lacks self-confidence. This, combined with the fact that self-confidence is an important leadership skill, leads us to believe that he's not likely to be a strong leader. This is unfortunate. We do need a strong leader for this position. Undoubtedly, it would be a mistake to hire this person.

Map these arguments before you look at the maps on the following pages. Perhaps you will have difficulties in mapping the entire argument for one or more of these three. Still, map as much as you can, then check your work.

Have you created a map for the arguments on the previous page? If you have, consider these accurate maps and the discussions of them.

1.

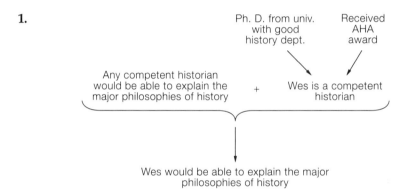

The word "because" occurs early and suggests that the preceding statement (several "statements" might be contained in one grammatical sentence) is a conclusion that is about to be supported by one or more premises that will then follow. The word "and" connects the next two statements, suggesting that they are of the same status—in this case, that they are both premises for that initially stated conclusion. The "after all" suggests premises, probably for the last statement. Indeed, the references to the doctorate from a good history department and the award do relate to Wes's competence specifically rather than the general point about *any* competent historian.

The two premises that support the ultimate conclusion must be joined with a plus and bracket because neither, without the other, would make a sensible case for the conclusion. The question of whether to use a plus and bracket or separate arrows for the two premises that support the claim that Wes is a competent historian is less clear. In the map above, separate arrows are used, in keeping with the instructions given earlier in this chapter that if separable points are made in the premises, they should generate separate arrows. However, an argument might be made that a plus and brackets might be used here if we understand the arguer to believe that neither point by itself provides really substantial support for the (transitional) conclusion apart from the other. On this account, while each premise is relevant, only together do they make a reasonably sufficient case for their conclusion.

2.

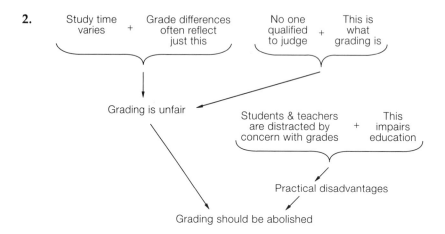

Notice that the point of the whole discussion is that "grading is unfair." The two main lines of support for this claim are indicated with the phrases "in the first place" and "second." These phrases suggest that the same kind of statement follows each; both are premises, in this case. The "besides being unfair" phrase tells us that separate arrows should be used from those two premises to the general conclusion that "grading is unfair." The statement that begins with the words "Both students and teachers can be distracted . . ." follows the claim that there are practical disadvantages, and is itself offered as evidence that there is such a practical disadvantage, along with the premise (join these with a plus and bracket) that "This distraction seriously impairs the educational process." Next, we have the helpful sentence, "Now back to the point of the unfairness." Although transition statements like this may not be necessary, they help listeners or readers track our remarks more clearly. The premise about varying study time and the premise that grade differences often "reflect just this" should be joined with a plus and bracket, because they combine to establish a single point of evidence. The remaining premise ("speaking of fairness") will have its own arrow, pointing to "grading is unfair" because that (questionable) claim that no one is qualified to judge the work of another constitutes a separate way of arguing that grading is unfair, quite apart from the issue of study time. Now, although some of this reasoning is not good reasoning, our present purpose here is simply the accurate presentation of someone's line of reasoning. If this were your own reasoning, the map would (we can hope) help you see that you need to revise some of your thinking, even if you continue to maintain the same conclusion.

3.

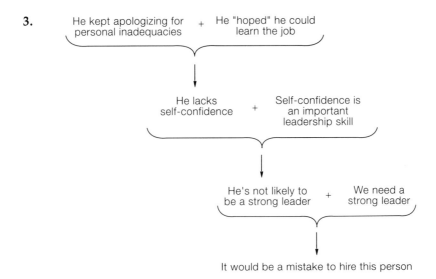

As you read the comments to be mapped, the first clear sign that an argument is being presented is the phrase "We can conclude." This signals a conclusion that is supported by the preceding claims. The next phrase — "from this display of insecurity" — refers back to those preceding premises and may be omitted from your map. (An alternative is to draw an arrow from the two premises to a transitional conclusion, "he is insecure," and then from this statement to the one that, it is said, "we can conclude": "he lacks self-confidence.") This statement should be joined with a plus and bracket to the next, because the phrases "combined with the fact" and "leads us to believe" show that this is a single step of reasoning, to be represented by a single arrow. Again, the new conclusion, "he's not likely to be a strong leader," is joined to the next statement, "We do need a strong leader for this position," by a plus and bracket, since each requires (or assumes) the other in providing support for the claim which is the ultimate conclusion: "it would be a mistake to hire this person." Notice that this line of reasoning flowed rather directly from the top of the map to the bottom, while other lines of reasoning you encounter or create may begin with a transitional or ultimate conclusion, or with premises that would not be at the top of a map.

■

PRACTICE ACTIVITIES

Set 5.1 *Create a basic map that displays the reasoning in the following conversational arguments.*

1. Mike has to take either algebra or statistics next year. Since Mike always takes the course with the shortest textbook and the algebra textbook is shorter, it's clear that he'll be taking the algebra course next year.

2. I deduce that the butler committed the crime. He was the only person besides Mr. Voigt who could possibly have committed the crime. It could not have been Mr. Voigt because he was away in New York on the day the crime was committed.

3. Contrary to the claims of some, there are people who have both quantitative and artistic talents. Scientists, for example, are without exception competent at math, and thus have a quantitative talent. Furthermore, there are many scientists who love the arts and have artistic talent.

4. Young children should receive much affection, since this contributes to secure, stable personalities, and it enables the children to develop affective skills of their own. You really should be gentler with little Erin.

5. Service in the armed forces builds a person's character. That's why you should join the army. It builds character by making you self-reliant and responsible. You really need some character development. You are still relatively immature.

6. You should major in history. There are good history professors at this school and you've always been intrigued by historical novels. I'll bet you would find the study of history to be interesting. As I said, the professors are good. Our university was recognized as one of the top schools in the country in historical studies.

7. That American history textbook was published in 1960, so it won't describe the controversial American military involvement in Vietnam. President Kennedy's 1963 assassination wouldn't be in it, either. I know the book was published in 1960 because the copyright date is indicated as 1960.

8. The third witness must have been bribed. If he had been telling the truth, he would have met my gaze as I stared at him. But he didn't meet my gaze at all. The only motive for him to lie in this situation is bribery.

9. No one who tries to be a good Christian would consider letting the helpless suffer. This should be recognized merely by noting *premise* that every American is a good Christian — or at least tries to be — but no American would even think of letting the helpless suffer. Torrey is a good Christian. That much is clear. So we know without a doubt that helpless people will not suffer if he can help them. *Conclusion*

10. *Conclusion* There is no question that ① drugs should be legalized. ② For one thing, taxpayers' money would no longer be wasted on ineffective drug interdiction programs. ③ Not only that, but legalized drugs would be subject to taxes which would provide additional revenue. ④ Also, the black market would disappear and the drug lords would no longer be getting rich from other people's misery. ⑤ Drug prices would drop, which would result in a reduction in crime because ⑥ people would no longer have to steal in order to support their drug habits. Besides all that, the choice to use or not use drugs should be left up to the individual, not government.

11. *Conclusion* It would be a mistake to legalize drugs. Legalization would be like giving in and admitting defeat in the war on drugs. We have only just begun this war on drugs, and I'm sure in time we will win. *premise* The illegality of drugs is itself a deterrent for many people. If drugs were legal, this deterrent would be gone and many more people might start using drugs. Another deterrent to drug use is the fact that it is so expensive. Making them more affordable through legalization will only make them more available to people who otherwise might not try them. There are too many drug addicts in this country already. We don't need more!

= 8

Set 5.2

Create a basic map that displays the reasoning in the following arguments that have been excerpted from magazines.

1. From an advertisement for Dr. Roark, a plastic surgeon, *San Diego Magazine*, January 1991:

   Performed by a qualified surgeon, cosmetic surgery can work wonders. Reshaping the body form not only enhances physical appearance, it can also rejuvenate one's spirit and self-esteem.

2. From *Newsweek*, January 14, 1991:

   Bankruptcy is a rotten choice for anyone who can possibly avoid it. The siren song of "starting fresh" may especially tempt the Yuppie class, which in its heyday had so much credit shoved into its pockets. But life after bankruptcy isn't the breeze that many a lawyer makes it sound. The blemish sticks to your credit history for 10 years — and forever, if you're being checked for a mortgage, an insurance policy or a job paying more than $50,000. "Employers look at credit reports and see them as signs of character," says Jay Muzychenko, vice president of the National Foundation for Consumer Credit. "It might cause you a credibility problem."

Bankruptcy doesn't liquidate student loans, tax liabilities or child support. It will probably block you from any future job that requires bonding and may cause a landlord to reject you as a tenant. You'll need a high down payment to buy a car (maybe 50 percent or more) and won't get other credit easily, now that lenders are tightening up.

3. From an article entitled "Arrival of the Corporate State," *Wall Street Journal*, January 19, 1990:

> Because the U.S. imports more than it exports, this is supposed to prove that the U.S. is losing competitiveness. This is another outright deception, as can be seen from the fact that during the past seven years (a period of record trade deficits) U.S. economic growth at 4 percent has been about the same as Japan's, with its extremely high "favorable" trade balance, and two-thirds more rapid than in Germany, with a favorable balance. In addition, U.S. growth in 1982–1989 was 44 percent faster than it was in the 1970s when the trade balance was positive.

4. An editorial in the *Los Angeles Times*, July 12, 1991, titled "Some Banking 'Cures' Are Not: The Administration would let industrial companies own banks — and that's foolhardy":

> With remarkable speed and efficiency, the Administration's ambitious package of bank reforms is moving through legislative committees. So far, so good — the troubled banking industry is in need of change. But progress should not be at the expense of prudence, especially when it comes to opening up bank ownership to just about anyone. That happened with the savings and loan industry, and the rest is nightmarish history.
>
> That's why the Administration's proposal to allow industrial companies to own banks for the first time would be a mistake. The need for new capital doesn't justify the potential risks. And the timing is poor, considering current weaknesses in the banking system.
>
> The Administration's banking package will soon go to the House Committee on Energy and Commerce. Overall, the legislation seeks to free banks of Depression-era laws that put them at a competitive disadvantage. That means allowing

banks to branch across state lines and enter new businesses, such as insurance and securities. Such welcome changes would enable banks to tap new revenue sources, as long as they establish separate units to sell the new services. Establishing "fire walls" between such activities is critical to making sure that insured bank deposits are not misused.

But opening up bank ownership to industrial companies needlessly complicates bank reform. Many commercial and industrial firms already are in the lending business and are doing just fine. The so-called non-banks operated by U.S. corporate giants such as General Motors, General Electric and others make a variety of loans to consumers and businesses.

These non-banks have been operating outside traditional bank regulations and are not protected by federal deposit insurance. The vagaries of the marketplace force discipline on the non-banks, which have prospered by competing with traditional banks.

The goal of banking reform is to make traditional banks more competitive with these new entities, not to make non-banks more like banks. Under liberalized bank ownership, opportunists could abuse their bank privileges, knowing that the government would pick up the tab for any misdeeds, as the S&L debacle so painfully illustrated. Imagine if some hard-pressed company decided to dip into the till of its government-insured bank affiliate and then it went belly up. Who would pay?

The proposal should be abandoned. Legislators ought to focus instead on imposing new, stricter deposit insurance limits. Banking reform must solve existing problems, not create new ones. Reprinted by permission of *The Los Angeles Times*.

5. From "Notebook" in *The New Republic*, July 15 & 22, 1991:

Last week Air Force spokeswoman Kathy Blevins helpfully explained the rationale behind the interrogation of Captain Greg Greeley, who was recently discharged from the Air Force for being a homosexual. Mr. Greeley was offered immunity from prosecution in exchange for naming fellow homosexuals in the Air Force. Ms. Blevins crashed in flames when, according to *The Washington Post*, she said, "We're questioning him because he had a clearance for classified information and the fact that we just found out. . . . he claims he is a homosexual. Somebody could use that against him. We're questioning him to make sure he is under no threats." If Mr. Greeley claims he is a homosexual, how exactly could someone blackmail him? By threatening to reveal that he's really a closet hetero?

6. From "Letters," *The Washington Monthly,* June 1991:

> Elizabeth Lesly's excellent article on tax exemptions for churches ["Pennies from Heaven," April] fails to mention one other serious difficulty with granting tax-exempt status to religious organizations. In order to determine which groups merit the exemption, the government must, of necessity, decide which are "legitimate" religions and which are not. Such a determination comes perilously close to the "establishment" of religions by the government. Government-approved religions realize substantial benefits under our system of taxation, while those that the government refuses to sanction do not. Simply treating religious organizations as corporations would avoid this pitfall. If such a corporation meets the standards for status as a non-profit or charitable organization, fine. If not, it should be taxed on the same basis as any other for-profit institution.

7. From "Tilting at Windmills," *The Washington Monthly,* June 1991:

> If you think George Bush's invasion of Panama was a good idea, consider the headline from the April 18 *Washington Post:* "Panama Said to Revert to Pre-Invasion Drug, Money Activity." And if you still, after realizing that hundreds of thousands died during and immediately after it, think that our war against Iraq was another good idea, ponder this headline from the April 20 *Post*: "Saddam's Power Seen Increasing."

8. From "Tilting at Windmills," *The Washington Monthly,* June 1991:

> It is unsettling to learn from Bob Woodward's new book, *The Commanders,* how little George Bush's extensive experience in Washington has taught him about decision making in a crisis. John Kennedy, on the other hand, was a quick study, able to absorb the painful lessons of the Bay of Pigs in April 1961 in time to apply them to the Cuban missile crisis in the fall of '62.
>
> Chief among these lessons was not to rely on a narrow group of advisors but to expand the circle to include able people outside the chain of command — people who are likely to argue with the president and bring original points of view to the discussion.
>
> For the Bay of Pigs, Kennedy relied almost solely on the advice of the CIA's Allen Dulles and Richard Bissell, who had been the original sponsors of the idea of an invasion by exiles and had a stake in defending that concept even when reality made it seem increasingly unlikely to succeed. By contrast, when the missile crisis began to unfold, Kennedy sought the

advice of a dozen or so people outside the chain of command, including his brother Bobby, Dean Acheson, and Ted Sorensen. The result was a wise decision that avoided war but attained our objectives.

So what does Bush do as the crisis in the Gulf unfolds? He relies on a small group that sometimes seems to include just himself and Brent Scowcroft and that, even when expanded, includes at most Cheney, Baker, and Powell. Instead of encouraging argument, he conducts the meetings in a way that does not encourage systematic deliberation. Only once is an argument, by Powell, heard in favor of sanctions instead of war. It is quickly brushed aside, not with any discussion of its merits but with Bush's ex cathedra pronouncement that it is not "politically" feasible. James Baker also seems to have favored allowing more of a chance for sanctions, but there is no evidence that he argued the case with the president in any of those meetings. Only Powell dared challenge Bush in the way that Acheson did Kennedy—in a group meeting that everyone knew history would record. After reading Woodward's revelations, *Newsweek's* Washington editor, Evan Thomas, concluded: If the war had ended badly, *The Commanders* would seem like . . . the story of a president plunging toward disaster, heedlessly dragging his armies over the cliff." But because the war ended in a military victory—although I'm sure history will view it as a human disaster—George Bush will not learn the error of his ways. I tremble to think how he would handle an equivalent of the missile crisis.

9. From "Tilting at Windmills," *The Washington Monthly*, June 1991:

    The headline of the lead article in the April 2 *New York Times* read: "Low Medicaid Fees Seen as Depriving the Poor of Care." Nowhere did the article mention that the greed of physicians — whose average annual income now exceeds $100,000 — might have something to do with the problem. Why aren't some of these well-paid doctors willing to accept modest fees in order to care for the poor?

10. From "Tilting at Windmills," *The Washington Monthly*, June 1991:*

    The top tax rate may be 31 percent, but last year George Bush paid only 22 percent. He paid zero in state taxes. The reason is that he claims Texas, which has no income tax, as his state of residence. One has to wonder just how many days Bush spent in Texas in the past 20 years compared to those he spent in Washington, or for that matter at Camp David, Maryland, or his vacation home in Kennebunkport, Maine.

For Further Reading

Barry, Vincent E., and Joel Rudinow. *Invitation to Critical Thinking.* New York: Holt, Rinehart and Winston, 1990.

A textbook that offers, in Chapters 5 and 6, a discussion of steps 1 and 2 of mapping.

Johnson, R. H., and J. A. Blair. *Logical Self-Defense.* New York: McGraw-Hill Ryerson Limited, 1983.

A textbook that offers "tree diagrams" for the reconstruction of arguments.

P A R T

THREE

Is My Reasoning Good?

C H A P T E R

SIX

Constructing Good Reasoning

"You're not making any sense."

"You missed the point completely."

"Well, that doesn't prove your point."

"You can't assume that."

How much easier it is to see what's wrong with someone else's reasoning, rather than our own. Partly because we are less than thrilled to recognize faults in our reasoning, most of us have had insufficient practice at it. It may hardly occur to us even to look for weaknesses in our own arguments.

Some people adore those talk-show hosts, politicians, or acquaintances who can "talk a good game" and flamboyantly outargue (in the competitive sense) almost anyone they encounter and oppose. Is this skill an essential or important part of a good life? Our intellectual heroes should not be people who almost always argue passionately for one view, demonstrating the ability to convince others of nearly any idea. Instead, our intellectual heroes should be people who are articulate, but demonstrate restraint and reflection, and argue a good — not just a rhetorically overwhelming — case. They should be people who qualify their claims and see the weaknesses in their own lines of reasoning, without losing the capacity for judgment and commitment.

To improve your own ability to construct good reasoning, you can (1) learn how to separate evidence from inference — that is, to distinguish between the truth of your premises and the relation of those premises to your conclusions, (2) practice identifying which kind of evidence it takes to support the different sorts of claims you make, and (3) practice distinguishing between strong and weak support for your conclusion. These are the topics of this chapter.

SEPARATE EVIDENCE AND INFERENCE

When does it makes sense to challenge someone's argument? Basically, there are only two kinds of logical challenge to be made. First, you might challenge someone's reasoning when one or more premises seem to you to be false or questionable. For example, as your friend tries to establish that he was justified in cheating on a test, he might claim that "It didn't really hurt anyone." You might find his argument unacceptable because that premise seems not completely true. Second, you might challenge someone's reasoning when the premises do not lead to the conclusion. For example, you might say that, even if that friend who tried to justify his cheating is correct in saying that it didn't hurt anyone, "That still doesn't make it right."

Thus, two kinds of errors can occur when someone is arguing the truth of a conclusion: errors of evidence and errors of inference. Either the premises (the items of evidence) are weak or the move from premises to conclusion (the inference) is weak.

The same will be true, of course, of your own reasoning. When your argument is a weak one, that weakness can be found in one (or each) of two aspects of that argument: its premises or the inference itself. You should check these aspects of your own reasoning as readily as you would check them in the reasoning of someone whose view (and perhaps whose style of presentation) irks you.

Why go to the trouble of distinguishing in our minds between "evidence" and "inference" when so many people so often reason quite well without any conscious awareness of that distinction? This is a good question. Perhaps learning about this distinction makes matters more difficult than they need to be.

It's true that we sometimes reason superbly without thinking about evidence and inference separately. However, on topics that seriously challenge our objectivity, or on topics that for other reasons we are prone to assess wrongly, it helps to check our reasoning against these two criteria of good reasoning. Otherwise, we are less likely to notice which of those kinds of errors we might have made. Ultimately, we are less likely to see that there is anything wrong with our reasoning at all.

You will reason reliably more consistently if you take care, for example, to ask if those premises you are rattling off are as certain as you would like to think. You will also reason reliably more consistently if you take care to produce evidence that is both relevant and sufficient, and you don't overstate how well your evidence establishes your conclusion.

Although this chapter focuses primarily on the construction of your own good reasoning, these same tools can be useful in assessing and challenging others' reasoning. In the first place, of course, you can apply the two criteria of good reasoning (1. Are the premises true? 2. Do the premises adequately support the conclusion?) to other people's arguments in order to determine for yourself whether to accept their reasoning. Second, however, it provides you with a tactic for getting someone to reevaluate his or her own reasoning. Consider the following.

Imagine that you're in one of those situations in which it seems desirable to question someone's argument. (This is not always a productive alternative.) If that person has offered *both* questionable evidence (at least one questionable premise) *and* a weak inference (the conclusion doesn't follow from the premises), you have a choice. You can begin by attacking evidence or inference. You can usually make your point more effectively if you focus on inference rather than evidence — on the "logic" rather than on the "facts." Why? The questionable premise will quite possibly express a belief that has been long and deeply held. It may concern a point of logical vulnerability for that person. Your contention of that premise may generate more heat than light, because it may be a point on which that person is *unwilling* to change. Besides, if it is a social, political, or religious issue, clear-cut proof of your view may be elusive. On the other hand, if you focus on form, suggesting that "even if everything you say is true, that still doesn't seem to prove your point," the other person may back off, admitting that at least some revision in the argument is required. This is a start. The person is reconsidering his or her argument.

Why does this work? As you know, some of our firm beliefs on the sorts of topics that we get contentious about become entwined with our identity and self-esteem. Very often, the most questionable premises in a person's argument will be one of these unnegotiable beliefs. Giving ground on these suggests to that arguer some personal inadequacy of character and some deficiency in what that person "stands for." On the other hand, most of us can admit that, at least on this one occasion, we jumped to a conclusion and didn't reason well. That is not the same as admitting that "I typically or usually don't reason well." Thus, a critique of a person's inference instead of evidence is less likely to feel like a personal attack.

In Chapter 9 you will learn to extend the mapping skills you developed while studying Chapter 5. You will learn to record your assessment of both inferences and evidence right on the map.

USE RELIABLE PREMISES

For your line of reasoning to be convincing, you have to provide premises that are reliable — that is, ones that are likely to be true. Why? If you are reasoning something out for your own sake without presenting the evidence to anyone else, the obvious reason for having reliable premises is to avoid coming to false conclusions. If you are trying to be persuasive with another reasoner, you certainly will be trying to offer dependable premises. However, to be convincing, those premises you offer must not only be reliable, they must be accepted as reliable by the other person. An argument with true premises that the other person does not accept is an argument that does not convince. Your purpose in reasoning aloud is to get your own point across clearly and in its best light. So your premises should be ones that are accepted by your "audience" or ones that you will then support (thus, in the language of Chapter 5, transforming basic premises into transitional conclusions) to demonstrate their reliability.

What kind of evidence would you need to support a premise that has been challenged? That depends on the kind of claim made in that premise.

Some claims are rather subjective assessments. Their truth is notoriously hard to establish, so they become matters of opinion that vary from one person to another and seem destined never to be proven to everyone's satisfaction. Some are merely reports about oneself and one's own preferences and perspectives. Consider these examples.

"Rare steaks are disgusting."

"Video games are a foolish hobby."

"Romance novels are not worth reading."

"It's better to be smart than to be happy."

"A true communism is fairer than any other economic system."

"God spoke to me."

It's not that these issues cannot be discussed intelligently. They are simply examples of the sorts of statements that are likely to result in a conversation-ending remark such as "Well, that's just your opinion" since they may reflect quite different tastes and basic views of life. Different people might not even agree on what kind of evidence it would take to prove such a claim (except, perhaps, for the first of those statements, which may simply amount to the expression of a wholly personal view). When you offer such statements as basic premises, you can expect to be challenged by some people, and you can expect some frustrating discussions.

Other premises cry out for definition of a key expression. If you are seeking legal representation on a very important issue, you might consider your friend's assurance that Jaspers is a competent attorney as a reason for believing that your case will be presented in its best light. However, the truth of that premise might depend on what she means by "competent." Your friend might use the term, as some people do, to refer to someone who is one of the best in her profession. On the other hand, she might use the term, as other people do, to refer to people who *are not clearly or usually incompetent*, but who do not rise above the category of the *merely* competent. (Defining terms was discussed in Chapter 3.) Is your friend's claim true or false? This may depend on how she uses the expression.

Still other premises can be supported rather straightforwardly with evidence of some sort. The kind of evidence that is necessary, of course, varies from one claim to another. Perhaps the contended claim is merely that "the Los Angeles Dodger pitcher Ramon Martinez had 20 wins, 6 losses, and an earned run average of 2.92 in the 1990 major league baseball season." Although some people may need a definition of "earned run average," there is only one common definition. This is not a matter of contended definitions; it's a matter of checking the records of the people who sat through the games he played in and recorded each pitch, out, and run. Perhaps the contended claim is something empirical in an obvious way: "There are more than fifty buildings on this campus." You can check a campus map or actually walk around campus counting the buildings. For simple matters like these, we know what sort of evidence would establish the point, and generally other people will agree with us about how to go about proving the point.

Of course, many of the claims we use as premises are a mix of the three categories just mentioned: subjective assessments, matters of definition, and straightforward — often physical — evidence of some sort.

"That's obscene!" pronounces a visitor to an exhibition of Robert Mapplethorpe's art. What definition of obscenity might the offended viewer be applying? Although we need to know *that* in order to see if we agree with this evaluation, the definition itself might still leave us with a subjective assessment that results in our disagreement, after we observe the physical evidence of the art itself.

"I have the hottest car in town!" boasts the youth, gunning the engine. Again, all three categories come into play. What is the definition of a hot car? Different people might use that expression differently. We can now examine the physical evidence of the car itself, and perhaps still be left with the subjective assessment of that owner who had an undefinable special feeling about that car which prompted the hot car claim.

DON'T OVERSTATE THE STRENGTH OF YOUR INFERENCE

It's a shame. Good reasoning is often transformed into incorrect reasoning because of overenthusiasm for the point of view that is presented in the conclusion, or just because of careless wording.

Have you ever done this? You present some relevant and persuasive evidence for your point of view, but you overstate how well this establishes your conclusion. For example, you assure the buyer of your now-used car that she will get "easily" another 20,000 carefree miles out of it because of how well it has run ever since you bought it and because of the good attention you have given its maintenance. She will be upset if major repairs are needed next month, as she remembers your assurances. Your evidence was relevant, but you were only justified in claiming a probability, with the proper qualifications, of 20,000 carefree miles. Sure, it's true she should know that you can't assure such a thing, and that you "just overstated." On the other hand, drawing an appropriately worded conclusion might spare both of you the trials that go along with the resentful accusations of the new owner. For another example, consider the case of someone who assures us that "the economic recession in our region will be over by mid-year." That person looks foolish when someone with a good memory reminds him — in front of workmates — of his confident prediction. Whether he was foolish or not perhaps depends on whether he based his prediction on reasonable economic predictors or on, to use an extreme case, superstitution. However, instead of being admired for his insight, our poor friend is reviled for his audacity. Of course, large-scale economic trends are notoriously hard to predict, but without overstating the probability of his conclusion, he might have come away from this without such damage to his reputation. Events of this sort are not rare. Our evidence is the right kind, but we overstate the likelihood it establishes for our conclusion.

It's worth encouraging sensitivity to the issue of how boldly or with which qualifications or limitations a conclusion should be offered. As one way of doing this, we will now examine a traditional contrast between "deductively valid" arguments in which the premises lead necessarily to the conclusion and "inductively strong" arguments in which the premises establish good reason to believe the conclusion without that ironclad sense of deductive proof.

Deductive Validity and Soundness

In some arguments, the premises lead with certainty to the conclusion. This is to say that they *prove* the conclusion. It is *not* to say whether the premises are true or false. Such arguments are deductively valid. Other arguments in which the premises fall short of proving the conclusion beyond any possible doubt are not deductively valid, even if their premises are true. Again, a judgment about the validity of an argument is made independently of a judgment about the truth or falsity of the premises. Of course, not all arguments that are correctly persuasive establish the conclusion beyond any possible doubt.

Clearly, your concerns as a thinker go beyond the issue of good inference. You know that any acceptable argument will have good evidence as well: the premises will be true. In a sound argument, the premises lead necessarily to the conclusion *and* the premises are true. The argument is unsound if either of these two conditions is not met. In other words, a sound argument has both good inference and good evidence. Its conclusion can be accepted as true.

To decide whether the reasoning in an argument is valid* (whether the evidence proves the conclusion), it is not necessary to concern yourself with the question of whether the premises are true. You can ignore the truth or falsity of the premises and still determine whether the argument is valid. *In a valid argument, if the premises were true, then the conclusion would have to be true.* This means that although the premises may or may not actually be true, you should *imagine* that they are, then ask if that shows beyond any possibility of doubt that the conclusion must be true. In other words, to determine whether an argument is valid, you ask, "If the premises were true, would the conclusion then have to be true?" A "yes" answer to this question indicates that the argument is valid. An answer of "no" or "maybe," or even "probably" indicates that the argument is not valid, a condition logicians describe by saying the argument is invalid.

Consider two more definitions of validity. They present the preceding point in different words.

1. An argument is valid when it is inconceivable for the premises to be true while the conclusion is false.

2. An argument is valid if, by accepting the evidence, we must also (to avoid contradicting ourselves) accept the conclusion.

The reasoning itself in the following argument would be valid, and the argument itself will be called a valid one, even though one of the premises is false.

> Earth must be the fourth planet from the sun because there are nine planets in our solar system, only five are farther from the sun, and no planet is the same distance from the sun as we are.

The conclusion, "Earth is the fourth planet from the sun," is stated at the beginning of the argument. The argument is valid because *if* the premises were true, then the conclusion would have to be true. The argument has a good inference; its premises establish its conclusion with necessity. How-

---

The terms valid and invalid will be used in this section to refer to deductively valid and deductively invalid arguments. In the next section deductive validity will be contrasted with inductive "strength." In an inductively strong argument, the premises render the conclusion probable but not necessary.

ever, since one premise, "only five [planets] are farther from the sun," is false, the argument does not have good evidence. This is not an acceptable argument, even though the reasoning is valid.

The following argument is also valid.

> Since all corporate executives are over fifty, and anyone over fifty has at least minor health problems, absolutely anyone who is a corporate executive will have health problems—at least minor ones.

The conclusion is stated last. Both premises in this argument are false, but the argument is valid because *if* it were true that all corporate executives were over fifty and *if* it were true that anyone over fifty had at least minor health problems, *then* it would necessarily be true that any corporate executive would have at least minor health problems.

Consider another argument.

> Neil Simon must have a vivid imagination because he's a dramatist and it's very common for dramatists to have vivid imaginations.

This argument is invalid because *even if* Neil Simon is a dramatist and *even if* it is very common for dramatists to have vivid imaginations (in other words, many of them have vivid imaginations), this would not prove that Simon is one of those with such an imagination. Notice that you might believe—or even *know* on other evidence—that the conclusion is true; you still would have to admit that the argument presented here is invalid.

To decide whether an argument is sound (and thus whether the conclusion should be accepted), you must determine whether it passes both of the following tests.

1. The argument must be valid.

2. All premises must be true.

Test 1 requires that the evidence actually prove the conclusion. Test 2 requires that the evidence be *good* evidence. Obviously, when good evidence proves the conclusion, that conclusion should be accepted as true. The argument has both a good inference (it has passed the first test) and good evidence (it has passed the second test). If the argument fails either test, it is unsound.

Call to mind the first two arguments used in the explanation of validity.

> Earth must be the fourth planet from the sun because there are nine planets in our solar system, only five are farther from the sun, and no planet is the same distance from the sun as we are.

Since all corporate executives are over fifty, and anyone over fifty has at least minor health problems, absolutely anyone who is a corporate executive will have health problems—at least minor ones.

Both arguments were valid; the conclusion followed from the premises. Thus, they pass the first test for soundness. But one premise in the first argument and both premises in the second argument are false. Thus, each argument fails the second test for soundness. Although these arguments have a good inference, they do not have good evidence.

The following argument is sound.

Earth must be the third planet from the sun because there are nine known planets in our solar system, only six are farther from the sun, and no planet is the same distance from the sun as we are.

To check its validity, we ask, "*If* there were nine planets in our solar system, and if only six were farther from the sun, while no planet was the same distance from the sun as Earth, *then* would it have to be true that Earth was the third planet from the sun?" The answer is "yes," showing that the argument is valid. This argument clearly passes the first test for soundness. The other question to be asked is this: "Are all the premises true?" Again, the answer is "yes." Since the argument passes both tests, it is sound, and the conclusion must be true.

Notice that it is possible for an argument to be valid and sound, valid and unsound, or invalid and unsound. Only one combination is impossible. It is impossible for an argument to be invalid and sound since, in order to be a sound argument, it must pass test 1, which requires it to be a valid argument. By the definitions of the terms, then, no argument can be invalid and sound. If the argument is invalid, it is necessarily unsound—you don't even need to determine whether the premises are true or false.

Inference	Evidence or Premises	Soundness of Argument
Deductively valid	All true	Sound
	One or more false	Unsound
Deductively invalid	All true	Unsound
	One or more false	Unsound

Notice also that unsound arguments will not always have false conclusions. For that matter, invalid arguments will not always have false conclusions. Here we see an example of an argument that is invalid and therefore unsound. The conclusion, however, is true.

> Coal production is a major industry in my home state of Pennsylvania, but Kentucky certainly produces even more coal than Pennsylvania. Why, when I spent a week in Kentucky last month, I saw coal mines and heard talk of coal almost everywhere. I was in Bell County, Harlan County, Letcher County, and Knott County. Coal seemed to be the major industry everywhere.

The conclusion of the person who is presenting this reasoning is that Kentucky produces more coal than Pennsylvania. While the conclusion is true and could be firmly established with the appropriate premises, this person has drawn the conclusion merely from casual observation on a week's trip to Kentucky. This is an invalid argument with a conclusion that happens to be true. (It can also be noted that Bell, Harlan, Letcher, and Knott counties are all located in the same part of the state; they are contiguous. They lie in the rich Appalachian Plateau mining area. Elsewhere in Kentucky, our rash thinker might not have made similar observations.)

Finally, bear in mind that an argument is not to be considered unsound merely because *you do not know* whether a premise is true. If the argument is valid, then it is sound if the premises are true but unsound if the premises are not true. If you are not certain about whether a premise is true or false, the argument's soundness is undetermined until you look into the matter sufficiently to establish whether it is sound. Further, if you incorrectly judge a valid argument's premises to be true or false, then you will be wrong when you assess its soundness. The soundness of deductive arguments does not depend on personal perspectives.

Inductive Strength

Either the available evidence proves the point being considered or it doesn't. If the evidence, once accepted, establishes the conclusion with certainty, the reasoning is deductively valid. If the reasoning falls short—even by a bit—the reasoning is deductively invalid. It's as simple as that. Isn't it?

Yes, it is. If we are concerned only with unqualified proof, we can reject as invalid any argument that falls short. Deductive validity was the topic of the previous section. Skill at this kind of argument evaluation is useful. Among those arguments that do fall short of unqualified proof, however, many are "good arguments" in the sense that they move reasonable people *closer* to an acceptance of the conclusion, and in many cases they are all that we can reasonably expect.

Although many arguments must be judged to be deductively invalid, some can still be judged worthwhile because of the *inductive strength* that they may have in varying degrees.

An inductively strong argument is one in which the evidence, once accepted, establishes a firm probability that the conclusion is true. This is one example:

Judge Burnet has dismissed the charges against every one of the hundreds of graffiti defendants he has seen over the past eight years.

The charge against me is the same, and there seem to be no special circumstances in my case.

∴ Judge Burnet will dismiss the charge against me.

If Judge Burnet does not dismiss the charge in this case, we cannot say, "That's impossible." We did not have deductive certainty. We can only say, "That's very surprising." It was simply unlikely, based on previous experience.

Here is another example of an inductively strong argument:

Coyotes are almost never found in this part of the country.

You have never seen a real coyote before.

∴ The animal you saw in the field was not a coyote.

It *could have been* a coyote, but it probably wasn't one. If the conclusion to this argument were "The animal you saw was a dog," the argument would not be as strong, since the animal may have been a fox or another kind of animal. Since coyotes do look much like dogs, and since dogs are probably more common in the area, the chances are reasonably good that it *was* a dog. The argument with this conclusion has some strength, but not as much as the original argument we considered.

If the conclusion to this argument were "You must have dreamed it," the argument would have very little inductive strength. In fact, we would have to say that the argument was inductively weak. Unless the person reporting the sighting has a habit of confusing dreams with reality, the evidence does not establish a *probability* that the conclusion is true. It does, of course, allow for such a *possibility*, but the chances are very good that this conclusion is false.

A distinction between an argument's inference and its evidence was discussed in the previous section. There, in the discussion of deductive validity, an argument was considered to have good form if the premises were of the right sort to establish the truth of the conclusion beyond any possible doubt, logically speaking; an argument was considered to have good evidence if all of its premises were true.

An inference/evidence (or form/content) distinction can also be used in assessing inductive strength. However, since the separation of good and bad inferences is not so clear here, the tidy concepts of validity and soundness are not used. When judging inductive strength rather than deductive validity, an argument can be considered to have a good inference (or "good form") if the level of probability established for the conclusion is high. An argument can be considered to have reliable evidence (or "good content") if its premises are true or likely to be true. Since we are not using deductive standards of acceptable reasoning now, both inference and evidence can allow for some possibility of error.

Assessing Inferences*

Deductive Necessity	Inductive Probability
Valid *Acceptable because necessity has been established.*	*There is no inductive correlate to deductive validity.*
Invalid *Not deductively valid. Necessity has not been established, although the argument may have a high or low degree of inductive strength.*	Very strong support/almost certain *Almost always acceptable because the conclusion has been established as very probable.* Strong support *Almost always acceptable.* Stronger Moderate strength, with various levels of probability Weaker Very weak support; does not establish a probability Worthless/no support *Unacceptable.*

When we assess an argument for deductive necessity there are two categories: valid and invalid. However, many arguments that do not establish deductive necessity still have acceptable form because they have sufficient inductive strength to make them useful.

ASK THE R-E-T QUESTIONS

In many everyday situations, the R-E-T method of evaluating reasoning might serve you better than the more technical concepts of deductive validity and inductive strength as you think through your own or someone else's arguments. The R-E-T method is simple and easy to remember. Essentially, it involves the steps you take whenever you think out a matter thoroughly.

There is certainly no way to avoid having to identify the conclusion and the evidence before assessing an argument. Once you have identified them, however, the R-E-T method involves simply asking yourself three questions:

1. Are these reasons the *Right kind* for supporting such a conclusion?

2. Are they *Enough* to warrant accepting the conclusion?

3. Are they *True*?

In short, you ask: Are the reasons . . . the *Right kind? Enough? True?* The letters *R-E-T* signal three questions to be asked when assessing your own or another's reasoning (R: Right kind; E: Enough; T: True). Let's briefly discuss each of the three questions.

R: *Are the reasons the right kind?*

In other words, is the evidence offered relevant to the conclusion drawn? Sometimes, the problem with an argument is that the very sort of evidence offered is not the sort required to establish the point at issue. As with most errors, this is more easily recognized in others' arguments than in our own. If the R question receives a "Yes," go on to the E question.

E: *Are the reasons enough?*

Sometimes the evidence, being the Right kind, or relevant, is also clearly sufficient for reasonable people to accept the argument. In other arguments, the evidence, even though it may be relevant, is clearly insufficient to make a good case for the conclusion. Because of the subtle and innumerable distinctions to be made, what seems sufficient to one person will fall short for a person who is more cautious on the issue being considered. However, the question must be asked. There is seldom a clear dividing line between inductively strong and weak arguments. If you honestly judge the case for the conclusion to be too weak, you must reject the argument—but not necessarily the conclusion.

If the E question receives a "yes," go on to the T question.

T: *Are the reasons true?*

A strong argument will have reliable premises. At this point, you ask if the evidence presented is to be accepted as true.

If all three questions receive a "yes," the argument is acceptable. The conclusion can be considered well supported.

Consider two examples of how the R-E-T method of evaluating reasoning may be used in practical contexts.

EXAMPLE

Practical context: Andrew has done poorly in his two previous philosophy courses. On this basis, he concludes that he will do poorly in the Introduction to Logic course, which is another philosophy course.

Application of R-E-T: Andrew's past performance in philosophy classes is not irrelevant. It is not at all obvious that he is considering the *wrong kind* of evidence for his conclusion. Still, while his concern about his previous performance is legitimate (it is, in this sense, "the right kind"), it is not alone sufficient ("enough") to lead persuasively to his conclusion. Although this additional philosophy class may involve some difficult abstractions like those in his other two courses, perhaps a "process-oriented" logic course will be significantly different from those "content-oriented" courses. If Andrew applies R-E-T, and does just a little casual research, might he not see that he doesn't have *Enough* evidence to justify his disturbing conclusion? Note again that it is usually easier to see the fault in another's reasoning than in one's own; it is easier to imagine Robert, let's say, who has already been exposed to the R-E-T method, helping Andrew reason this out. Also, perhaps this particular instructor will teach in a way that makes it easier for Andrew to learn. Here again, in applying R-E-T, we identify the problem as we find that the E question yields a "no." We need more evidence than we have if we are to make a really strong case for Andrew's conclusion, although his concern is not wholly without foundation. ∎

EXAMPLE

Practical context: Daniel, age fifty-eight, works in a factory, attending college at night. Simon, his working partner for thirty years, has just retired. Upon hearing that his new workmate will be someone who is "hardly more than a youngster," Daniel is tempted to declare his refusal to work with the boy, whom he expects — although he doesn't know him — will not do the job well.

Application of R-E-T: Put in terms of logic, Daniel's reasoning runs thus:

Premise: He is young.

Conclusion: He won't do his job well.

First, we ask (we can imagine Daniel assessing his own reasoning or having it assessed by a family member or a fellow worker) whether the reason given for accepting Daniel's conclusion is the *Right kind*. Our answer is probably "no."

However, what if, on further information, Daniel considers a different reason for coming to that conclusion?

Premise: He is forgetful.

Conclusion: He won't do his job well.

This is perhaps the *Right kind* of reason to consider. If Daniel had heard this about his new workmate, and especially if their job is dangerous, he might quite justifiably want to know more. This information alone, however, is not *Enough* to show that his conclusion is warranted. Perhaps the new worker is forgetful "only about certain things," but never about job-related matters. This is certainly not inconceivable. To satisfy the E requirement in the R-E-T test, Daniel must have additional evidence before accepting his conclusion. This would do it:

Premise: He is often forgetful about important aspects of his job.

Conclusion: He won't do his job well.

Is the reason the *Right kind* — is it relevant? Yes. Is it *Enough*? Yes (unless the boy can change his ways). Is it *True*? Daniel would certainly have to substantiate any such rumor before justifiably accepting his conclusion. If the information is reliable, if the new person indeed "is often forgetful about important aspects of his job," the conclusion is warranted. If the information is determined to be very probably true, Daniel has at least good grounds for concern. ∎

Sometimes an argument clearly fails the R-E-T test. If this happens, you at least know something about what is wrong with the argument because you know which of the three questions didn't warrant a "yes." The evidence is irrelevant (if it failed the R test), insufficient (if it failed the E test), or unreliable (if it failed the T test). Often, however, the argument won't simply and neatly fail or pass the R-E-T test. *Only some* of the evidence will be irrelevant, the evidence will be marginally relevant, or the evidence will be sufficient only for a rather tentative conclusion. With careful attention, especially to the E question, you can decide whether the likelihood that the conclusion is true has been overstated. Based on this evidence, you ask, would the conclusion have to be true, would it probably or very probably be true? Does this evidence support the conclusion at all? Your decision on this will determine whether the warranted conclusion is introduced with a "possibly," "probably," "no doubt," or another such expression. It's the same result that you get with a deductive and inductive analysis, but there are no technical terms to apply. That's why the R-E-T method is useful for everyday life.

PRACTICE ACTIVITIES

Set 6.1 *Decide whether each of these arguments is valid or invalid. If it is invalid, decide on the degree of inductive strength it has. Remember to disregard the truth or falsity of the premises as you assess inference rather than evidence.*

1. Angelo is an Italian, and he's intelligent. Vasco is an Italian, and he's intelligent. In fact, Vasco's whole family is intelligent. I know five other Italians. Each of them is intelligent. Obviously, then, Italians are all very intelligent people.

2. It is clear that Harcourt is the one who murdered Fleisch. After all, he had hated Fleisch for years, he needed money to pay off a gambling debt, and his fingerprints were found on the murder weapon.

3. Mesa College must have courses in anthropology, since it is a community college and most community colleges have courses in anthropology.

4. Psychology is not worth studying, since none of the behavioral sciences is worth studying, and psychology is one of the behavioral sciences.

5. At least one nation in the Western Hemisphere is headed by someone over the age of seventy. After all, George Bush is over seventy and he heads the United States, which is certainly in the Western Hemisphere.

6. Joan's next baby will be a girl because girl babies always follow boy babies when the mother is in her later childbearing years. Joan *is* in her later childbearing years and her last baby was a boy.

7. Kohlrabi must be nutritious because it's a vegetable and most vegetables are nutritious.

8. Nixon was undoubtedly guilty of serious political crimes. So many people think he was guilty — he must have been.

9. No one under the age of eighteen can vote legally in our nation, so a child of twelve would not be able to vote legally in our nation.

10. Some Republicans are politically conservative, and some Republicans advocate liberal abortion policies. So some political conservatives apparently advocate liberal abortion policies.

11. Since we know that some Democrats vote in every election, it must also be true that there are teachers who vote in every election, because some teachers are certainly Democrats.

12. California must be a desert, because it never rains in California, and anywhere that it never rains has to be a desert.

Set 6.2 *Evaluate the reasoning in each of the following situations. Write down your reasons for giving either a "yes" or a "no" for each of the three questions to be asked in the R-E-T method. Stop at the first "no." Then assess the overall inductive strength of the reasoning and the acceptability of the argument. (Inductive strength is determined by answers to the R and E questions. The actual acceptability of the argument is determined by answers to all three R-E-T questions. In some of the fictional examples, however, you won't have an answer to the T question.)*

1. The *Chicago Tribune* must be a top-notch newspaper. My daughter-in-law is an editor there, and she is one of the most intelligent and principled people you will ever meet.

2. There's no doubt that Dr. Hackney would know about the important issues in higher education today. After all, he has a doctorate, he has taught at universities, and he is currently the president of the University of Pennsylvania.

3. "Arnie, you would be a *great* teacher," concluded his sister Gail. "You're smart and you always think of a good way to get your point across."

4. Lonnie regularly shies away from difficult courses. Today he decided not to register for the abnormal psychology course that he had earlier planned on taking. "I found out that the professor

for that course has two Ph.D.s! There's no way I could ever pass a course as difficult as that one is bound to be."

5. "But I need a top-notch architect who knows his stuff," snorted the company president. "And what do you send me? A woman barely into her thirties. This is obviously not someone who will do the best possible job for our company."

6. In the past, the Iraqi government lied to the United Nations about their resources for making nuclear weapons. Obviously, they're just lying again, as they once more say how very limited their resources are.

7. I didn't get a very good elementary school education in the Badlands Unified School District. So I figure that my kids won't get a good education there either.

8. My daughter is not getting a good education in the Badlands Unified School District. So I'm sure that your daughter isn't, either.

9. That's my jacket you're wearing. Take it off! So you're the one who stole my jacket.

10. UFOs that are alien spaceships do exist. Hundreds of people have reported seeing unexplained lights and shapes in the night sky.

Set 6.3

1. Create an argument that would not receive a "yes" answer to the R question. Avoid silly arguments; use an argument that someone might actually offer.

2. Create an argument that would receive a "yes" answer to the R question, but a definite "no" answer to the E question.

3. Create two arguments that would receive a "yes" answer to the R question and a "yes" answer to the E question (to establish at least a strong inference). The first argument should have at least one questionable premise; the second argument should have no questionable premises.

For Further Reading

Lambert, Karel, and William Ulrich. *The Nature of Argument.* Lanham, MD: University Press of America, 1988.

A study in deductive validity that explores the application of symbolic logic to practical argument.

Mayfield, Marlys. *Thinking for Yourself: Developing Critical Thinking Skills Through Writing*. Belmont, CA: Wadsworth, 1991.

A book on reflective writing that has good observations on premise and inference evaluation, and on critical reasoning in general.

Scriven, Michael. *Reasoning*. New York: McGraw-Hill, 1976.

A classic discussion of the practical evaluation of reasoning.

Skyrms, Brian. *Choice and Chance*. Belmont, CA: Wadsworth, 1986.

An exploration of inductive logic. The deductive-inductive distinction in *Open Minds and Everyday Reasoning* is consistent with that distinction in *Choice and Chance*.

SEVEN

Recognizing Fallacies

Y ou undoubtedly make errors in your reasoning from time to time. We all do. Sometimes we even make the same error repeatedly. Such repetition of a single pattern of bad reasoning can be avoided in many cases by learning to recognize the most common logical fallacies.

A **fallacy** is an incorrect pattern of reasoning. There are many such patterns. Each fallacy is given a name that, in some way, describes the error. The same fallacy can be committed on different occasions and in reference to different topics. It would be the *same* fallacy (with the same name) in the sense that the same erroneous pattern of moving from evidence to conclusion was present in each case.

Finding a fallacy in your own or someone else's reasoning does not show that the conclusion is false. It shows only that the conclusion has not been adequately supported by the evidence. In most cases the fallacy identifies a particular kind of inadequate evidence.

The type of fallacy that we are now discussing is technically called an *informal* fallacy. It is to be distinguished from *formal* fallacies, which we will examine later. (In this book, the word *fallacy* will refer to informal fallacies unless otherwise indicated.) An important difference between formal and informal fallacies is that their persuasive power has a different basis. The formal fallacies persuade us because they so closely resemble arguments whose form is deductively valid. The informal fallacies persuade us because the evidence offered can be mistaken as having more bearing on the issue than it really does.

AVOID COMMON FALLACIES

Many fallacious patterns of reasoning exist, and names have been given to dozens of them. The eleven fallacies that are defined, explained, and illustrated through examples in this chapter are among the most frequently committed ones.

Attacking the Person

The fallacy of **attacking the person** is committed when we reject a person's reasoning or position by criticizing the arguer instead of the argument.

Premise: An irrelevant attack on the person's character or circumstances.

We conclude that: That person's reasoning or position is wrong.

In Chapter 2, we observed that people sometimes get off the original track in their thinking and reasoning by "getting personal"—that is, by making critical comments that shift attention from the line of reasoning to the person who is presenting it. It is best to avoid calling this a fallacy, because questionable *reasoning* is not necessarily involved. However, if it is carried one step further, a fallacy is indeed committed, since a questionable conclusion is drawn.

If, on the basis of an irrelevant personal comment, we draw the conclusion that the person's reasoning is flawed or that the person's position is incorrect, we commit the fallacy of attacking the person. Here is an example.

EXAMPLE

After her exercise class, Kim found herself discussing the coming local elections with several of her classmates. Kim confessed, with some embarrassment, that she hadn't thoroughly researched the candidates. In fact, she reported, there was one candidate for the city council about whom she knew nothing: Al Kaplan.

"Oh, he's the one to vote for," Helen, the teacher, called from across the room. She had overheard Kim's last comment and now hurried over to the small group that Kim was in. "Kaplan has more political experience by far than any of the other candidates. He is very intelligent and he's always fair, looking at all sides of an issue. Once I heard him . . ." Helen detailed Kaplan's experience and fairness, then went on to mention a few more of the candidate's strong points. Kim was impressed with the report she received. In fact, while thanking Helen for the information, she commented that she believed she now had a candidate to vote for.

Kim then looked for her friend Marie, and the two of them left the building. As they walked down the sidewalk toward the bus stop,

Marie asked what the conversation with Helen had been about. "Oh, Helen was just giving me some reasons for voting for Kaplan for city council," Kim explained.

"What?!" Marie stopped in her tracks and stared at her friend with wide-eyed amazement. "*Helen* was giving you reasons for voting for *Kaplan?*"

"Yes. Why?" asked Kim, physically backing off from her still wide-eyed companion.

A knowing smile came to Marie's face as she relaxed a bit. "Didn't you know? Helen is Kaplan's *sister-in-law*! You would expect her to be in favor of Kaplan in the election."

Kim felt foolish. In the classroom, she had been embarrassed that she hadn't thoroughly researched the candidates. That was nothing when compared with the embarrassment she felt now. "How stupid I was," she confessed. "There I was, nodding my head and taking it all in. I was actually convinced. I had no idea that she had such a personal investment in how I voted. Now I have to forget everything she said. One thing is certain—I'm not going to vote for Kaplan." ∎

Kim's reaction is perhaps understandable. She felt that Helen had taken advantage of her ignorance. Nevertheless, Kim commits the fallacy of attacking the person because she draws the conclusion that Helen's conclusion about Kaplan is unreliable solely on the grounds that Helen's circumstances suggest that she would *want* Kim to believe it. Notice that Kim is not, at this point, considering the evidence that Helen has presented. Kim's rejection of the conclusion that Kaplan would be the best choice for the city council is based on a fact about the arguer; it should be based on an examination of the arguer's premises.

Consider the possibility that the same reasons Helen had presented were now presented by Marie, who has no personal interest in the outcome of the election. Would the reasons that were insufficient to establish the conclusion now become sufficient? Would Helen's reasoning now become good reasoning? Does the soundness of an argument vary, depending on who produces the argument? Certainly logic is more objective than this. To justifiably reject someone's reasoning or position, you must examine the reasons themselves, not the characteristics of the person who is presenting the reasoning.

Sometimes there *is* a reason to doubt someone's word, and Kim may be justified in questioning the reliability of Helen's premises. However, there is usually a possibility of checking those claims through other sources. It is still fallacious to reject the reasoning or position on personal grounds.

Let's look at one brief additional example of the fallacy of attacking the person.

EXAMPLE

Watching a videotape of a convict in a federal prison arguing for certain changes of policy for all American penal institutions, your friend elbows you and comments, "Don't listen to that criminal argue for his point. You know that anything he says will be self-serving." ∎

Your friend commits the fallacy of attacking the person because he is encouraging you to dismiss the convict's entire argument without looking at it. He apparently presumes that nothing the convict says—regardless of what it is—will have any merit. What if the same argument about penal institutions were presented by a noted law-enforcement official or your friend's favorite politician? That same argument might look more credible. Again, to evaluate the merit of an argument, we must at least consider the argument.

The fallacy of attacking the person has also been known as the genetic fallacy (referring to the source or "genesis" of the argument), the fallacy of poisoning the well (fouling the source of the water or argument), and the *ad hominem* fallacy (Latin for "against the man").

Argument from Ignorance

The fallacy of **argument from ignorance** is committed when we suggest that our position is proven by a lack of conclusive evidence against it.

Premise: A claim that a certain position has not been disproven.

We conclude that: That position must be correct.

Sometimes, instead of presenting actual evidence for our own position, we focus on the opposition's inability to *disprove* our point. We may do this by discrediting their arguments to an opposing position or by simply observing that they have no evidence at all to offer. In either case, we commit the fallacy of argument from ignorance if we conclude that this lack of counterevidence is itself proof of our position.

Observe how the fallacy of argument from ignorance is committed in the following example.

EXAMPLE

David and his wife, Nara, have much in common. On the topic of psychic phenomena, however, they are worlds apart. Usually, they avoid the topic for the sake of peace in the family. Today, however, they have slid into heated debate. "Denying that a belief in psychic phenomena has some basis in fact is just closed minded," David charges. "Despite all the many efforts of skeptics around the world, no one has ever been able to show that all of these sincerely reported experiences have other possible explanations or that the realm of the psychic is an impossibility. Doesn't that tell you something?" David is becoming sarcastic and believes that with his last statement, Nara must concede that he is right, or she will indeed settle for being "closed minded." ∎

Perhaps it does not occur to David that conclusive evidence is elusive on *both* sides of the issue. While a belief in psychic phenomena is not easily disproven, neither is the opposite belief easily disproven. Considering the nature of the topic, the kind of proof that would establish a deductively sound argument appears, at the present time, simply unavailable.

Nara could now show David that his reasoning is inadequate by using **parity of reasoning** (the same kind of reaoning) to "prove" the opposing position. After all, a person could argue like this: "Insisting on a belief in fairy tales about super powers of the mind is just irrational. In spite of all the experimentation, no consistent verification of psychic powers has ever been provided through laboratory experiments. Doesn't *that* tell you something?" By at least pointing out how, with the same kind of reasoning, we could produce the opposite conclusion, Nara could show David that his argument is definitely fallacious.

It is often the case, when a person commits the fallacy of argument from ignorance, that this person has a notably limited range of specific evidence to support the original position. The argument-from-ignorance fallacy may be used simply because nothing better comes to mind. It is not surprising that we often see this fallacy committed in discussions and articles on issues for which conclusive evidence is difficult to come by: the existence of spirits, life on other planets, the existence of God, and pseudosciences like astrology.

The elusiveness of evidence should not suggest, however, that in such cases one belief is as reasonable as its opposite. The "burden of proof" — the primary obligation to justify one's claim — often rests more with one side than another. For example, when the existence of something (such as psychic phenomena, extraterrestrial life, or leprechauns) is being claimed, the burden of proof rests more heavily with the person who is making the claim than with the skeptic. Ultimately, of course, both believer and skeptic should remain receptive to new evidence.

The fallacy of argument from ignorance is not completely limited to such mysterious topics. Here is an example of the fallacy in a quite down-to-earth matter.

EXAMPLE

The boss's wallet, which had been lying in the top drawer of his desk, is missing. He is certain that the secretary, whom he has come to dislike, is the thief. *"Of course* I'm sure he did it," the boss proclaims. "I've already questioned him about it, and there's no way that he can prove that, as he claims, he never came into my office while I was out."

∎

This is perhaps a more obvious example of the fallacy of argument from ignorance. The boss's thinking is certainly muddled. Still, whether anyone in the office wants to show the boss, by parity of reasoning, that the opposite ("The secretary did not steal the wallet") could also be shown to be true, remains to be seen. One would hope that *someone* would choose to point out to the boss that the burden of proof rests with him.

Questionable Cause

The fallacy of **questionable cause** is committed when, on insufficient evidence, we identify a cause for an occurrence that has taken place or a fact that is true.

Premise: A statement of fact or an observation that an event has taken place. (This is generally an uncontentious claim.)

We conclude . . . by naming a cause. (This is a contentious claim because there are other possible causes.)

Quick judgments are sometimes necessary. They are often made, however, even when they are unnecessary, and quick judgments can involve oversights.

In naming the cause for something, people sometimes latch on to the first possibility that comes to mind and never give serious consideration to other possible causes. At other times, the problem is not that what has been named as a cause is not one at all; the problem is that the person is seeing only one of several contributing causes. In judgments of either kind, the fallacy of questionable cause is committed.

The fallacy of questionable cause is committed in the following example.

EXAMPLE

Brad recently rented a new apartment that was one of six in a small apartment building near the store where he worked. One morning, about a month after Brad moved in, he was locking his door from the outside. He had to be on the job in fifteen minutes. Suddenly he heard someone shouting. He turned and saw his new landlord running toward him, waving some paper overhead. The landlord, as he approached Brad, slapped his right hand against the papers he held in his left and demanded to know why the water bill (which was not itemized by apartment) was so high. "Every month, it's within ten bucks of the same figure. Now you move in, and the bill almost doubles! What do you do—leave the water running day and night?" The landlord was seething and threatened to add the excess amount to Brad's rent next month.

Brad didn't say anything. He didn't know how to respond. He climbed into his car and drove away. ■

You don't know Brad. Maybe the landlord was right about him. Maybe he *does*, for some reason, leave the water running "day and night." Still, the landlord, even if he happens to be right, reasons dangerously and fallaciously if he fails even to consider alternate possible causes.

What could explain the sudden rise in the water bill? Could it be that the landlord didn't notice that the rate the Municipal Water District charged had increased sharply? Could it be that there is a serious leak in apartment #6, while the tenant there is on vacation? Could it be that the landlord forgot about the sprinkler system that was on every day now that the weather was hot, or about some extensive tree plantings that were being watered heavily? If the landlord did not give sufficient consideration to other possible causes, he committed the fallacy of questionable cause.

Here is another example.

EXAMPLE

Jonathan was in his second year of college, and he had earned all A's and B's up to this point in his college career. He lived at home with his parents. One morning during breakfast, Jonathan mentioned — as casually as he could — that he would be moving out of his parents' home at the end of the semester. He had found an apartment near the college.

His parents conceded that he was old enough to move out. They were concerned, however, that the many household activities that Jonathan would now have to perform — shopping, cooking, washing clothes, and more — would take too much time from his studying.

Jonathan moved out, but his parents insisted on keeping track of his grades. At the end of the following semester, Jonathan's grade report showed a C and a D. When his parents saw this, they exclaimed, almost in unison, "We told you so!" Jonathan's parents insisted that he return home. The evidence showed that he could not handle both his studies and independent living. ∎

Considering only the information given here, Jonathan's parents may have been right. However, like Brad's landlord, they reason dangerously and fallaciously if they do not ask Jonathan about, or otherwise consider, different possible causes for the drop in grades.

What could account for the lower grades? There are many possibilities. This may have been the semester that Jonathan enrolled in the difficult chemistry course that so few students even pass. Perhaps, as bad luck would have it, this was also the semester when Jonathan began studying a foreign language. Foreign languages can be difficult, even for many bright students. To some, they come easily; to others, it seems as if the thousands of bits of information are just challenging them to be memorized. If Jonathan's parents have not given sufficient consideration to — if they have not even asked about — other possible causes, they commit the fallacy of questionable cause.

The fallacy of questionable cause is common in everyday life. We rashly determine a person's motivation when she makes a comment or acts in a certain way. We attribute to the distrusted politician the worst intentions when he votes against the bill we favor; we attribute to the trusted politician the best intentions when his actions could as easily be conceived differently. We draw hasty conclusions concerning why a job was lost, why the media reported in a certain way, why we succeeded, why we failed, why crime is increasing, why a particular Third World nation seems determined to humiliate the United States. We are sometimes more enamored of opinions than of the careful rational processes that bring about insight and true beliefs.

Begging the Question

The fallacy of **begging the question** is committed when we assume the truth of our conclusion in a premise.

Premise: A statement that, in order to be true, requires that the conclusion be true.

We conclude . . . what we have already assumed to be true.

We occasionally hear a person make the charge that someone else is "arguing in a circle." One form of arguing in a circle is the fallacy of begging the question. By assuming, in the evidence offered, the very point we wish to prove, we end up proving nothing at all.

Follow the argumentation in this conversation.

EXAMPLE

Ben casually mentions God in his conversation with Theresa. "Wait a minute," Theresa interrupts. "You seem to think that it's just obvious that God exists."

"Well, it's true," Ben responds with surprise. "God certainly *does* exist."

The conversation continues:

Theresa: What makes you so sure of that?

Ben: It's right there in the Bible.

Theresa: And just how does that prove that it's true?

Ben: The Bible is infallible — it has no errors.

Theresa: And what makes you think that the Bible is perfect? Do you believe everything you read in *Reader's Digest*? Or *Newsweek*? Or the morning newspaper? What makes the Bible so different?

Ben: The difference is that the Bible is the Word of God. ∎

What is Ben's point? His point — the conclusion that "God exists" — is stated at the beginning of the argument. Actually, this statement was originally just a claim—not a conclusion—since no evidence was being presented to support it. When his statement was challenged, however, Ben began to give reasons in support of his position. As soon as he offered the first premise ("It's right there in the Bible"), the statement that "God exists" became a conclusion.

Let's reconstruct Ben's argument. Since his last statement is offered as evidence for his previous one, the statement "The Bible is infallible" is a transitional conclusion and not just a premise.

Premise: The Bible is the Word of God.

Transitional Conclusion: The Bible is infallible.

Premise: The Bible says that God exists.

Conclusion: God exists.

Has Ben proven his point? His argument does seem to be valid: *if* its premises were true, the conclusion would follow and be true as well. There is a problem with this attempt to persuade, however. The conclusion is already *assumed* to be true in one of the premises. The conclusion that "God exists" must be accepted as true *before* the premise that "the Bible is the Word of God" is accepted. This makes the argument useless. If Ben were addressing someone who already accepted the existence of God, the argument would be unnecessary. He or she would need no argument. If, however, he addresses someone who does not already accept the existence of God, he should be unable to persuade that person: if he or she cannot accept the conclusion that "God exists," then neither will that person be able to accept the premise that "the Bible is the Word of God."

Ben's argument requires a certain type of circular reasoning. The premises are intended as evidence to establish the conclusion but, in order to accept one premise, the conclusion must already be established. The preceding example does not show that reference to the Bible is irrelevant to a belief in God, but it *does* show that, worded as it is here, this argument should be unconvincing to the unbeliever.

Another version of the fallacy of begging the question can be shown through the following example.

EXAMPLE

Sam and Jed are discussing the National Football League's next season.

Sam: Seattle will be the strongest team at running the football next year—at least in the American Conference.

Jed: What makes you think so?

Sam: It's just that all of the other teams — however good they may be — will be unable to produce the same effectiveness at running the ball that we'll see with Seattle. ■

In this case, the single premise is merely a rewording of the conclusion. The conclusion is that "Seattle will be the strongest team at running the football next year (in the American Conference)." The premise states that the other teams will not be as effective at running the ball. The premise not only assumes the truth of the conclusion; it echoes the very same statement in different terms.

In each kind of example, the truth of the conclusion is assumed in a premise. We believe we have proven a point that we have merely *assumed* to be true. This is the fallacy of begging the question.

Two Wrongs Make a Right

The fallacy of **two wrongs make a right** is committed when we suggest that an act is morally permissible, offering as evidence the claim that someone else has done something similar.

Premise: A claim that someone has performed an act that is similar to this one.

We conclude that: This act is not morally wrong.

The scene is classic. Little Timmy is perched on a kitchen stool. On his tiptoes, he can just manage to reach the cookie jar. He is elbow-deep in the cookie jar when . . . Who walks into the kitchen? Yes. It's Mommy. Knowing quite well that cookies before dinner are not allowed, Timmy can only come up with the defense that "Johnny did it first!"

The desperation in little Timmy's voice is enough to show that even *he* knows that this response will not get him out of trouble completely. Pointing the finger of blame will, at the most, allow Timmy to share the spotlight of guilt with someone else. *The fact that another person — in this case, Johnny — has done the same thing does not prove that the act is proper.*

Timmy does not use fallacious reasoning — he does not commit a fallacy. It is not clear that he misunderstands or reasons incorrectly. Sometimes, however, people draw unjustified conclusions using Timmy's approach; they commit the fallacy of *two wrongs make a right*. On the grounds that someone else has done something similar, they conclude that a particular act is not morally wrong. Here is an example of *two wrongs make a right*.

EXAMPLE

Charged with campaign improprieties, the politician huffily responds with the following defense: "I've done nothing wrong. Why, look at my opponent. He's done the very same thing for years!" ■

The speaker's conclusion is that he's "done nothing wrong." His only premise is his claim that his opponent has behaved in the same way. This kind of evidence does not establish the conclusion.

What kind of evidence does establish such a conclusion? This is certainly difficult to say. People do not always agree on what kind of evidence it takes to establish a *value claim* such as the conclusion in the preceding example. Still, despite such disagreement, we would be rather universal in our agreement that a particular act is not right simply because it has been done before. The fact that a president of the United States has used public funds for private purposes, for example, does not justify the same behavior by a subsequent president. It may have been morally wrong in the first place and, as the common saying puts it, "two wrongs don't make a right." The logical error, then, is made in offering the wrong kind of evidence to establish the conclusion.

Two wrongs do not make a right. Nor do *many* wrongs make a right. Sometimes, in attempting to justify an act, we may offer as evidence the claim that many people have done something similar. Examine this example.

EXAMPLE

A wife and her husband are driving through the parking lot at the Food Basket market, looking for a parking space. At first they see none. Suddenly, the wife, who is driving, spies a space that is conveniently located near the sliding-glass entry doors of the market. She quickly pulls into the parking space and turns off the ignition. She feels the burning gaze of her husband. Perturbed by his apparent disapproval, she turns to him and snaps, "Don't look at me as if I've done something terrible by parking in a 'Handicapped Only' space. People do it all the time!" ■

The wife commits the fallacy of *two wrongs make a right* because her suggested conclusion that parking in a "handicapped only" space is acceptable is supported only by her claim that "people do it all the time." She means, of course, that it is done *very often*. This evidence is, by any common standard, insufficient to establish that the act is morally permissible.

Although there are more than just two "wrongs" in cases like this, the reasoning is similar, whether the argument refers to one or to many other instances, and we can say that the same fallacy is committed: *two wrongs make a right* — or, for brevity, "two wrongs."

Division

The fallacy of **division** is committed when we conclude that any part of a particular whole must have a certain characteristic, using as evidence the claim that the whole has that characteristic.

Premise: The claim that a whole has a certain characteristic. (This is generally an uncontentious claim.)

We conclude that: Any part of that whole must have the same characteristic. (This is generally a false conclusion.)

A basketball team is nothing more than all of its players. A committee is nothing more than all of its members. A stamp collection is nothing more than all of the stamps *in* that collection.

Certainly, in one sense, each of these statements is true. In each case, the whole (the team, the committee, and the collection) is being considered as the sum of its parts (the players on the team, the members of the committee, and the stamps in the collection). In each case, we have a *part-whole relationship*; the similar parts completely constitute the whole, which usually has a name of its own. The fallacy of division is committed only when reasoning about part-whole relationships. Consider other examples of part-whole relationships.

Whole	Part
Encyclopedia set	Its volumes
News article	Its paragraphs
Family	The members
Pack	The wolves
Orchestra	The musicians
Deck of cards	The individual cards

When we reason that whatever is true of the whole must therefore be true of each of the parts, we commit the fallacy of division. Consider this example.

EXAMPLE

The army sergeant was walking through the lounge of the Officers' Club to deliver a message when he was seen by several officers at one of the tables. "Hey, sergeant!" a young lieutenant at the table called out, "I see from your organizational patch that you're from the Fighting Fourth Division, the bravest combat unit in this country. Sit down and have a drink and some conversation with us. We're always glad to share our table with a brave soldier." ∎

Do you see how the fallacy of division is involved in the lieutenant's thinking? The lieutenant knows or accepts the perhaps common belief that the Fighting Fourth Division is the bravest fighting unit in the country and concludes that the sergeant must be brave since, for a unit to perform bravely, its soldiers must. The characteristic of being brave is attributed to this *part* simply because of its membership in the *whole*. This shows that the lieutenant would expect the same of any — and therefore all — of the "parts." His reasoning is faulty, however, because it is not necessary for every soldier in the unit to have acted bravely in order to justify the unit's label of "bravest." Consider another example of the fallacy of division.

EXAMPLE

The young man was clearly perturbed. "I've heard that the BBC's dramatic series 'Great Lives' was one of the most notable productions for television in the past twenty years," he complained. "Well, last night I took the time to see one of the programs in that series. It was good but it wasn't great. 'One of the most notable productions in twenty years'! These critics sure get carried away with their rhetoric sometimes." ∎

While it may be true that the series is one of the most notable productions for television in the past twenty years, a reasonable expectation is that some of the programs in that series will be better than others. It is even possible that particular programs in the series are, considered alone, not especially noteworthy at all. Thus, while the whole—the series—may be a very notable production, not each program will necessarily be so notable. The characteristic of being "one of the most notable productions for television in the past twenty years" may be true of the whole but not be at all appropriate to a particular part of that whole (even though the series is nothing more than the sum of the programs).

False Dilemma

The fallacy of **false dilemma** is committed when we consider too few of the available alternatives and assess all but one as impossible or unacceptable.

Premise: A statement of available alternatives (omitting at least one that is worthy of consideration).

Premise (often unstated or indirectly stated): A suggestion that all but one of these stated alternatives are impossible or unacceptable.

We conclude that: The remaining alternative must be accepted. (The conclusion is often unstated also.)

We sometimes hear people complain that they are "in a dilemma." They often seem to mean they must make a choice between two or more alternatives, none of which is wholly desirable. Literally, a person faces a dilemma whenever there are multiple alternatives to choose from, whether desirable or not.

You are being presented with a dilemma when you are told, "There are only two routes you can take to get to the top of Mount Rennen—Archer's Road, which is winding and treacherous, or Route 74, which is a very steep climb." This is a true dilemma—the statement that there are only two alternatives is true—if, indeed, there is no other route to the top. However, if there is another route, the dilemma is a false one. Your alternatives have been incorrectly limited to two.

Let's examine an obvious example of the fallacy of false dilemma.

EXAMPLE

The father, thinking that a college education is essential to his son's, or any child's, success in life, demands an answer to his question: "Are you going to go to college and make something of yourself or are you going to end up being an unemployable bum like me?" ∎

The father is presenting his son with a false dilemma. The dilemma is his son's supposed choice between college, on the one hand, and personal failure, on the other. The dilemma is a false one because it is quite possible to "make something of yourself" without a college education. The father has suggested that his son has two alternatives: "go to college" or be an "unemployable bum." An alternative not considered is that of being employable — indeed, even being quite successful financially — but not going to college. Tens of thousands of real-life cases in business and industry confirm this possibility.

People may set the trap of a false dilemma (also called the *either/or fallacy*) for themselves by their tendencies to adopt extreme views and to distort others' views into extremes. Consider the following comment.

EXAMPLE

"Look, the choice is simple. It's either capitalism pure and simple, as it was meant to be, without any government interference through regulation . . . or else you have the government having complete control over not only business, but also political and private affairs." To the speaker, a businesswoman, the choice did, indeed, seem to be simple.

∎

Each alternative, as presented here, is an extreme. There are certainly alternatives between these extremes. You need look no farther than the American economic and political system to find an example of limited government control over business. While there is government regulation of American businesses, such regulation falls short of "complete control" of business or of "political and private affairs." The speaker in the preceding example, along with many other businesswomen and men, may believe that government control over business is too extensive, but they should admit that it is not without limit.

Colloquially, a person sometimes writes or says that another person has gone "between the horns" of a dilemma. A person goes "between the horns" when he or she recognizes the dilemma as a false one by identifying a position that is *between* the extremes of the stated dilemma. It's as if you were backed to a wall with a mad bull racing toward you. With the bull just five feet away, you seem to have only two alternatives: lunge to your right and be gored by the left horn or lunge to the left and be gored by the right horn. It seems that you will be caught on one horn or the other. Perhaps, however, by turning sideways or positioning yourself just right, you may avoid both horns. To avoid being caught on one of the "horns of the

unreasonable certainty about the results. Of course, pondering such might-have-been circumstances usually serves no good purpose.

When we can learn from the past, and thus serve our future, reflection on what might have been is worthwhile. It may be worthwhile to speculate on the results of having gone to a different school, having accepted a different job offer, or having responded differently in a personal crisis. It is also worthwhile to avoid hasty judgments about those results — in other words, to avoid the fallacy of contrary-to-fact hypothesis.

Common Belief

The fallacy of **common belief** is committed when we accept a statement as true and offer as evidence the claim that many other people believe it.

Premise: The claim that many people accept a certain statement.

We conclude that: That statement is true.

We know that other people can be wrong even when they are absolutely convinced that they are right. We also know that *many* people can be wrong about the same belief. The fact that a certain belief is held by dozens or hundreds or thousands of people is not sufficient to prove that the belief is a true one. Nevertheless, people occasionally suggest that we accept this kind of evidence in particular cases. Often, when such reasoning is offered, the arguer had been inclined to accept that conclusion in the first place.

How would such clearly fallacious reasoning ever be effective when discoursing with another person? The following example suggests an answer to this question.

EXAMPLE

She knew about President Nixon's 1974 resignation from hearing her parents talk and from her high-school history class. Willa knew that the impeachment process had never begun. Perhaps, she thought, Richard Nixon was not guilty of all the charges that had been informally made against him. When she ventures this comment to two friends at school, however, one of them scoffs, "Of course Nixon was guilty. Everyone knows that!"

Willa hesitates. "Well, I guess he *was* guilty . . . actually. I just think it would be interesting to know more about political scandals like that." ∎

Copyright © 1991 by Tom Tomorrow. Reprinted by permission.

The friend who insists on Nixon's guilt offers only one reason to get Willa to agree with his position. He says, "Everyone knows that." Certainly he doesn't mean that, literally, *no one* thinks otherwise. He does mean that since so many people believe Nixon was guilty, it must be true. At this point, Willa's friend commits the fallacy of common belief.

Why does Willa back off from her suggestion, immediately conceding that she was wrong? She quickly admits, "Well, I guess he *was* guilty," despite a glaring lack of evidence in this conversation for either position. She probably backs off for reasons of esteem rather than logic. When someone says, "Everyone knows that!" an implication seems to be that any person who doesn't possess this common information must be especially dense or poorly informed. In the company of peers or those who are perceived as superiors, many people will relinquish even the most secure positions. In this instance Willa's was not particularly secure.

Have you ever been the only person in a crowded room who didn't agree on a particular emotional issue? In this kind of situation, most of us would be uncomfortable about raising a hand and actually voicing our dissent. On some topics and in some situations, many of us simply would not do it. Research done by Solomon Asch shows that a person who draws a conclusion based on *personal observation* can come to reject that conclusion after hearing that others have drawn a different conclusion.* Asch brought the person to be examined, along with seven others, into a room. Each of the eight was shown three lines of easily distinguished length. The person who was to be examined was placed last when all were lined up. This person did not know that the others were part of the study and had been previously instructed on how to respond to questions. When subsequently shown a single line to determine whether it matched previous line A, B, or C, the eighth person often answered incorrectly *when the first seven did not answer correctly*. In fact, this happened in one-third of all such cases. However, when studied individually, without the distorting influence of the others, those examined responded correctly in 98 percent of their judgments. If the pressure of conflicting conclusions is so great when people are reporting on the basis of personal observation, how much more readily will people relinquish their conclusions if they are based wholly or in part on less secure grounds?

Consider the following exchange as another example of the fallacy of common belief.

EXAMPLE

Jovine sits at the breakfast table, shuffling the morning newspaper much longer than on most mornings. It's a day off for her. It's Lincoln's Birthday. She looks up from her paper. Her roommate is at the stove. "You know, it's interesting that some presidents get immortalized and others don't."

"Immortalized?" Terry's voice reflects no great interest.

"Yes. We get a day off for Lincoln and Washington, but there are other presidents who lots of Americans have never heard of. I wonder if there's really such a big difference between them. For example, maybe old Honest Abe wasn't such a great man after all. . . ."

Terry is suddenly awake. "*Of course* Lincoln was a great man. Any schoolchild knows that!" ∎

"Any schoolchild knows that." This single premise suggests that if Jovine is not aware of that which is common knowledge even to little children, she must be a sad case, indeed. Terry has given no actual evidence for the conclusion that Lincoln was a great man; instead, he commits the fallacy of common belief.

*S. E. Asch, "Studies of Independence and Conformity: A Minority of One Against a Unanimous Majority," Psychological Monographs 70 (1956).

"Everyone knows that." "Any schoolchild knows that." Other familiar phrases are also called on in the commission of this fallacy: "No one seriously doubts that" or "No one in his right mind could doubt that" or "No educated person would doubt that." The latter two are especially intimidating. "It's just common knowledge." "That's obvious to anyone who gives it any thought." You can probably add to the list.

How does the fallacy of common belief differ from the fallacy of *two wrongs make a right*? They *are* different. Review the definitions. The *two wrongs* fallacy dealt with action; the fallacy of common belief deals with belief. *Two wrongs make a right* gave rise to the conclusion that something was right—morally permissible; common belief gives rise to the conclusion that something is true.

Past Belief

The fallacy of **past belief** is committed when we accept a statement as true and offer as evidence the claim that it has been believed in the past.

Premise: The claim that a certain statement has been believed in the past.

We conclude that: That statement is true.

The phrase *tried and true* reflects the common view that whatever stands the test of time must have some merit. Perhaps this common view is well based. When someone takes this to an extreme, however, the result can be fallacious reasoning. We do not actually hear people say, "It's been believed in the past, so it must be true." Still, we do hear something very close to that.

EXAMPLE

Luis does not believe in the immortality of the soul. In fact, Luis does not believe that anything like a soul exists at all. This bothers his brother, Leon, who is quite religious and pleads for Luis to try to see the issue differently. "Look," argues Leon, "human beings must have souls. This belief goes back for centuries and centuries!" ∎

Leon commits the fallacy of past belief. It is certainly possible for false beliefs to be held for long periods of time. Even if you insist that humans do have souls, you should recognize that the preceding argument is fallacious.

"People have accepted [or *believed* or *known*] that for centuries." Whenever such a statement is offered as a premise to support the conclusion that the belief at issue is true, the fallacy of past belief is committed. After all, some beliefs that had been popularly held for years turned out subsequently to be false. An example is the ancient belief that in humans, only the male contributes hereditary characteristics to an offspring. With this in mind, follow this example of faulty reasoning.

EXAMPLE

Mona is wondering whether the Holistic Clinic in St. Louis might provide successful therapy for her bad back. Her son is skeptical, insisting that holistic health is just a fad without any scientific basis. Mona disagrees, saying, "But there *must* be something to this holistic health business. Did you know that the ancient Greeks had a holistic conception of health?" ■

It may well be true that there is, as Mona puts it, "something to this holistic health business." However, the Greeks' possession of a similar view does not prove that this is so. The Greeks, after all, were wrong—from our present perspective at least—about many other things. Might they not have been wrong about this as well? Mona needs evidence of a different kind if she is to avoid the fallacy of past belief in arguing for her present belief.

The modern Western world has revered the ancient Greeks. Our view of the history of civilization has endowed some groups of people with a halo of honor. Different characteristics are applied to different groups, and with some, such as the ancient Greeks and the ancient Egyptians, the aura is that of a special, though primitive, capacity for insight into the truth. However well or poorly founded such a view might be, our reverence for such cultures is excessive if it curtails our independent reasoning about particular topics.

The preceding example is correctly referred to as an example of the fallacy of past belief rather than the fallacy of common belief because, while many people may have believed this conclusion, it is the ancient Greeks' special place in history that seems to warrant their credibility. The earlier example of people "believing that for centuries" exhibits the fallacy of past belief because the notion of the longevity of the belief is a crucial element in the persuasive attempt.

False Authority

The fallacy of **false authority** is committed when we accept a statement as true and offer as evidence the claim that it was accepted by a particular person whose knowledge or reliability on this issue is questionable.

Premise: The claim that person X accepts this statement. (This person's knowledge or reliability is questionable.)

We conclude that: That statement is true.

If we were to rely only on information based on our personal experiences and not at all on reports of others' experiences, we could claim much less knowledge than we do. Those who did not have firsthand knowledge of the politics of the White House staff or the Vatican or the Kremlin would have to profess ignorance of the subject and leave the consideration of the matter to those who did have such knowledge. Those who hadn't been to the meetings of the U.S.-Soviet summit would have to do the same. Those without extensive experience in nuclear weaponry would forfeit the possibility of making intelligent comments on that topic.

Actually, we do rely on information provided by others when we think about both global and mundane matters. It seems silly to suggest that we do otherwise. We are fortunate to have books, newspapers, magazines, acquaintances, and other sources to expand our horizon of understanding.

Still, not everything that is reported to us is true, and it's not clear whether it's worse to believe too little or too much. As information users, we need to be able to distinguish between more and less credible sources. This is often difficult, since there is not always a clear line of distinction between the justified authority and the unqualified source. Nevertheless, we can make a beginning with the fallacy of false authority.

When the argument for the truth of a statement rests on the testimony of someone who is not in a position to know or, for some other reason, is likely to convey incorrect information, the fallacious reasoning may be branded as false authority. Let's examine an obvious example of the fallacy.

EXAMPLE

"I'll let you in on a hot financial tip," the bartender confides in his already glassy-eyed regular. "When you're deciding where to invest your money, keep in mind that the economy is going to take a sharp and long-term upswing in April."

The customer manages a question, but his gaze doesn't wander from the neon advertising lamp. "How do you know?"

"My neighbor told me." The bartender leans closer. "And he's been very involved in financial dealings for years — stocks and bonds and real estate and things like that." ■

Initially, the bartender does not argue for his claim that the economy is going to take a sharp and long-term upswing in April. He offers no evidence. In response to his customer's question, however, he does offer a single premise: "My neighbor told me." At this point, it seems that we are dealing with a rumor. Having no reason to believe that the neighbor has any special insight, we should recognize the fallacy of false authority. The bartender does go on to describe the neighbor's credentials ("he's been very involved in financial dealings . . ."), but this is insufficient to eliminate the fallacious character of his reasoning. Many people "are very involved with financial dealings," and even within this group there is wide disagreement concerning economic forecasts. Contrary to the bartender's suggestion, the neighbor's claim about the upswing was not qualified in any way. Economics is a social science that notoriously produces divergent predictions even from the experts. Even the word of an expert economist should not be taken as proof of such a conclusion.

It is true, then, that the fallacy of false authority can be committed even when an expert is speaking within his or her own area of competence. Examine this passage.

EXAMPLE

Mike is in a lazy sprawl across his favorite TV chair, watching a talk show on which an astrophysicist is being interviewed. "And what about the interesting question of intelligent life on other planets?" asks the host. "Dr. Wexler, being an astrophysicist, you must have considered the issue of this possibility. Tell us, *is there* intelligent life elsewhere in the universe?"

"Yes, I'm certain that there are creatures whose capacity for intelligence is at least equal to ours. . . ."

Mike presses the off button on his remote control box and walks out of the room. Talking to no one but himself, he says quietly, "How interesting. I guess she knows what she's talking about. She's an astrophysicist. I never thought there was life out there, but this isn't the first time I've been wrong." ■

■
Comments on the Fallacies

Fallacies can occur in spoken or in written communications. In some instances they will be obvious; in some they will be hard to recognize. Although the pleasure of the successful recognition of another person's fallacious reasoning may incline you to bring it immediately to that person's attention, you should first consider the probable reaction to, and results of, your comment. If your comment undermines your intentions for your overall interaction with this person, you must exercise self-discipline by withholding or rewording it.

Who commits the fallacy — the person who presents it or the person who "falls for it"? Generally, both the person who originates and the person who accepts fallacious reasoning commit the fallacy. The first person *argues fallaciously* by presenting the reasoning, regardless of whether he or she is aware of the error. The second person *reasons fallaciously* (as does the first person, if the fallacy is committed unwittingly) by accepting the reasoning as adequate.

While most of the patterns of reasoning in these fallacies are erroneous when judged by the standard of deductive validity (begging the question and false dilemma are exceptions), some arguments that are examples of these fallacies may have a degree of inductive strength. For example, the fallacy of division may yet allow inductive strength, especially if the whole has few parts.

Dr. Wexler does not commit the fallacy of false authority. Even if she is wrong about extraterrestrial beings, she displays no fallacious argumentation in the preceding example. In fact, the television set is turned off so soon that we do not even know whether she offers any argumentation at all.

On the other hand, Mike *does* commit the fallacy of false authority in concluding that he has been wrong and that there is, after all, intelligent life in outer space. Although the issue does, at least partially, fall within the range of Dr. Wexler's expertise, no one, as far as we know, possesses any evidence that would establish a conclusion such as this with certainty. Therefore, despite Dr. Wexler's knowledge in the general area and on related topics, Mike should realize that unquestioned acceptance of this conclusion is unjustified. Unless it is a closely guarded secret, news like this would have lit up the pages of books, magazines, and newspapers, and provided seemingly endless hours of television coverage. Mike should certainly not just dismiss Dr. Wexler's comment, but he should pay close attention to the evidence before passing judgment. Perhaps Dr. Wexler holds this belief on religious or other grounds, rather than on the basis of scientific evidence. Perhaps she makes this point after Mike's television is off. Whatever the case, Mike has judged hastily.

Often there is no good reason to doubt that someone's testimony assures the truth of a certain conclusion. If the baseball coach says that his star pitcher has a sore arm, we should believe him unless there is a good reason to doubt it. If the psychology professor says that phobias have been re-classified, we should believe her unless there is a good reason to doubt it. We are not committing a fallacy every time we accept someone's word. Still, it is important to remember that there is a difference between knowing that something is true "on good authority" and knowing that something is true on the basis of personal observation and reasoning. The latter is almost always a firmer knowledge than the former.

In technical areas such as nuclear power, ecology, governmental budgets, health care, automobile safety, and urban design, we need to use information provided by people who have special knowledge. We should also listen carefully to their reasoned judgments concerning probabilities. Their expertise is valuable. When listening to the experts, however, remember the following:

1. *It is sometimes difficult to identify the most qualified authorities.* Some people who have much experience in one area or who have advanced university degrees (M.A., Ph.D.) may nevertheless be barely competent in that area. The *quality* of a person's work in that field is relevant but often unknown to the casual inquirer. Persons who head organizations with impressive names sometimes gain unwarranted respect and credibility. For a nominal fee, however, a person can file for a "fictitious name." That person can then identify himself or herself as, for example, the president of the National Association of Taxpaying Americans. Such an "association" might have one or several members. We should thus avoid being impressed by mere "expert appearances."

2. *Experts can be biased.* Anyone, including scientists, priests, psychologists, historians, and statisticians, can have points of logical vulnerability that draw them toward or away from certain kinds of data or certain conclusions even in their own specialties. Sometimes a person's previous positions in research publications incline him or her toward that same position or a similar one. Few people are willing to encourage the perception that their previous work is seriously flawed.

3. *The conclusions of even the best experts can conflict.* When the most credible authorities disagree, there is no reasonable alternative to weighing the evidence for yourself. Even if the issue is highly specialized, you will need to evaluate the strength of each position by examining the authorities' expressed reasons for settling on their positions. You should seek information that is in "layman's terms," or nontechnical language. At last, sometimes there is no choice but to make a provisional decision on the basis of partial information and that dangerous sensibility called intuition.

DON'T BE FOOLED BY "LOOK-ALIKES"

Beware of look-alikes. By knowing the definitions of the fallacies, you can determine whether the fallacies are committed in particular cases. On occasion, a person's reasoning may resemble an actual example of a certain fallacy, but the resemblance will not be sufficient to qualify that reasoning as another example of that fallacy. In cases like this, either the similarity is incidental and does not fit the definition, or the reasoning conforms to part but not all of the definition. One logic textbook writer has actually named "False Charge of Fallacy" as a fallacy itself, committed when a person incorrectly charges that another has committed a specific fallacy.*

Consider some examples of how an overzealous fallacy-spotter might incorrectly label a comment or written passage as fallacious.

The fallacy of *attacking the person* might be incorrectly specified when a relevant claim about the person's background has been made and no questionable conclusion concerning the person's reasoning or position has been drawn. Example: "George will certainly know something about prison routine. He's an ex-convict who served eight years in the state prison."

The fallacy of *attacking the person* might be incorrectly specified when the person has sidetracked the matter by "getting personal," but has drawn no questionable conclusion concerning the person's reasoning or position. Example: "You just like to argue for the sake of argument, don't you? I hate it when you do that."

The fallacy of *argument from ignorance* might be incorrectly specified when a lack of evidence for an opposing view has been mentioned, but that position has not been rejected on this basis. Example: "We have found no evidence to support the claim that he acted in self-defense."

The fallacy of *questionable cause* might be incorrectly specified when a well-justified claim has been made concerning the cause of something. Example: Extensive hair loss immediately following certain kinds of chemotherapy would quite reasonably be attributed to that therapy.

The fallacy of *begging the question* might be incorrectly specified when a second claim has repeated or assumed an earlier claim, but there is no premise-conclusion relation between the two claims. Example: "You'll get the raise you asked for. Your boss knows he can't replace you, and he

---

Howard Kahane, in Logic and Contemporary Rhetoric *(Belmont, CA: Wadsworth, 1992).*

thinks you'll quit if he turns you down. There's no doubt about it. He'll give you the raise."

The fallacy of *two wrongs make a right* might be incorrectly specified when claims concerning the success of past practices have been offered as reasons for adopting the practice, but no issues of right and wrong are concerned. Example: "My attorney, Mr. Carr, has served me well in the past. So I intend to use his services again this time, even if this area of law is not his specialty."

The fallacy of *division* might be incorrectly specified when a characteristic has been determined to be possessed by a member of a whole on the basis of the claim that this characteristic was possessed by "every one" of the members rather than by the whole considered collectively. Example: "*Of course* he's a brave soldier. *All* soldiers in the First Division are brave."

The fallacy of *false dilemma* might be incorrectly specified when the omitted alternative was not a workable or viable one. Example: A friend says, "You're not really limited to the alternatives of passing this final test or failing the course. Just get the teacher to let you do an extra-credit assignment." This teacher, however, does not accept extra-credit work.

The fallacy of *contrary-to-fact hypothesis* might be incorrectly specified when the result that has been named is actually a necessary result rather than a merely possible result. Example: "If you had joined the army last year, as I suggested, you wouldn't be out of work with no paycheck and no place to live, like you are now."

The fallacy of *common belief* might be incorrectly specified when, although widespread acceptance of a belief has been noted, this has not been offered as proof of its truth. Example: "Interest in extraterrestrial beings is greater than ever. Tens of thousands of people actually believe in UFOs."

The fallacy of *past belief* might be incorrectly specified when, although past acceptance of a belief has been noted, this has not been offered as proof of its truth. Example: "Many cultures of the past have believed in some form of karma."

The fallacy of *false authority* might be incorrectly specified when a person who is not in a position to be knowledgeable about a claim nevertheless makes such a claim, but there has been no third-party acceptance of the claim on the basis of that testimony. (Speaking without justification does not necessarily involve fallacious reasoning.) Example: Your brother describes the "secret war plans" of the Soviet Union.

These are by no means the only ways to mistake a look-alike for the actual fallacy. There are many ways for two comments or passages to "look alike." You must simply know the fallacies so well that you recognize the essential aspects of each one and seldom get "taken in" by a look-alike. While this is not easy, it is important.

Finally, there will be cases in which the line separating a fallacy and a look-alike is not clear, even to the competent fallacy-spotter. You must, in these cases, be able to analyze the comment or passage so well that you are at least *aware* of the ways in which the wording is similar to exact examples of the fallacy and the ways in which it is dissimilar.

■

PRACTICE ACTIVITIES

Set 7.1 *For each of the following examples of reasoning, name the fallacy that is committed. These are the possibilities: attacking the person, argument from ignorance, questionable cause, begging the question, two wrongs make a right, division, false dilemma, contrary-to-fact hypothesis, common belief, past belief, false authority. Then explain how that particular example of reasoning conforms to the definition of the fallacy that you have named.*

Example: Since there's not a bit of objective evidence to show that spirits exist, we must conclude that they belong only to the realm of fantasy.

Correct answer: Argument from ignorance.

Explanation: A lack of proof for the belief that spirits exist is insufficient to prove the opposing belief that spirits do not exist.

> *The explanation can be worded differently, but you should show that you know the definition of the fallacy and that you know which elements of the example play a part in that definition.*

1. The closing paragraph from a letter to the editor of *The Desert Sun*, criticizing opponents of the death penalty, May 5, 1990:

    If the individuals or groups who profess to be against the death penalty were asked to support this belief with money out of their pockets instead of just supporting this position verbally, it might be difficult to find enough of them to support this program.

attacking a person

2. From a letter to the editor of the *San Diego Union*, March 5, 1989:

   false dilemma

   Do we want another memorial wall in Washington or are we willing to stop all aid to the [Nicaraguan rebels] . . . ?

3. Two excerpts from "[Pete] Rose Has Suffered Enough, He Doesn't Deserve to Go to Jail" by Thomas Boswell, syndicated by the *Washington Post*, April 1990:

   #1. He was sent to prison for neglecting to pay taxes on his fees for signing thousands of autographs. Ironically, in a time when many corporations paid no taxes at all, Rose paid a dozen times more to the IRS than he evaded.

   #2. If U.S. Judge S. Arthur Spiegel sends Rose to jail, as he has already sentenced Rose's friend Tommy Gioisia to five years, then Rose will have been imprisoned for neglecting to report about three percent of his income. How does that compare to the national average?

4. From a column in the *Telescope*, May 4, 1990:

   questionable cause

   It is . . . fear of failure that motives the American student[s].
   motivates

5. From "She Who Must Be Obeyed," *Newsweek*, January 15, 1990:

   cause + effect = questionable cause

   Panamanians . . . believe that Felicidad [Noriega's wife] pushed one of Noriega's mistresses out a window to her death. The woman's death had been ruled a suicide, but Felicidad was said to have been the last to see her alone.

6. From *Weekly World News*, May 14, 1990:

   2 wrongs make a right

   She said Di Gregorio had said that in recent months his deranged daughter had refused to take the medication that kept her fits of rage under control.
   Miss Rodriguez recalled one especially violent outburst two years earlier when Carol attacked her father with a knife.
   "I think he did everything he could for her. You can't blame him for killing her," she said.

7. From an article in the *San Diego Union*, May 5, 1990:

   false authority (or attacking person)

   Gilliam is serving an 18-month sentence at Lompoc federal prison in California after pleading guilty to accepting bribes in connection with HUD projects. . . . Following the hearing [at which Gilliam testified about the involvement of Mr. Pierce], Pierce's attorneys . . . attacked the credibility of Gilliam's testimony, describing it as "the words of a convicted felon."

questionable cause

8. From a movie review by Michelle Pollino in *Preview* for the week of May 14, 1990:

> Rosalie rationalizes, "He's Italian, so he flirts a little."

9. From the *Escondido Times-Advocate*, February 28, 1990:

division

> A candidate in the state senate race accused his opponent of murder because his law firm had defended a nursing home that was sued for negligence. The TV ad showed the patient's tombstone.

10. A columnist's comments in the *Escondido Times-Advocate*, May 20, 1990:

questionable cause

> Ah, but it is the distinctions between men and women that have made the world go 'round for so many millennia. And it is the breaking down of these distinctions that has led to the breakdown of the home and the enormous social consequences we now face because of it.

11. From *The Sun*, May 14, 1990:

> Jesus Christ has returned to Earth! And he's now working miracles for the betterment of all mankind.
>
> "There is overwhelming evidence that Christ's return has already taken place and that an announcement of this only awaits a final decision by the Pope," says a Vatican source.

questionable cause

> "There are indicators all around us that Jesus is living again and working miracles today just as he did 2,000 years ago," says Monsignor Alexandrini Biaggi.
>
> "It's the only explanation for remarkable events that are happening throughout the world. How else can you explain what we're seeing? Who would have dared dream that the people of Eastern Europe would suddenly be free after more than four decades of living under tyranny? And who would expect peace in long-embattled Nicaragua? Who would expect a change of government, not by revolution, but by ballot?"

12. From the *National Examiner*, May 14, 1990:

(or is missing)
false dilemma

> The convicts said they kill to ease crowded prison conditions. ". . . We have to kill [other convicts]. It's the only way we can get attention."

13. From a letter to the editor of the *San Diego Union*, May 22, 1989:

contrary to fact hypothesis

> . . . the salesmen and women of America provide a valuable service to the consumer and are responsible for the high standard of living we enjoy in the United States today. If it weren't

for the telemarketer making the calls, then we salespeople would not have customers. With no customers — no sales; if there are no sales nothing gets produced, no production means no jobs.

14. A quote from R. Gregory Nokes, Associated Press diplomatic writer, July 1986:

    . . . administration officials, risking new controversy over their South African policy, are saying freedom for blacks might be possible without black majority rule or a system of one-man, one-vote.

    "There are a lot of different ways they can go about it that will work," Secretary of State George P. Shultz told Congress this week. He said one-man, one-vote isn't perfectly practiced in the United States and need not be a model for South Africa to follow.

15. Had it not been for Abraham Lincoln, black people would still be slaves today. (*Missing 'if'*)

16. A passage by George F. Will that appeared in *Newsweek*, August 18, 1986:

    This summer the administration has agreed to subsidize grain sales to the Soviet Union. American taxpayers wil pay to enable the invaders of Afghanistan to buy grain cheaper than Americans can. Why? Because 22 of the 34 seats contested this year are in farm states. Bob Dole, senator from the breadbasket of the Soviet Union, a.k.a. Kansas, rationalizes this blunder by recalling Eisenhower's statement that we should sell the Soviets anything they cannot shoot back at us. Alas, dumb thoughts, unlike wine, do not improve with age.

17. From a television commercial for Public Insurance Corporation:

    No one else can give you such low rates because no one else represents our company.

18. If John F. Kennedy had not been assassinated, he would not have been such a famous president.

19. There's nothing wrong with misrepresentation on tax forms. You can be sure that most of the people holding government posts are doing the very same thing.

20. A financial advisor to a client:

    You can either invest as I suggest or you can lose your money to inflation.

[margin note: attacking]

21. Speaking in English in a tent at Tripoli's Al Fatah University, [Libyan leader] Qaddafi told reporters the following statement that appeared in *The Tribune*, (AP), April 11, 1986:

> I don't worry about his [Reagan's] declarations, particularly what he said about me personally. He's an old man.

22. From *Good News, etc.*, April 1986:

[margin note: false dilemma]

> . . . most families [in this area] feel the need for two incomes in order to live comfortably. This creates an artificial choice of either loss of parental guidance or loss of added income.

[margin note: division]

23. I heard that the nation's educational community is opposing the new tax bill. George, you're a teacher. Just why do you think the bill is a bad one?

[margin note: past belief]

24. Despite constant criticism of the Electoral College system, it's clear that this is the best method for selecting a national leader. After all, it has been accepted as a fair and good method for a couple of centuries now.

25. From *The Plain Truth*, June 1985, back cover:

[margin note: false dilemma]

> Will the next 15 years bring human extinction — or the dawn of a new world of peace and incredible achievement?

[margin note: false dilemma]

26. What will *you* do? Will you give every penny you can afford for helping the pathetically starving people in Africa? Or will you clutch desperately to each dollar you earn, using all of your abundance of wealth for personal comfort and convenience?

[margin note: two wrongs make a right]

27. I see nothing wrong with doing my civic duty and casting my vote in a local election even if I am uninformed on the issues. Why, I'll bet that half of the people who vote have done essentially no research prior to election day.

[margin note: attacking the person]

28. Just disregard Ralph Nadar's latest list of reasons to require stricter safety standards on new cars. He has been critical of the United States auto industry for years. Why should we expect anything different now?

[margin note: contrary to fact]

29. Were it not for a handful of brave colonists in the eighteenth century, we would still be paying taxes to the English crown!

30. A driver of a car to a companion:

[margin note: questionable cause]

> "That fellow up ahead is weaving. He must be drunk."

31. Sportswriter Jerry Magee questioned whether it was proper for television (through instant replays) to be used to help in the refereeing of games in the National Football League. His comment on the subject appeared in the *San Diego Union*, August 1, 1986:

> Should television, with a mission only to report, help police games?

argument of ignorance

32. You can't prove he was to blame for her misfortune, so it must actually have been someone else who was responsible.

33. *Bank officer:* You say, Dr Scott, that you will repay this unsecured loan. How does my bank know that you are honest and trustworthy so we can take your word for that?

circular reasoning

Dr. Scott: You can ask my department chairperson, Dr. Aldape.

Bank officer: But how do we know we can rely on the word of Dr. Aldape?

begging the question

Dr. Scott: Oh, don't worry about that. I can vouch for him without reservation!

34. A high-school teacher comments:

> My students don't seem to be doing as well on the tests I've been giving lately. Students are apparently not as smart as they used to be.

35. Altruism, the view that people do not always act out of self-interest, is clearly false. There is no proof that, when you consider ultimate motivations, any motive other than pure self-interest is at work.

36. Were it not for the Watergate scandal of the 1970s, the American people would never have discovered the extent to which corruption had gone on in our government.

37. From a letter to the editor of the *Morning Press*, October 8, 1985:

> I get so fed up with [Speaker of the House of Representatives] Tip O'Neill's prattle about Africa.
> Does he want the Commies to take over Africa and South America? He has lived off the taxpayer all his life. Take a look at the big pension he will receive.

38. *Of course* women are more emotional than men. Everybody knows that! Since nobody—or almost nobody—really doubts this, it's just silly for you to challenge this simple fact. Of course it's true.

39. From *Time*, September 9, 1985:

> When a British Tory asked him about religious freedom in the U.S.S.R., [Soviet leader] Gorbachev testily replied, "You persecute entire communities. . . ."

40. Even the ancient Egyptians believed in a form of life after death. So there must be some truth in that idea.

41. In the movie *The Bishop's Wife*, the bishop (played by David Niven) asks the angel (played by Cary Grant) who he is. The angel replies, "I'm an angel." The bishop's challenge, "How do I know that?" meets with the following reply: "Surely you, of all people, know you can believe an angel."

Set 7.2 *Using the list of fallacies from Practice Activities Set 7.1, name the fallacy for which each of the following examples might be mistaken. Then explain, through reference to the definition, why this is not a good example of that fallacy. Each of these is a fallacy look-alike.*

1. From "Passive Smoke Boosts Heart-Disease Risk," *San Diego Union*, May 21, 1990:

   The Tobacco Institute, which represents cigarette makers, said the surgeon general had failed to find proof that passive smoking causes heart disease.

   Brennan Dawson, a spokeswoman for the institute, said in a telephone interview there have been only three studies since the surgeon general's 1986 report, "and they continue to support the conclusions" that there is no proven link between passive smoking and heart disease.

2. From the *Autobiography of Malcolm X:*

   "The devil is also a man," Reginald said. . . . "The white man is the devil." . . . I said, "Without any exception?" "Without any exception."

3. A columnist from the *San Marcos Courier* reported the following on August 8, 1985:

   Bradley says Justice [Rose] Bird is interpreting [the Constitution] to her own prejudice against the death sentence. If that is true, it has not been proved to me.

4. You wouldn't be in such misery defending yourself against charges of medical malpractice, Arlene, if you had gone into financial planning, as I had advised you, instead of medicine.

5. From *Time*, September 29, 1986:

   Augustine more than any other writer defined Roman Catholic teaching on the Trinity, conditions for waging a "just war" and the "original sin" of Adam and Eve that corrupts all humanity.

With the latter teaching, complains French philospher Jean Guitton, "he weighed down Christianity with his pessimism."

6. From the article "Coping with Anxiety" by Carol Tavris, *Science Digest*, February 1986:

   "In spite of promising successes in treating some anxiety disorders with medications, there is a complete lack of evidence that drugs alone will do the job," says [David] Burns [founder of the Behavioral Sciences Research Foundation].

7. Arthur Schlesinger, Jr., after arguing his case in "Against a One-Term Six-Year President" (*The New York Times*, January 10, 1986), observes at the end of his article:

   The Founding Fathers were everlastingly right when they turned down this well-intentioned but ill-considered proposal 200 years ago.

8. John is a liar and a cheater.

9. If I hadn't had a serious motorcycle accident when I was a teenager, I might have been a concert pianist.

10. Dr. Stanley Weiss of the National Cancer Institute was quoted in *Newsweek*, November 10, 1986, with reference to AIDS:

    What happens in the next five years will depend on our success in changing people's attitudes and behaviors. If we don't succeed, the virus will continue to spread.

11. In the same issue of *Newsweek* as the previous example, there was an article on our ancestors of the late Ice Age. In this article, we read:

    . . . mammoth bones were stacked in precise ways. One hut was made primarily of long bones; in another 95 jawbones are stacked above skulls in a herringbone pattern. [Olga] Soffer [of the University of Illinois] speculates that the architecture may have been the result of ritual. . . .

12. You have two choices. You can either do military service or you can remain a civilian all your life. There might be advantages with each choice.

13. An increasing lack of public trust in, and political support for, former President Richard Nixon was the cause of his resignation.

14. You have lied on the application form for financial aid in college, just as thousands of others have. It's a very common practice; people are learning how to make themselves appear poorer than they are.

15. You cannot prove your claim that human souls are immortal. Nor can you prove your claim that God will ultimately save all of humankind. From this evidence, I conclude that you are more attracted to opinions than you are to rational investigation.

16. President Duarte of El Salvador is a heavy-handed dictator who is ruthless in his attempts to maintain power. I reject his approach to the political realities.

17. A mother to her daughter over breakfast:

    "You wouldn't have to deal with this problem of coming up with enough money to repair the car if you hadn't taken the car last night. I *told* you to stay home and leave the car in the garage. You got just what you deserved for not listening to me."

18. From *National Geographic*, December 1985 ("How We Found *Titanic*," by Robert D. Ballard):

    It was from [the crow's nest of the *Titanic*] that lookout Fred Fleet, who survived, first sighted the iceberg one-fourth of a mile dead ahead. Instinctively he gave three rings on the bell above the crow's nest. . . . Fleet warned the bridge [by telephone], "Iceberg right ahead!"

    Ironically, Fleet's words doomed *Titanic*. In response to the warning her officer-in-charge tried to reverse engines and turn hard to starboard. The reversal actually turned the ship slowly to port, and she suffered the fatal gash in her starboard side. Had she rammed the berg head-on, she would likely have flooded only two or three compartments and remained afloat.

19. From a letter to the editor of *The New York Times*, February 25, 1986:

    There is not an iota of evidence to suggest that Moslems in North Africa have been involved, directly or indirectly, in any terrorist activity.

20. From an Associated Press release concerning political unrest in the Philippine Islands:

    "There has been widespread speculation that Mr. Salvatierra's death was politically motivated by pro-Marcos supporters. Our ongoing, thorough, and exhaustive investigation has discovered no evidence whatever to support that position," Thompson told a news conference at police headquarters.

Set 7.3 *Which of the following involve fallacies? Explain why each is either an actual fallacy or merely a look-alike that might be mistaken for one.*

1. From *Newsweek*, May 21, 1990:

   > Since 1983 more than 700 Thai workers in Singapore and else-where have died of what local health authorities call Sudden Unexplained Nocturnal Death Syndrome. Health experts sus-pect the deaths are caused by poor diet resulting in too much insulin and not enough potassium and vitamin B-1. But the men, believing that a widow's spirit is snatching men from their marital beds, have begun wearing lipstick and painted nails to bed in order to trick the ghost. But recently a man, dressed like his wife, died in bed. Back in one village, a 22-pound phallic symbol — thought to ward off spirits — has al-ready been made.

2. From the *Escondido Times-Advocate*, March 3, 1989, regarding John Tower's nomination for Secretary of Defense:

   > No concrete evidence has been offered that excessive drinking will affect Tower's performance as secretary of defense. There-fore, Tower's confirmation would not be a detriment to the national security of the United States.

3. Written by Susan Van Raalte, author of *Apply Yourself: Writing College Applications That Get Results:*

   > Students frequently tune out their parents at [college] applica-tion time because they fear their parents' advice will be out-of-date, unrealistic or simply incorrect. One mother recounts how her daughter rejected her advice by exclaiming: "What do you know about college? You went to an all-girls school. No one goes to an all-girls school anymore!"

4. After the space shuttle *Challenger* exploded and fell into the sea, debris was found afloat in the Atlantic Ocean. One private citizen found a bone and tissue fragment with blue fabric attached. The following excerpt is from the *San Diego Union*:

   > NASA officials in Houston said the astronauts were issued blue flight suits, but the officials said no link to the shuttle explosion had been established.

5. *David:* But how do we know that he *meant* to kill the old man?

   Mark: It's a matter of intentions. It's clear that he intended from the outset to kill him. It was his purpose in the first place. That's how we know.

6. DRGs (Diagnosis Related Groups) are being instituted to limit health care costs. These will limit Medicare's reimbursement to hospitals according to the type of health care problem. I read an article in Sunday's *L.A. Times*. It was written by a physician and it opposed the DRGs as undesirable for the patient. But I'm not listening to a word of it. It's clear to me that physicians oppose the DRGs because they'll end up making less money themselves.

7. From an interview with Daniel Ellsberg that appeared in *The Progressive*, July 1985:

> Our Presidents have come close to using nuclear weapons — close in the sense that they passed the trigger to our opponents. Whether there would be an explosion was up to what our opponents did.
>
> They were *not* bluffing. If the Chinese had attacked Quemoy, or if the blockade had been fully effective, I think Eisenhower would have done what he told the Joint Chiefs of Staff he intended to do — he would have used nuclear weapons. That scares me, and I think it would scare a lot of people to know that we almost went to war over Quemoy, if the Chinese had not been mature enough, cautious enough, to back down. If the Chinese had been like Khomeini, let's say, we would have had a nuclear war.

8. From a promotional brochure for *The Plain Truth*:

> "What Next? Prosperity or Economic Depression? Peace or Another World War?"

9. From a columnist for the *San Marcos Courier*, August 15, 1985:

> The four-page election sheet that came from [Assemblyman] Ron Packard was obviously written by a Reagan propagandist who does not think the rest of us know much. No economist I ever read . . . could have made such a mindless, illogical mess of mishmash. If anyone falls for this pack of trash they are also mindless.

10. You are insisting vehemently that nuclear accidents are avoidable in a world in which nuclear power plants are common. I refuse to accept that unless I have proof of it. To date, I have seen none.

11. Yes, I cheated on the test, but so did a lot of other people. To be fair, you should punish all of the offenders equally.

12. The only life in the universe may be right here on this planet. On the other hand, there *may be* life elsewhere in the universe. Who

knows which of these claims is true? Certainly one or the other is true.

13. Written by Henry Kissinger and quoted in *Harper's*, July 1985:

    If the United States had not suffered a tragic loss of executive authority in the early 1970s, which, in creating the oddest coalition of liberals who disliked President Nixon and conservatives who disliked the Russians, destroyed the political basis for further negotiations, the superpowers would surely have completed agreements on mutual restraints [on nuclear arms]—which might or might not have worked.

14. We know that Pope John XXIII was moved by compassion, since all popes have been moved by compassion.

15. Don't look to your physician for sympathy on medical costs, George. Dr. Diaz will undoubtedly be unsympathetic. The medical community has strongly opposed virtually all significant cost-containment efforts and shown no practical concern to limit the costs of health care to the public.

16. The Atlanta Braves are going to win the National League pennant this year. It's true! I heard Ted Turner, the owner of the team, say so himself.

17. I don't see how you can think you have a moral obligation to feed the starving masses overseas. No one else seems to feel that way.

18. How can you doubt that good and right will eventually triumph? This has been a basic assumption of Western thought for ages.

19. Reported in *The Sporting News: 1986 Pro Football Yearbook*:

    Later someone asked [Miami Dolphins coach] Don [Shula] how he would have reacted if his son [playing for the opposing Baltimore Colts] had broken away on a long punt return.
    "I would have chewed out my coverage team," he said. "It could have cost us the game."

20. There will be no World War III. A famous novelist has explained that the new and inevitable direction of the world community is toward cooperation among people, factions, and nations.

21. It's all just talk. The Schusters aren't going to sue the school district. The superintendent of schools just told me yesterday that no one would *dare* sue the district over such a small issue.

For Further Reading

Acock, Malcolm. *Informal Logic Examples and Exercises*. Belmont, CA: Wadsworth, 1985.

A collection of quotes and written passages that exemplify certain concepts in logic. Chapters 13, 14, 15, and 16 cover fallacies.

Damer, T. Edward. *Attacking Faulty Reasoning*. Belmont, CA: Wadsworth, 1987.

An extensive listing of fallacies, with examples and advice on attacking each fallacy.

Engel, S. Morris. *With Good Reason*. New York: St. Martin's Press, 1990.

An introduction to the fallacies.

Kahane, Howard. *Logic and Contemporary Rhetoric*. Belmont, CA: Wadsworth, 1992.

An introduction to persuasion in politics, advertising, and the public media. The three chapters on fallacies are illustrated with examples from these sources.

■

C　H　A　P　T　E　R

EIGHT

Recognizing Other Kinds of Faulty Reasoning

D o you sometimes sense that something is wrong with "the reasoning"—your own or someone else's—but you can't put your finger on just what it is? This is a bothersome feeling that can result in the acceptance of the suspect reasoning since "I can't find anything specific that's wrong with it." People are sometimes embarrassed to admit that, although they sense an error, they can't find it.

Some faulty reasoning follows the pattern of one of the eleven informal fallacies that were explored in Chapter 7 or one of the less common informal fallacies that occasionally mislead.*

Other kinds of faulty reasoning follow different patterns that you can examine in this chapter (although some dangerous or erroneous reasoning doesn't follow any particular pattern). You can also master, if you haven't already, the art of creating counterexample "logical analogies" to demonstrate the invalidity of some reasoning. Don't resign yourself to accepting weak reasoning because you don't recognize the logical mistake. Learn about some of those mistakes.

SPOT THE FORMAL FALLACY

With the informal fallacies or Chapter 7, the kind of evidence offered (the "content" of the argument) is inappropriate for the conclusion drawn. With formal fallacies, something about the structure of the argument (its "form") allows you to recognize that it's invalid apart from any other consideration

---

*For accounts of those other fallacies and different versions of the Chapter 7 fallacies, please see "For Further Reading" at the end of this chapter.

of the relation between the premises and the conclusion. These formal fallacies can be convincing because they resemble arguments whose form is deductively valid. However, these formal fallacies regularly produce invalid reasoning. The ones described in this section are *affirming the consequent* and *denying the antecedent* (which are forms of conditional arguments), the *false universal syllogism*, and the *false universal-to-particular syllogism*.

Conditional Arguments and Their Counterfeits

It is important for us to take a special look at the question of validity in one particular kind of argument — the conditional argument. The reason is simple: Although conditional arguments are used continually in everyday reasoning, people consistently make mistakes when deciding whether the conclusion follows from the premises.

How many times do you say the word *if* in an average day? Since this little word is so familiar, we do not become especially alert to the logic involved in its use. We should. *If* is the traditional sign of a conditional statement, and conditional statements are often presented within deceptive conditional arguments.

An if-then statement such as "If your candidate is elected, then our country is doomed" is called a **conditional statement**. Part of the statement is offered as a *condition* for the other part. In the example just mentioned, the speaker is claiming that the existence of the condition ("your candidate is elected") guarantees the existence of a certain result ("our country is doomed").

In a conditional statement, the phrase that follows the word *if* is called the **antecedent**. The phrase that follows the word *then* is called the **consequent** of the conditional statement. In the example, the antecedent is "your candidate is elected" (the condition); the consequent is "our country is doomed."

Conditional statements sometimes vary from the regular if-then form. Here are three variations:

1. The word *then* may be omitted. The meaning of the statement is not changed when we say, "If your candidate is elected, our country is doomed."

2. The word *if* may be presented in the middle of the sentence instead of at the beginning. When we say, "Our country is doomed if your candidate is elected," the antecedent "your candidate is elected" comes after the consequent "our country is doomed."

3. Other words, such as *when* or *whenever*, sometimes introduce the antecedent instead of *if*. The meaning of the statement "If I drink too much

alcohol I get sick" is basically the same as the meaning of the statements "When I drink too much alcohol I get sick" and "Whenever I drink too much alcohol I get sick."

Conditional arguments, by definition, involve conditional statements. Here is an example of a conditional argument.

Whenever Aunt Mary visits us during the summer, I have a miserable time. But I won't have a miserable time *this* summer because Aunt Mary is fortunately not going to visit.

The first premise is a conditional statement. Then the conclusion is stated and another premise is stated. Is the argument valid? No. Certainly other factors may cause the speaker's summer to be miserable. So even if the premises were true, the conclusion might not be true. This argument does not have good form, even if it appears to at first sight.

Here is another conditional argument.

Kim must not have known the material for this test, because if a person really knows the material, then that person will get an A, but Kim wasn't one of the students who got an A.

Here the conclusion is tested first. Then comes a conditional premise and another premise. Is this argument valid? Yes. If the premises were true, the conclusion would have to be true. So the argument passes the test for validity. Perhaps, however, this sounds like bad reasoning to you, and perhaps the previous argument sounded as if it were good reasoning. You should indeed sense something wrong with the argument, but the problem is not one of validity — it is not a lack of good form. The problem is that the argument is not sound. The problem you may sense is that the conditional premise is false. There are good grounds to doubt the truth of the statement "If a person really knows the material, then that person will get an A." Almost all of us remember situations in which someone "really knew" the material, yet did not receive an A. One possibility is that the person was nervous or very tired or distracted during the test and did not perform well for that reason. The reasoning is valid; our argument is not sound because the conditional premise is false.

Validity is the thorny problem in conditional arguments, however, because even short and simple conditional arguments are regularly evaluated incorrectly in this regard. Think of how often we use conditional arguments in everyday reasoning: "If I take that course, then . . . ," "If the car could be fixed by tomorrow morning, then . . . ," "If you had changed your approach, then. . . ." Let's consider how mistakes are made in such reasoning and how they can be avoided. After all, if the conditional argument you judge wrongly has a conclusion that is important to you or to someone else, the price for that mistake might be high.*

Examine the following four arguments. They are similar in that each has the same conditional premise, but they are not identical. Each is different from the others. In each of the four cases, decide whether the argument is valid or invalid.

1. If Mr. Rivera is the instructor for that course, then the students are enjoying themselves and learning a lot.

   (And) Mr. Rivera *is* the instructor for that course.

   (Therefore) the students are enjoying themselves and learning a lot.

2. If Mr. Rivera is the instructor for that course, then the students are enjoying themselves and learning a lot.

   The students *are* enjoying themselves and learning a lot.

   (Therefore) Mr. Rivera is the instructor for that course.

3. If Mr. Rivera is the instructor for that course, then the students are enjoying themselves and learning a lot.

   (But) the students are not enjoying themselves and learning a lot.

   (Therefore) Mr. Rivera is not the instructor for that course.

4. If Mr. Rivera is the instructor for that course, then the students are enjoying themselves and learning a lot.

   (But) Mr. Rivera is not the instructor for that course.

   (Therefore) the students are not enjoying themselves and learning a lot.

Stop here. Do not read the next paragraph unless you have already determined, to your own satisfaction, whether each of the preceding arguments is valid or invalid.

*Notice that the conditional arguments with which we are concerned in this section have one premise that is a conditional statement and one premise that affirms or denies the antecedent or consequent of the conditional premise. The conclusion then affirms (if the nonconditional premise affirms) or denies (if the nonconditional premise denies) the other part of the conditional premise (antecedent or consequent).

The argument in the top box is valid. When we accept as true the statement "If Mr. Rivera is the instructor for that course, then the students are enjoying themselves and learning a lot," and when we also accept as true the statement that "Mr. Rivera is the instructor for that course," we must, to avoid contradicting ourselves, accept the statement "the students are enjoying themselves and learning a lot." If the premises were true, the conclusion would have to be true. This, of course, does not show that the argument is sound. Still, the argument *is* valid.

The argument in the second box is invalid. Even if the premises were true, the conclusion might not be true because of the probability that other instructors might also provide enjoyable courses in which the students learn as much. This argument is actually a counterfeit of the argument above it on the chart. It is a counterfeit because, while it is similar to the "real thing" (the form of the reasoning appears enough like the first version to be mistaken for it), it is unacceptable (it is invalid). In conversation, the invalid form may be mistaken for the similar-sounding valid form. Having the premises and conclusion occurring in different locations from argument to argument makes this error even easier to commit.

The argument in the third box is valid. When we accept as true the statement "If Mr. Rivera is the instructor for that course, then the students are enjoying themselves and learning a lot," and when we also accept as true the statement that "the students are not enjoying themselves and learning a lot," we must, to avoid contradicting ourselves, accept the statement "Mr. Rivera is not the instructor for that course." If the premises were true, the conclusion would have to be true.

The argument in the fourth box is invalid. As in the second argument, the premises do not prove the conclusion, since there may be other instructors who could provide enjoyable courses in which the students learned as much. Furthermore, as in the second argument, this argument is actually a counterfeit of the argument above it on the chart. It may be mistaken for that valid argument form because it is similar, but this last argument is definitely invalid.

There is one short word that, if added to the arguments in the second and fourth boxes, would transform them into valid arguments. The word is *only*. People sometimes think that when they say "only if," they are merely being emphatic about their "if" statement. Actually, however, that phrase can change the whole argument. These two alternate versions (with *only if*) of the two previously invalid arguments can be seen now to be valid.

Only if Mr. Rivera is the instructor for that course will the students enjoy themselves and learn a lot.

(Or: The students will enjoy themselves and learn a lot only if Mr. Rivera is the instructor.)

The students *are* enjoying themselves and learning a lot.

∴ Mr. Rivera is the instructor for that course.

Only if Mr. Rivera is the instructor for that course will the students enjoy themselves and learn a lot.

(But) Mr. Rivera is not the instructor for that course.

∴ The students are not enjoying themselves and learning a lot.

Now, going back to the original four sample arguments, we need a way to determine when a conditional argument is valid because, although you may have seen clearly whether each of the four arguments in the boxes was valid, this is not always such an easy matter. Conditional arguments invite confusion when we fail to distinguish between form and content.

The following chart parallels the chart on page 160 and shows the form of each argument.

1.	If A then C A —— C
2.	If A then C C —— A
3.	If A then C Not C —— Not A
4.	If A then C Not A —— Not C

Each of the four arguments from the first chart — the one on page 160 — is valid or invalid because of its form. By looking at the structure of the argument rather than the content, we can tell whether a conditional argument is valid. The chart on page 162 shows the form of each of the original arguments. The letter A stands for the antecedent of the conditional premise and the letter C stands for the consequent of that premise.

Compare this chart with the preceding one. Each box here corresponds with the appropriate box on that chart. To understand this second chart, note the following:

1. The phrase that follows the *if* of the conditional premise is represented on this chart by the letter A wherever it occurs in the argument. The phrase that follows the *then* of the conditional premise is presented on this chart by the letter C wherever it occurs in the argument.

2. *Not A* represents the denial of whichever statement is represented by the letter A; *Not C* represents the denial of whichever statement is represented by the letter C. If, for example, A represents the statement "Mathematics is an exact science," then *Not A* represents the statement "Mathematics is not an exact science." If A represents the statement "Physics is not an exact science" then its denial, "Physics is an exact science," is represented by *Not A*.

If you look from this second chart back to the first, you will notice that, since the antecedent of the conditional premise is "Mr. Rivera is the instructor for that course," this statement can be represented by the letter A. Since this statement is also the nonconditional premise, we can use the letter A to represent that entire premise. Since the statement that is the consequent of the conditional premise is also the conclusion, we can use C to represent the entire conclusion.

Any argument with the form shown in the top box of the second chart will be a valid one, regardless of the content.

The counterfeit version of that form may be seen in the second box, where the conditional premise and the conclusion are reversed. Any argument with this form will be an invalid one, regardless of the content — that is, regardless of whether the premises are true.

When we think of the premises as coming before the conclusion as in the order displayed in the example, the error in constructing the argument occurs with the nonconditional premise. With this premise, instead of affirming the antecedent of the conditional statement to produce a valid argument, we *affirm the consequent* and produce an invalid argument. The logical error that we make is called **affirming the consequent**. It is a *formal* fallacy. In other words, it is a common error that is due to the form independently of the content of the argument.

Any argument with the form shown in the third box of the second chart will be a valid one, regardless of the content.

The counterfeit version of that form may be seen in the fourth box, where the nonconditional premise and the conclusion are reversed. Any argument with this form will be an invalid one, regardless of the content. When we think of the premises as coming before the conclusion (in the order displayed in the example), the error in reconstructing the argument occurs with the nonconditional premise. With this premise, instead of denying the consequent of the conditional statement to produce a valid argument, we *deny the antecedent* and produce an invalid argument. The logical error that we make is called **denying the antecedent**. Like affirming the consequent, it is a formal fallacy.

Two formal fallacies, then, are sometimes committed in conditional arguments: affirming the consequent and denying the antecedent. You should be able to recognize these when considering someone else's reasoning and when you are reasoning on your own.

Finally, here are the answers to four reasonable questions about conditional arguments.

1. *Are these formal fallacies common in everyday reasoning?*

Yes.

Reason from if-then premises is a common and casual part of everyday thinking. This makes quite notable the research suggesting that people *more often than not*, given certain common patterns of conditional reasoning, identify as valid arguments ones that exhibit the formal fallacies of affirming the consequent or denying the antecedent.*

2. *Do the two valid forms of conditional reasoning also have names?*

Yes.

Certainly we could name them by referring to what happens in the nonconditional premise, as we do with the invalid forms. They would then be called affirming the antecedent and denying the consequent. However, they are more often known by their Latin names, *modus ponens* (first box) and *modus tollens* (third box).

3. *Do I need to memorize the second chart?*

No.

The chart should have helped you understand the forms of conditional arguments. You do not, however, need to keep a mental picture of it in order to distinguish between valid and invalid conditional arguments.

---

*In his article "Selective Processes in Reasoning," Jonathan St. B. T. Evans refers to a 1981 Evans and Beck study that found 54 percent of the respondents accepting the reasoning of the fallacious denial of the antecedent and 53 percent accepting the affirmation of the consequent. He also refers to a 1977 Evans study that yielded 38 and 67 percent results, respectively. From Jonathan St. B. T. Evans, Thinking and Reasoning: Psychological Approaches (London: Routeledge & Kegan Paul, 1983), pp. 135–63.

If you encounter a conditional argument of the sort that we have been examining, you need only identify the conditional premise, the nonconditional premise, and the conclusion. Then, looking at the nonconditional premise (not the conclusion!), determine first whether it is similar to the antecedent or the consequent of the conditional premise, and then whether it affirms or denies that part of the conditional premise. Then you will know whether, in the crucial nonconditional premise, the argument involves affirming the antecedent, affirming the consequent, denying the antecedent, or denying the consequent. The two errors to watch for are affirming the consequent and denying the antecedent.

4. *Are there exceptions to these rules of logic?*

An apparent exception occurs when a speaker or writer casually words an "only if" statement as if it were simply an if-then statement. Consider this example. A person wistfully observes, "If we had some money, we could go out to eat at a restaurant tonight." Perhaps this is the simple if-then statement it appears to be. In this case, by denying the antecedent, we create an invalid argument because there may be ways of eating out that do not require cash in hand; credit cards are one possibility, for example. Perhaps, however, we can envision the possibility that the speaker is really (and correctly) suggesting that *only if* they had money could they go to a restaurant. Here he or she is implying that there are no other ways to manage to dine out. If this is what is intended — and sometimes we do word the "only if" statement with a simple *if* — then by denying the antecedent through claiming that "we don't have any money," we *validly* produce the conclusion that "we can't go out to eat at a restaurant tonight."

Two Syllogisms and Their Counterfeits

Some simple and valid patterns of reasoning have look-alike or counterfeit forms that might be mistaken for them. In the previous section, we found that *affirming the consequent* is a counterfeit of the valid *modus ponens* pattern of reasoning, and *denying the antecedent* is a counterfeit of *modus tollens*.

These are not the only simple and valid patterns of reasoning that have such counterfeits or look-alikes. Some syllogisms have such counterfeits, too. Syllogisms are valid argument patterns with two premises, in which the premises and conclusion can be worded to start with "all," "no," or "some," and two categories of things are compared. For example, one of the statements might be "All generals are experienced military officers." "No lizards are mammals," "Some children are very reasonable people," and "Some criminals are not psychopaths." Let's examine two valid syllogisms and their counterfeits.

Universal Syllogism   Although the following argument is unsound, it is valid because its pattern is that of a universal syllogism:

All religious fundamentalists are political conservatives.

All political conservatives are Republicans.

∴ All religious fundamentalists are Republicans.

By accepting these (false) premises, we bind ourselves logically to an acceptance of the conclusion.

Make up your own example of this pattern of reasoning. Here is the pattern:

All A is B (or: All A's are B's)

All B is C (or: All B's are C's)

∴ All A is C (or: All A's are C's)

If you choose obviously false premises, your argument will be a silly one. Still, it will be valid.

This **universal syllogism** is a common pattern of reasoning, and to many people its validity will be simply obvious. However, that obvious validity can itself be a problem. Being familiar with this useful pattern, *a person may mistake a similar but invalid pattern for the valid one.* Consider another argument form in which two premises and the conclusion begin with *all*.

All A is B

All A is C

∴ All B is C

This is the form of one kind of invalid reasoning. Here is an argument with that form:

All religious fundamentalists are political conservatives.

All religious fundamentalists are Republicans.

∴ All political conservatives are Republicans.

If you are at all tempted to say that this argument is valid, you can understand how careful you must be to distinguish between these two patterns of reasoning. If, however, you easily recognize its invalidity, consider whether either different argument content or the occurrence of these premises in a casual conversational setting (with parenthetical comments) might not invite error. Finally, even if you would not offer such reasoning yourself, don't be amazed if someone else does.

There is one more invalid look-alike that might be mistaken for the valid universal syllogism. Here is the form:

All A is B

All C is B

∴ All A is C

Try to create a valid argument that has this form. You can't.

Universal-to-Particular Syllogism   The following reasoning is valid:

All major league baseball players are people who earn over $100,000 a year.

Some major league baseball players are people who feel they are extremely underpaid.

∴ Some people who earn over $100,000 a year feel they are extremely underpaid.

The conclusion follows necessarily from the premises. In other words, if you accept those premises, then you cannot consistently deny the conclusion. It would have to be true, too. The pattern of reasoning for this universal-to-particular (or "all-to-some") syllogism goes like this:

All A is B

Some A is C

∴ Some B is C

An invalid counterfeit of this pattern of reasoning has similar opening words for its premises and conclusion: *all, some, some*. However, the categories are presented in a different order. The deceptive pattern is this:

All A is B

Some B is C

∴ Some A is C

The following reasoning follows this counterfeit pattern, but is too obviously invalid:

> All major league baseball players are people who earn over $100,000 a year.
>
> Some people who earn over $100,000 a year are incompetent at baseball.
>
> ---
>
> ∴ Some major league baseball players are incompetent at baseball.

Despite the cries of some baseball fans, that conclusion is not true. The point to be made here, however, is that the argument is invalid. However, this example *is*, as mentioned in its introduction, too obviously invalid. Consider another invalid argument:

> All major league baseball players are people who feel they are extremely underpaid.
>
> Some people who feel they are extremely underpaid are frequent complainers.
>
> ---
>
> ∴ Some major league baseball players are frequent complainers.

Perhaps all three of these sentences—the two premises and the conclusion—are true. Still, the argument is invalid because the premises don't validly support the conclusion. Those underpaid (or so they feel) people referred to in the second premise—the ones who are frequent complainers—might all be people in other lines of work. Thus, the conclusion doesn't follow from the premises.

UNDERSTAND WHEN AND WHY ANALOGIES FAIL

Sometimes you can best make your point by comparing the situation being discussed with something quite different. Comparison with something else—something simpler, more familiar, or less controversial—can free a mind that is struggling with or resisting the original argument. The issue can be seen in a new light. Occasionally, an analogy is even used as the *initial* way to convey a point.

Later in this chapter, you will learn about logical analogies, which are also called counterexample arguments. These show the similarity between the *structures* of two arguments. Analogies generally — not the special argumentative device called the logical analogy — focus instead on the *content* of an argument. One situation is claimed to be similar to another. Since the one situation typically illuminates the other but does not provide uncontestable proof, the objective should be to establish inductive strength rather than deductive necessity.

An **analogy** is a comparison of two generally dissimilar things that are similar in one way, with the inference that they must be similar in a second way. It is often true that two generally dissimilar things have something in common. This is, of course, not sufficient proof that some *other* characteristic that one has is shared by the other. Thus, analogies can be misleading. Nevertheless, careful attention to the analogy — and sometimes insight into the functioning of analogies — can help you recognize analogies that sound good but actually mislead.

This is the general structure of an analogy.

Item X	**Item Y**
Premise:	Premise:
. . . has characteristic #1	. . . has characteristic #1
Premise:	Conclusion:
. . . has characteristic #2	. . . has characteristic #2

The suggestion is that these two things (for example, people, situations, organizations) that are alike in one respect will also be alike in a second specific respect. Here is an example of an analogy.

EXAMPLE

A conscientious and indignant employee, wagging a finger, scolds his lazy fellow worker, saying "Anyone who wastes time on the job, just loafing around like you do, should be fired . . . or, for that matter, arrested! It's the same as stealing money from the company." ∎

Wasting time on the job and stealing from the company are different sorts of activities. They are the same in the sense that in each case the lazy employee ends up with the company's money, through wages or stealth, and does not give anything in return. The speaker concludes, then, that since dismissal or arrest is appropriate in one instance (actually stealing the money), dismissal or arrest will also be appropriate in the second instance (wasting time on the job).

The indignant worker uses an analogy to deliver his condemnation clearly and powerfully. How good is his reasoning? Specifically, the question is, "Is this a fair analogy?" Up to a certain point, this is not an unreasonable analogy. If we ignore the reference to arrest, the reasoning in the analogy has this structure.

Stealing	**Wasting Time on the Job**
Premise: Money is taken but no appropriate services are returned.	*Premise:* Money is taken but no appropriate services are returned.
Premise: The offender should be fired.	*Conclusion:* The offender should be fired.

Although we might first want to know, in the case of wasting time on the job, whether this problem is chronic and whether management has warned the worker, the reasoning is worth consideration. The manner in which the two situations are similar may well suggest the appropriateness of the same management response.

The worker who issues the scolding does not, however, limit himself to the endorsement of a dismissal. He adds that such an offender should be arrested. This is a second conclusion. The reasoning in the analogy now has this structure as well.

Stealing	**Wasting Time on the Job**
Premise: Money is taken but no appropriate services are returned.	*Premise:* Money is taken but no appropriate services are returned.
Premise: The offender should be arrested.	*Conclusion:* The offender should be arrested.

When carried this far, the analogy breaks down. This conclusion does not follow plausibly from the premises. The two situations—stealing and wasting time on the job—are similar in the first way, but they are not similar in the second. The evidence clearly should not lead us to believe that a person should be arrested for wasting time. Perhaps there is *no* evidence that would establish this. In fact, we can be more specific about the *disanalogy*—the crucial difference—between the two arguments. The "stealing argument" has an unstated second premise: "This way of taking money is prohibited by law." This second premise is not true for the "wasting time argument."

Thus, a point that is essential to establishing the conclusion in one case is simply absent in the other.

Here is another example of an analogy.

EXAMPLE

Jacob is criticizing his younger brother Greg for spending "every minute" of his free time playing video games. Jacob claims that Greg will grow up to be a narrow-minded person if he doesn't investigate more aspects of life around him and listen to other people's views. Greg, especially annoyed by criticism from his older brother, gets personal, responding angrily, "What about *you*? You spend all *your* time in the library. That's just like spending time in the video arcade. You spend all your time doing one thing: studying in the library. That must lead to just as narrow a mind as anything else that a person gives so much time to." ∎

Like many analogies, including the one in which wasting time was compared with stealing money, this analogy is good only up to a point. Greg's analogy has the following structure.

Video Games	Library Study
Premise:	*Premise:*
A person's spare time can be spent entirely on this activity.	A person's spare time can be spent entirely on this activity.
Premise:	*Conclusion:*
Narrow-mindedness would be the result.	Narrow-mindedness would be the result.

Greg is using this analogy in an interesting way. He is trying to show that Jacob, by using his own premises, would have to admit that his dedication to library study shows the same narrowness with which he is charging his brother. Greg intends for Jacob to withdraw his objections to his younger brother's fun in order to avoid that conclusion.

The analogy itself suggests that complete dedication of free time to library study will produce the same narrow person who does not investigate different aspects of life and does not expose himself or herself to other persons' views. There is only a little merit in the analogy and its conclusion.

The person who spends *all* of his or her free time in the library certainly may miss some worthwhile experiences in life. Generally, it seems wise to moderate even a passion for scholarship. However, this analogy is a weak one because, far from being "just like spending time in the video arcade," library work—if it is sufficiently varied—will actually yield the knowledge of many aspects of life and many points of view on issues. The narrowness that Jacob warned against can be defined as an ignorance of such perspectives. Greg's conclusion that Jacob would end up "just as narrow" is not well supported. Note that to evaluate the reasoning thoroughly, we would consider the truth of Jacob's crucial premise concerning the kind of person Greg would become.

Few analogies will provide perfect matches between the dissimilar elements or prove the conclusion with deductive certainty. Fair analogies are effective up to a reasonable point of comparison. In these cases, the premise claims are true or probable and the conclusion is a reasonable product of the comparison. Unfair (often called "bad") analogies are those that do not provide reasonable grounds for strengthening a person's belief in the conclusion or those that present only an illusory parallel.

Guidelines for Evaluating Analogies

Analogies can be subtle, enlightening, and ingenious. They can also be elusive, misleading, and frustrating. No set of rules for the analysis of analogies can replace the need for thoughtful attention to the unique character of each analogy. Still, general advice on the evaluation of analogies may be helpful.

When you are deciding whether an analogy is good, bad, or acceptable up to a point, you can ask yourself these questions.

1. *Are* the two items similar in the first stated way?

2. Does this similarity increase the probability that the two items will be similar in the second way? (This is usually difficult to answer. Asking the question, however, may lessen our gullibility by encouraging careful evaluation of the *relation* between the two stated similarities.)

3. Even if the answer to the second question is "no," is there a parallel between the two items that strengthens the conclusion?

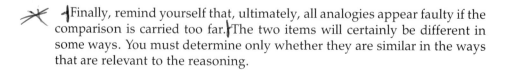

Finally, remind yourself that, ultimately, all analogies appear faulty if the comparison is carried too far. The two items will certainly be different in some ways. You must determine only whether they are similar in the ways that are relevant to the reasoning.

Analogical Explanation

Our focus has been on the analysis of argumentative analogies, which have a premise/conclusion structure. Analogical comparisons can also have an explanatory function. Sometimes we want to *explain* an idea or set of facts rather than to *convince* someone of a conclusion. Here, mere understanding rather than persuasion is the object. Occasionally an analogy may fall somewhere between these two categories.

Here are some examples of how analogical reasoning can be used in explanation. Certain computer processes might be explained through comparison with common functions of the human mind. Certain functions of the human body might be explained through comparison with the workings of a machine. Methods of detecting bad study habits might be explained through comparison with a mechanic's assessment of a car engine that is performing poorly. In cases like these, the comparison is intended to clarify a process or relationship rather than to lead a person to accept a specific belief.

An excerpt from Edward Bellamy's classic book, *Looking Backward*, provides a detailed example of analogical explanation. In the novel, a gentleman from nineteenth-century Boston has awakened in that same city in the year 2000. The advanced society he encounters knows no strife or poverty. In the following passage, the gentleman is describing the nineteenth-century society he has left behind.

> By way of attempting to give the reader some general impression of the way people lived together in those days, and especially of the relations of the rich and poor to one another, perhaps I cannot do better than to compare society as it then was to a prodigious coach which the masses of humanity were harnessed to and dragged toilsomely along a very hilly and sandy road. The driver was hunger, and permitted no lagging, though the pace was necessarily very slow. Despite the difficulty of drawing the coach at all along so hard a road, the top was covered with passengers who never got down, even at the steepest ascents. These seats on top were very breezy and comfortable. Well up out of the dust, their occupants could enjoy the scenery at their leisure, or critically discuss the merits of the straining team. Naturally such places were in great demand and the competition for them was keen, every one seeking as the first end in life to secure a seat on the coach for himself and to leave it to his child after him. By the rule of the coach a man could leave his seat to whom he wished, but on the other hand there were so many accidents by which it might at any time be wholly lost. For all that they were so easy, the seats were very insecure, and at every sudden jolt of the coach persons were slipping out of them and falling to the ground, where they were instantly compelled to take hold of the rope and help to drag the coach on which they had before ridden so pleasantly. It was naturally

regarded as a terrible misfortune to lose one's seat, and the apprehension that this might happen to them or their friends was a constant cloud upon the happiness of whose who rode.

But did they think of themselves? you ask. Was not their very luxury rendered intolerable to them by comparison with the lot of their brothers and sisters in the harness, and the knowledge that their own weight added to the toil? Had they no compassion for fellow beings from whom fortune only distinguished them? Oh, yes, commiseration was frequently expressed by those who rode for those who had to pull the coach, especially when the vehicle came to a bad place in the road, as it was constantly doing, or to a particularly steep hill. At such times, the desperate straining of the team, their agonized leaping and plunging under the pitiless lashing of hunger, the many who fainted at the rope and were trampled in the mire, made a very distressing spectacle, which often called forth highly creditable displays of feeling on top of the coach. At such times the passengers would call down encouragingly to the toilers of the rope, exhorting them to patience, and holding out hopes of possible compensation in another world for the hardness of their lot, while others contributed to buy salves and liniments for the crippled and injured. It was agreed that it was a great pity that the coach should be so hard to pull, and there was a sense of general relief when the specially bad piece of road was gotten over. This relief was not, indeed, wholly on account of the team, for there was always some danger at these bad places of a general overturn in which all would lose their seats.

It must in truth be admitted that the main effect of the spectacle of the misery of the toilers at the rope was to enhance the passengers' sense of the value of their seats upon the coach, and to cause them to hold on to them more desperately than before. If the passengers could only have felt assured that neither they nor their friends would ever fall from the top, it is probable that, beyond contributing to the funds for liniments and bandages, they would have troubled themselves extremely little about those who dragged the coach.

> *Edward Bellamy,* Looking Backward: Two Thousand to Eighteen Eighty-Seven, *1888.*
> *Reprinted with permission of Hendricks House, Inc., from their 1960 edition.*

The author is not presenting argumentation. He is *describing* in order to *inform* with clarity and power. His efforts to leave us with the impression of injustice are obvious, but the passage is still primarily explanatory. We are being told what society was like;* we have not been offered the argument that, since one characteristic is shared by two items, a second characteristic is likely to be shared as well.

Explanatory analogies sometimes also are used to relate why an event has taken place in a certain way. For example, a chemistry teacher might explain the reaction between two substances through analogical comparison with something quite different.

PREPLAN YOUR STRATEGIES FOR CRITICISM

Do you usually handle contention well, so that you're happy about what you said? Or do you often figure out only afterwards what you could have or should have said? Do you finally think of the way to approach the point that was being argued only as you drive home or late at night when you're alone with your thoughts?

It's almost impossible to eliminate this kind of frustration completely. The best *general* approach is to work on being more reflective during those discussions. Don't react too quickly, rushing to respond to other people's comments. Listen carefully and thoughtfully. Don't interrupt. Usually, when a person gets emotionally tied up in knots and feels pressure to make a quick defense or comeback, the resulting interchange is not the best.

Besides simply slowing down the pace of the discourse and letting yourself be more reflective (even if you express fewer ideas), you can plan some of your behavior ahead of time. This doesn't mean that you will have specific, stock comments to lie in wait with. It means you will prethink both (1) some ways of making your point clearly as you criticize a certain kind of argument, and (2) when it is worth pointing out errors and when it isn't. Let's now examine one method of criticism for certain statements and arguments — the counterexample — and then turn to a basic question of civility — when to criticize and when not to.

Using Counterexamples to Make Your Point

We all know what *examples* are. They are specific cases that stand for something that's more general. Bianca might be referred to as an example of a conscientious student. Keiko might be referred to as an example of an unmotivated student. Vancouver might be given as an example of an attractive city. The savings and loan crisis is sometimes offered as an example of government shortsightedness and inefficiency (in its failure to adequately oversee these institutions).

When someone cites an example, you can respond by:

(a) accepting the example as characteristic of what is being described ("Yes, the savings and loan crisis *is* a good example of government shortsightedness and inefficiency.");

(b) disagreeing that this is a true example of it ("The savings and loan crisis may display human greed, but the government can't be expected to have foreseen the problem early enough. I don't think it shows either short-sightedness or inefficiency."); *or*

(c) offering a *counterexample* ("This may or may not be a good example of government incompetence, but that doesn't mean that our government is always like that. The veterans' home loan program is run very well, for example, and even makes a profit.").

Sometimes you may not be sure whether the other person's example is intended to establish a universal claim (suggesting there are no counterexamples), whether it is intended to establish a general claim (suggesting that there are few counterexamples), or whether it is merely intended as an example of something that should be considered although it isn't widespread.

When someone makes a universal statement (for example, "All technical manuals are poorly written"), all you need is one counterexample ("The manual for my home computer was very well written") to disprove that claim. (Of course, you have only made your point if that counterexample is acknowledged as a true one by the person you're talking with!) The same is true when no explicit universal claim is made, but is suggested by someone's example: one counterexample refutes the implied universal claim. When a person complains by saying, "Technical manuals! Look at how poorly these instructions are written," any implied condemnation of *all* manuals is countered by your one counterexample.

To your counterexample, the original speaker might respond, "Well, *most* of them are like this." Now you have a general statement rather than a universal statement. A single counterexample doesn't disprove this modified claim. You would have to come up with lots of counterexamples to show that this qualified claim should be rejected. As you know, several examples out of hundreds of possibilities neither establishes that "most are" nor that "most aren't."

Sometimes an example will be given wtihout any intention to suggest that all or most other items are similar. "The technical manual for this gasoline-powered model airplane is an example of poor writing." The speaker here has not suggested anything about other technical manuals or manuals for other model airplanes. The only kind of counterexample that could be used here would be samples of good writing from the same manual, casting doubt on whether the manual as a whole displayed poor writing.

So far the term "counterexample" has been used to refer to evidence that counts against a *statement*. Another kind of counterexample — the *counterexample argument* or *logical analogy* — can be useful as well. Let's consider why, when, and how it works.

Sometimes a person will make only one error in a long list of reasoning, and to notice it you must be alert. At other times, the errors and questionable moves are unbelievably numerous. When there is more than one weak point in an argument, and you have decided to question that argument, you need to determine which point or points to address. It is tedious and usually inadvisable to attack every one of an arguer's many errors. Besides, in conversation at least, we normally want to allow the other person to preserve the self-esteem necessary for him or her to eventually change positions. Crucial to the issue of which point to address is the question of whether you want to focus on a problem with the *form* of the argument (a weak or worthless inference) or a problem with the *content* of the argument (a false or questionable premise). Obviously, there is sometimes no choice. When there is, keep this general rule — as mentioned earlier — in mind: *It is usually advisable to question inferences (form) rather than premises (content).*

When the form is bad the evidence does not adequately support or "prove" the conclusion; when the content is questionable or bad, there is reason to doubt the truth of one premise — or more than one. Questioning the premises themselves often leads to a face-off with the other person. Since the premise is so strongly maintained, progress toward seeing its weaknesses is not easily made. People will more readily admit that their reasoning in a particular case was hasty than that an old and dearly held premise is false.

Sometimes you realize that another person's argument is invalid and you want to communicate this insight to that person. To demonstrate that an argument is invalid, you can sometimes make up another argument — one that has the same structure as the original argument but has obviously true premises and an obviously false conclusion. This second argument is called a **logical analogy** or *counterexample argument.*

Consider the following argument. It is invalid, but some people don't easily see that it is invalid. Sometimes almost no amount of talking about the reliability of the inference enables a particular person to see the invalidity of such an argument. Occasionally, you may resort to a logical analogy to make your point.

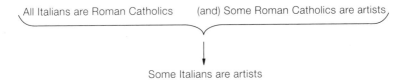

This argument can be shown to be invalid by stating the argument clearly and then suggesting that "that's like saying . . . ," then offering a parallel argument such as this one.

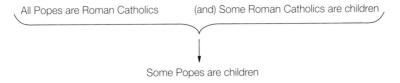

The arguments are parallel—they have the same structure—because each is constructed on this pattern:

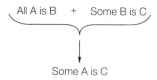

All A is B   +   Some B is C

Some A is C

In each argument, then, we have the same kind of reasoning. Words like *all* and *some* cannot be changed, and the order of the terms *A, B,* and *C* must be preserved. In the logical analogy (the second argument), however, the premises are obviously true and the conclusion is obviously false. This shows that, *with this kind of reasoning, even the most reliable premises can produce an unacceptable conclusion.* There must, therefore, be something wrong with the original reasoning.

Let's review briefly. Presented with the "Italians" argument, someone who wants to communicate its invalidity says this: "You are saying that, since all Italians are Roman Catholics and some Roman Catholics are artists, some Italians must be artists. But that's like saying that, since all popes are Roman Catholics and some Roman Catholics are children, some popes must be children." Yes, the second argument sounds ridiculous, but it's *supposed* to. With your reasoning, the speaker is suggesting, true premises can lead to a false conclusion. Thus, you should reevaluate your reasoning.

In the preceding example, one of the terms, *Roman Catholics,* was kept when the logical analogy was constructed. This is not necessary; all the terms can be new ones. It is important, however, that the premises be uncontentious and beyond discussion (not even inviting a passing comment or joke) and that the conclusion be so obviously false, even ridiculous, that it could not be construed as true. The purpose in constructing the logical analogy is to direct attention to the form and away from the content. The person being addressed is sure to miss the point if attention is now inadvertently drawn to the *content* of the logical analogy. Consider an example.

What if the following argument had been offered as a logical analogy for the "Italians" argument?

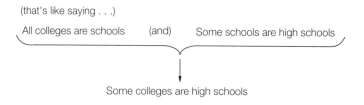

(that's like saying . . .)

All colleges are schools   (and)   Some schools are high schools

Some colleges are high schools

This argument has the same structure as the original argument. It has obviously true premises and an obviously false conclusion. However, if a person was attending, or knew of, a college that he or she considered to be academically weak, the conclusion of the logical analogy may draw a sarcastic comment: "Well, some colleges *are* high schools!" If this happens, attention has been drawn away from the form of the arguments. The point of your logical analogy will almost certainly be missed.

Let's examine one more invalid argument for which a logical analogy could be useful.

Original argument: Some teachers are Democrats and most Democrats are political liberals. So some teachers must be political liberals.

This argument is invalid. In fact, it's "like saying . . ."

Logical analogy: Some children are professional actors and most professional actors are adults. So some children must be adults.

The premises of the logical analogy are true and uncontentious. The structure or form of the arguments is identical. We are showing that with reasoning like this, even good evidence can lead to an unreliable conclusion.

Logical analogies can be used to show another person that his or her reasoning is invalid — that the conclusion being offered does not follow from the premises. There are both advantages and limitations to a reliance on logical analogies to do this job.

Advantages of Logical Analogies

1. We can avoid a discussion of sensitive premises by focusing completely on the form of the argument.

2. No technical terms such as *invalid* or *premise* are necessary to make your point.

3. Successful logical analogies present their point with great psychological power.

Limitations of Logical Analogies

1. Although the preparation of written responses to an argument allows time to create logical analogies, for immediate spoken responses the ability to think on your feet is crucial. Some people are better than others at creating logical analogies, and sometimes you simply can't think of one.

2. Having a good logical analogy is not enough. If the person or persons you are addressing do not, for whatever reason, see the similarity in the structure of the two arguments, you have failed to convey the intended message. Note also the following advice on this matter: Use the same voice inflection and body movement when articulating each of the two arguments. If you raise the tone of your voice, for example, or wave your

hand in a certain way at the end of each premise of the first argument, do the same when you give the second argument. Use any such tools that may help the listener to sense the similarity.

Remember, finally, that in actual conversation—or in writing, for that matter—the conclusion may be stated first, last, or elsewhere, and that many parenthetical statements may separate the premises from each other and from the conclusion. When you use a logical analogy, however, you should first offer a clear reconstruction of the other person's argument by eliminating all parenthetical statements and by placing the conclusion last.

■
_____

PRACTICE ACTIVITIES

Set 8.1 *Evaluate the following analogies by indicating the ways in which the two items are being claimed to be similar, then by assessing the accuracy of those comparisons.*

1. Elizabeth Cady Stanton, who published the *Woman's Bible* in the 1880s, referred to the New Testament passage (Mark 12:43–44) in which Jesus praised a widow for giving the last of her money to the church. Stanton wrote that this praise of the woman's self-sacrifice had been used by organized religion in defense of the subordination of women.

   > This woman, belonging to an impoverished class, was trained to self-abnegation; but when women learn the higher duty of self-development, they will not so readily expend all their forces in serving others. Paul says that a husband who does not provide for his own household is worse than an infidel. So a woman, who spends all her time in churches, with priests, in charities, neglects to cultivate her own natural gifts, to make the most of herself as an individual in the scale of being, a responsible soul whose place no other can fill, is worse than an infidel. "Self-development is a higher duty than self-sacrifice," should be woman's motto henceforward.

2. In "A Civil Rights Bill Attacks Sound and Unsound Policies," *Chicago Tribune*, May 30, 1991, Stephen Chapman suggests that the more severe penalties of the Civil Rights Act of 1991 will transform times of discrimination against minorities and women into times of discrimination in favor of minorities and women.

Just as imposing the death penalty on parking violators would discourage not only illegal parking but the ownership of cars, allowing unlimited damages for civil rights transgressions will mean an end to legitimate as well as illegitimate disparities.

3. The Carnegie Council on Children (1977) described parents as coordinators of their children's out-of-home activities, while these activities are shaped and directed by a myriad of professionals who claim to know their fields and how they apply to children. The parent becomes like . . .

> a maestro trying to conduct an orchestra of players who have never met and who play from a multitude of different scores, each in a notation the conductor cannot read.

4. From Christina Hoff Sommers's "Once a Soldier, Always a Dependent," *Hastings Center Report*, August 1986:

> Why are [armed service] veterans entitled to special benefits, such as free medical care? Not because such a benefit is an inducement to military service, or because a soldier accepts risk. Rather, the relationship of the Army, to use one service as an example, to a soldier is like that of a parent to a child. The right to health care, even carried beyond the term of service, is an extension of this quasi-familial relationship.

5. In November of 1985, the Associated Press reported that the State Education Assessment Center plans to develop new state-by-state comparisons of public school achievement. Here is one reported reaction to these plans:

> Florida's Ralph D. Turlington, whose state was a pioneer in competency testing, said the move "will significantly impact upon achievement in our schools."
>
> "What would happen if you took down from our athletic fields the scoreboards?" he asked. "If you do not keep score, it is not important."

6. President Reagan reportedly did not remember whether he had approved the 1985 Israeli arms shipment to Iran. On December 10, 1986, *USA Today* reported the following defense of the Reagan claim:

> Do you recall what you had for lunch on the first day of September, 1985?

7. From a letter to the editor of *Newsweek*, August 18, 1986 (responding to a National Affairs article in the July 28 issue):

> It's sad that the seven fundamentalist families in Tennessee are so insecure about their own beliefs that they feel obligated to

bad

shield their children from the incredible richness of science and human history. They are like totalitarian governments, which seek to control their populations by limiting the information allowed in from the outside world.

good

8. It's amazing that the human race is allowing the world to be increasingly polluted. Birds don't foul their own nests. People don't dispose of their garbage on the living room floor. The consequences in each case threaten healthy survival. It doesn't make sense to ruin your own habitat.

9. On the new proposals for science education in California schools (from the *San Diego Union*, November 16, 1985):

> While a majority of local educators say they are excited about teaching the new curriculum, a few are concerned that the rigorous subject matter will force some students who are weak in the sciences out of academia.
>
> "Our drop-out rate in the schools already is very high," said Richard Robinson, head of textbook selection for the Ocean-side Unified School District. "I have a great concern for the nonacademic student, and we have a great many of them. We need to have more regional occupation classes for those students who just can't cut it in the classroom.
>
> "The curriculum next year is going to be a lot tougher, and for the kids who are just barely making it, it might mean they'll drop out. I hope we learned a long time ago that we can't cut one suit and have it fit everybody."

10. A Seattle man whose cancerous spleen was removed by UCLA specialists is suing the University of California system, which could make millions of dollars off cells cloned from his tissue. His attorney's comment on the issue was reported in the *San Diego Union*, August 23, 1985:

> Our position is that Mr. Moore provided the work of art and [the medical researchers] simply put a frame around it.

11. In a campaign advertisement in the *Vista Press*, November 3, 1986, voters were urged to vote out an incumbent candidate for the Tri-City Hospital Board of Directors:

> She has brought public infighting and distrust to the Board of Directors severely impairing its ability to compete and progress in today's complex world of hospital management. As a supervisor of a competing hospital, she has a clear conflict of interest. Certainly other multi-million dollar public corporations would not tolerate such activity, or obvious lack of business

acumen on their Board! (Does G.M. place on its Board an employee from Ford?)

12. In William Shakespeare's play *Julius Caesar*, Brutus is attempting to convince Cassius that they must immediately engage in combat with the opposing armies of Octavius and Antony. Brutus says the following:

> There comes a tide in the affairs of men
> Which, taken at the flood, leads on to fortune;
> Omitted, all the voyage of their life
> Is bound in shallows and miseries.
> On such a full sea are we now afloat,
> And we must take the current when it serves,
> Or lose our ventures.

Set 8.2 *Each of the following arguments has a special form that ensures its validity (modus ponens, modus tollens, universal syllogism, universal-to-particular syllogism), or it is a counterfeit of one of these. Identify each by name.*

1. All lawyers are intelligent and some lawyers are wealthy. Therefore, some intelligent people are wealthy.

2. All Coast Guard personnel are government employees, and some government employees are spies. Therefore, some Coast Guard personnel are spies.

3. All Coast Guard personnel are government employees, and some government employees work on ships. Thus, some Coast Guard personnel work on ships.

4. If a person is rich, then he or she is certain to be well dressed. The fellow I met last night was certainly well dressed. Therefore, he must be rich.

5. If you had had a good logic course, you would not have been misled by my "argument from ignorance" fallacy. But you *were* misled by my use of that fallacy. Thus, you cannot possibly have had a good logic course.

6. Since some Europeans are artists, and all Spaniards are Europeans, at least some Spaniards are artists.

7. All teachers are college-educated, so all college-educated people can do basic math, since all teachers can do basic math.

8. All physicians are college-educated. All physicians can read and write. Clearly, then, all college-educated people can read and write.

9. When the person viewing an artwork understands the personal and cultural influences on the artist, that viewer can find meaning in the artwork. But you don't know anything about the personal and cultural influences on Picasso. Therefore, you will be unable to find meaning in his painting *Guernica*.

10. When the person viewing an artwork understands the personal and cultural influences on the artist, the viewer can find meaning in the artwork. And you are finding meaning in Picasso's *Guernica*. I conclude that you understand the personal and cultural influences that affected Picasso.

11. If a person is very deeply moved by the victims of famine in Africa, then that person will contribute to the effort to alleviate the suffering. You have contributed to that cause. I know, therefore, that you have been deeply moved by this tragedy.

12. All Americans are materialistic, and anyone who is materialistic misses the true meaning of life. Consequently, Americans all miss the true meaning of life.

13. Each and every Iraqi is an adherent of Islam, and some adherents of Islam are engineers. Consequently, we can conclude that some Iraqis are engineers.

14. Jennifer is broke again. She must have been to the racetrack yesterday because she's always broke whenever she's spent the previous day at the track.

15. There must be (some) good thinkers who are highly emotional, since all computer programmers, for example, are good thinkers and some computer programmers are highly emotional.

16. There is no God. There would be no evil in the world if God existed. Yet, alas, there is indeed evil in this world!

17. God must exist because there is an intricate pattern of interdependent designs in this world. Certainly, if such a pattern exists, then God must also.

18. He would understand things like this if he had really been raised on a farm. So we can safely assert that he was, after all, raised on a farm since he *does* obviously understand these things.

19. Yes, I did hear that the boss gets violent when he feels threatened. But don't worry. He won't get violent with you, since I'm sure he won't feel threatened by you in any way.

20. A quote from G. Gordon Liddy that appeared in *Newsweek*, November 10, 1986:

   Obviously crime pays, or there'd be no crime.

Set 8.3 *Determine how many conditional arguments, obvious or subtle, are in each of the following passages. Then determine whether each conditional argument is valid or invalid. For each invalid conditional argument, name the formal fallacy that is committed.*

1. *Terry:* Where's Dad? It's time to leave for the ball game.

    Chris: I don't know. Maybe he went into the bedroom to lie down. He said he felt dizzy.

    Terry: Oh, no! He must have taken his twice-a-week medicine this morning. Doctor Herndon said that he would feel dizzy for hours whenever he took that medicine.

    Chris: Well, if he took it just this morning then he's not going to be alert enough to go to the game at eleven-thirty. Dad didn't get out of bed until nine. He must have just taken it.

    Terry: You're right. Dad won't be alert enough to go to the game. But who can we sell his tickets to?

2. At a meeting of the Administrative Council of the National Veterans Organization, the officers of the NVO are discussing the Presidential Awards Banquet. Their organization must select someone to represent them when the president presents them with the American Service Award. Part of the discussion follows:

    Sanders: You say that this McReynolds fellow would be a fitting representative for the NVO?

    Jameson: Yes, we think so. He has seen combat action and earned the Purple Heart award for his war injuries.

    Sanders: Well, someone who has earned the Purple Heart would certainly be a good representative for our group.

    Harrell: Wait a minute, fellows. You've made a mistake, Jamie. McReynolds *is* the man we've recommended, but he never earned a Purple Heart. That was Tarantino, the other man we were considering seriously. So I guess, Colonel Sanders, from what you said about the Purple Heart, you don't now think that McReynolds is a fitting representative. Do you want us to look at the list of candidates again?

3. A letter to the editor:

    Editor:

    The letter from Mr. Springer (dated August 8, 1987) shows his lack of appreciation for the small farmer.
    For the past two years, small and medium-sized family farms have been going bankrupt at an alarming rate. Unless a broader program of aid to such farms is enacted, this rate will not only continue but

actually increase. This is a matter of personal tragedy for thousands of our hardest-working, traditional-valued Americans. Mr. Springer's cold reference to "the necessary displacement of persons during social change" reflects his low regard for farmers and for people in general.

It is now clear—listen to so many politicians backing off from their long-standing support for farmers—that no further programs of significance will be initiated. My sad conclusion is that the rate of defaults will continue to rise. Still, although I have no illusions, I have nothing but contempt for the Mr. Springers of this nation.

Signed,

A sad but angry soul.

Set 8.4 *For each of the following invalid arguments, create a logical analogy to demonstrate its invalidity.*

1. Some Republicans are politically conservative and some Republicans advocate liberal abortion policies. So some political conservatives apparently advocate liberal abortion policies.

2. All scientists are college educated and some college-educated people have artistic talents, so there must be some scientists who have artistic talents.

3. Since some teachers are scholars and many scholars are humanists, some teachers must be humanists.

4. There aren't any priests who are dishonest (or: "No priests are dishonest"), but some priests aren't intelligent. Therefore, some intelligent people must be dishonest.

5. Since all socialists are political leftists and all communists are also (or: "All communists are political leftists"), anyone who is a socialist is also a communist (or "All socialists are communists").

6. Physicians are all quite wealthy, so some of them must not be compassionate people, since many wealthy people are not compassionate.

7. Some people with good memories must be interpreters, since all interpreters are bilingual and some bilingual people have good memories.

8. In college, different types of students are drawn to different subjects. Take psychology majors, for example. With them, however, it's more complex. Here you see multiple characteristics. Some very intelligent people are psychology majors. This is easily documented. Observation will tell you something else: Some very disturbed people are psychology majors. One interesting side conclusion here is that some very intelligent people are also very disturbed.

9. It's not possible that any Italians are atheists. Think of it. The Vatican is right there in Rome. Most Italians, as you might guess, are Roman Catholics. Certainly, whoever is a Roman Catholic is not an atheist.

10. In all schools, there are some discipline problems. What kind of student poses such a problem? Observe, first, that some children with behavior problems are kids who are abnormally active. The clinical term is *hyperactive*. Now, many hyperactive children are quite intelligent. This proves what many educators have known for years: Many children with behavior problems are really quite intelligent children.

For Further Reading

Copi, Irving M. *Introduction to Logic.* New York: Macmillan, 1986.

A general logic textbook that includes a full discussion of conditional arguments and syllogisms.

Govier, Trudy. *A Practical Study of Argument.* Belmont, CA: Wadsworth, 1988.

A study of reasoning that includes an excellent section on analogies.

Hurley, Patrick J. *A Concise Introduction to Logic.* Belmont, CA: Wadsworth, 1991.

A general logic textbook that includes a clear explanation of logical forms.

NINE

Evaluative Mapping

I t's embarrassing to be unable to keep track of reasoning—someone else's or your own. That this is embarrassing is surprising, since, as it turns out, tracking a line of reasoning is *not* a simple skill that seldom fails us. It's sometimes difficult and we are often unsuccessful. To help with this important but elusive skill, the concept of *basic mapping* was presented in Chapter 5.

Basic mapping can help you (1) keep track of the main points in someone's spoken or written reasoning, and (2) remember what was offered as evidence for particular statements. This deceptively challenging skill of keeping track can be useful.

However, our complicated lives call for us to do more than just "keep track" of the efforts to persuade that surround us daily in advertising, magazine articles, workplace rhetoric, and the conversations of both friends and less friendly acquaintances. What would we think of someone who remembers reasoning but cannot evaluate it? The person who can recite preceding points, but who doesn't competently distinguish between strong and weak inferences or reliable and questionable premises will not get far.

Evaluative mapping builds on basic mapping. You start with a basic map that displays the line of reasoning. Then you write something beside each arrow to show your assessment of the strength of the inference, and you mark each basic premise to indicate your assessment of the reliability of each basic premise.

Like a road map that shows how you get from one location to another, a basic map of an argument shows how you (or someone else) got from one point in the argument to another. Like a topographical map that shows high points and low in a landscape, an evaluative map adds to this by identifying the strong and weak points in a line of reasoning.

Knowing the weak points in your own reasoning can enable you to strengthen your argument and can keep you from appearing silly in an indignant defense of reasoning that other people recognize as faulty in ways that elude you. Knowing the weak points in someone else's reasoning can prevent you from dismissing an entire line of reasoning because of an error that is only incidental to the main thrust of the argument. Generally, the object is to safeguard against overassessment of your own arguments and underassessment of others' arguments.

The finished map then serves as an aid in the reevaluation of the mapped line of reasoning rather than a final judgment about it.

EVALUATE INFERENCES ON YOUR MAP

Each arrow on your map stands for an inference: a step of reasoning in which one or more premises are offered as evidence for ("reason for believing") a conclusion. In evaluative mapping, you write beside any arrow your own assessment of the strength of that inference.

Ask yourself the following question for each inference: "If the immediately preceding premise(s) were true, how certain could we be that the conclusion is also true?" In its simplest form, it's a question of whether or not the evidence offers strong support for the conclusion—whether the reasoning is good or bad, reliable or suspect.

Examine the following two single-inference maps.

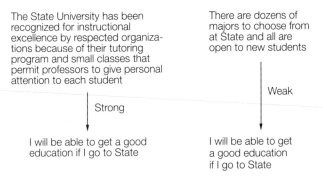

The inference at the right is a weak one. Since most universities have dozens of majors, this doesn't set State apart from the pack. It's nice that students are not kept out of certain major areas of study because of over-enrollment, but that can be true of the less impressive schools as well as the good schools. The inference on the left is much stronger. Of course, the premise doesn't include all the things a person would want to check before arriving at the conclusion, and we don't know at this point which "respected organizations" are referred to, but this is the sort of evidence that makes that conclusion quite likely to be true. Certainly we can agree that you have much more to go on as you draw the conclusion in the "strong" inference than in the "weak" one.

If you try to brand each inference as either strong or weak, you will probably end up frustrated by those numerous inferences that seem to fall short of the one label and warrant more than the other. Ultimately, you will probably resort to creating at least one more category. Let's use the term "moderate": The premises offer moderate support for the conclusion — not impressively strong and not notably weak. Perhaps the following little map displays an inference of moderate strength.

The State University has an impressive program that brings their most distinguished professors into the introductory courses, allowing more students to benefit from their expertise

Moderate

I will be able to get a good education if I go to State

This sounds like a good program. Still, it's only one program and may not reflect the general character of the campus. Besides, just how good are the classes in this program? A good research professor is not necessarily a good teaching professor. Is that program deemed "impressive" because of its basic intent or its ultimate effectiveness? The inference mapped here appears stronger than the "weak" one already mentioned, and weaker than the "strong" one.

Certainly, with this kind of inference evaluation, each assessment will be subjective. What one person calls "moderate," another will call "weak." To achieve more precision, let's refer back to the categories of argument assessment discussed at the end of Chapter 6 and tie those in with evaluative mapping.

The most obvious connection casts the terms "strong," "moderate," and "weak" in terms of inductive assessment, that is, in terms of how likely (i.e., probable) the conclusion would be if the premises were true. Now, although some assessments will still vary, we can establish a loose standard for each category:

Inductively strong — If the premises were true, the conclusion would be *highly probable*.

Inductively moderate — If the premises were true, the conclusion would be *probable* (i.e., more likely to be true than false).

Inductively weak — If the premises were true, they would contribute *relevant evidence* for drawing that conclusion, but would not alone establish a probability.

Still, one argument may be branded with different labels when sized up by different people. However, we wouldn't expect different ends of the spectrum, with one person saying "strong" and another saying "weak," unless the two people were somehow looking at the argument in different lights, accepting different assumptions about unstated elements of the situation being described.

Now you can easily extend your on-the-map inference assessment to deductive validity. Here is how to do it.

As before, you ask how strongly the premises support the conclusion. In other words, you ask, "If the premises were true, how likely would it be that the conclusion is also true?" If your answer is that the conclusion would *have to be* true if the premises were, then you will write "Deductively Valid" beside the arrow. For the moment, you do not concern yourself with the issue of whether the premises are actually true; you ask how well the premises would support the conclusion if they *were* true. (You may refer back to Chapter 6 for a review of the concept of deductive validity.) Here is an example.

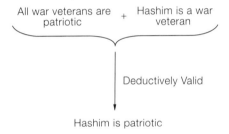

Although at least one of the premises is open to challenge and the term "patriotic" begs to be defined, we can say with assurance that the inference is deductively valid. Assuming that the basic terms are used in the same sense when they are repeated in the conclusion, the premises lead necessarily to the conclusion.

One aspect of this inference assessment warrants restatement for emphasis: You do not, for the inductive or deductive assessment, concern yourself with the truth of the premises. Even if the premises are false, the inference can be a good one. Again, you ask yourself, "If the premises were true (though they might not *actually* be true), how likely would it be that the conclusion would also be true? Here we are assessing the form of the argument rather than its content.

You can be more specific than this in the notation you write next to an arrow on your map. Examine the following list of possible abbreviated notations. Two of the argument structures listed — hypothetical syllogism and deductive syllogism — have not yet been presented. The brief discussion of these two basic structures will follow this list.

Kind of Logical Move You Find	Your Notation Beside Arrow
Deductive certainty (validity):	
—Deductively valid	Ded. Val.
—*Modus ponens*	D.V. — M.P.
—*Modus tollens*	D.V. — M.T.
—Disjunctive syllogism	D.V. — D.S.
—Hypothetical syllogism	D.V. — H.S.
—Universal syllogism	D.V. — U.S.
—Affirming the consequent	NO — A.C.
—Denying the antecedent	NO — D.A.
—Disproven by logical analogy	NO — L.A. disproves
Inductive Strength:	
—Inductively strong	Strong
—Inductively moderate	Mod.
—Inductively weak	Weak
—No support	No support
—Good analogy	OK? — Good anal.
—Weak analogy	NO — Weak anal.
Fallacies	NO — False auth. (for example)

Do not restrict yourself to this list. You may want notations that detail your rejection, reservations, or even acceptance of the logical moves. You may want to indicate that an inductively weak move was rejected because the *E* question of the R-E-T test failed or that unstated counterevidence weakens the argument. Be creative in detecting strengths and weaknesses in arguments. The skills discussed in this book cannot alert you to the whole range of specific challenges you will encounter in everyday reasoning, so don't go to the chart to discover whether an argument is good. First determine the legitimacy of the argument; then decide on your notation. There's often a wonderful subtlety to human reasoning, a subtlety that continually breaks through the patterns we previously noticed. You will detect more kinds of errors than you have learned about in this book.*

*To make evaluative mapping more elementary, avoiding the various technical terms, you can use the notation "Nec." to indicate the necessity of deductive validity ("If the premises were true, the conclusion would necessarily be true."), "V-Prob." to indicate that the inference is inductively strong ("If the premises were true, the conclusion would very probably also be true."), "Prob." to indicate that the inference is inductively moderate, and "Rel." to indicate that the inference is inductively weak (The premises are relevant as we compile evidence for the conclusion, but they don't establish probability.).

Two additional patterns of reasoning—both deductively valid—can be introduced here: the hypothetical syllogism and the disjunctive syllogism.

Hypothetical Syllogism The following argument is valid though not sound:

> *If* you like the art of Jackson Pollock, *then* you really know your art.
>
> *If* you really know your art, *then* you will like the sculpture of Rodin.
> ───────────────────────────────
> ∴ *If* you like the art of Jackson Pollock, *then* you will like the sculpture of Rodin.

By accepting the premises we bind ourselves logically to an acceptance of the conclusion. Thus, the argument is valid.*

Make up your own example of this pattern of reasoning. Here is the pattern:

> If A, then B
>
> If B, then C
> ─────────
> ∴ If A, then C

Your example will be valid, too! This can be predicted because *any* argument with this form is necessarily valid. Such arguments are called **hypothetical syllogisms**.

Some arguments with "if" premises and an "if" conclusion are not valid, however. If the repeated expressions occur in the wrong location, the form is not a standard hypothetical syllogism. These two forms of argument are invalid:

> If A, then B   If A, then B
>
> If C, then B   If A, then C
> ─────────   ─────────
> ∴ If A, then C   ∴ If B, then C

A chain of valid hypothetical syllogisms produces a valid overall argument. This form displays valid reasoning:

---

*Recognizing that the phrase "really know your art" is a casual expression suggesting your overall sophistication in the art world, we see that the first premise is false. It is certainly possible for a person who is ignorant of art styles and traditions to like any artist's work. Thus, the argument is unsound. The second premise is almost certainly false as well.

If A, then B

If B, then C

If C, then D

If D, then E

∴ If A, then E

The premises might not have been presented in this order in the actual argument. As long as the reordered chain displays linked premises (*then B* followed by *if B, then C* followed by *if C*) and the appropriately structured conclusion, the argument is valid. The principle of the basic hypothetical syllogism applies whether the argument has two premises or twenty.

Disjunctive Syllogism   The following argument is valid and sound:

The flag of China shows white stars on a red background *or* it shows yellow stars on a red background.

The stars on China's flag are not white.

∴ The stars on China's flag are yellow.

By accepting the premises, both of which happen to be true, we bind ourselves logically to an acceptance of the conclusion.

Make up your own example of this pattern of reasoning. Here is the pattern:

A or B

Not-A

∴ B

Your example will be valid, too. Even if one or both of the premises you choose is false, the argument will be valid because of its form. Such arguments are called **disjunctive syllogisms**.

There are acceptable variations from the preceding form of disjunctive syllogism, but in each the basic structure is the same: if an "or" statement is accepted as true, and the statement on one side of the *or* is denied, the statement on the other side must be accepted.

EVALUATE PREMISES ON YOUR MAP

In evaluative mapping, you assess each basic premise. You write Ⓣ above any basic premise that can be reliably accepted as true; these premises are to be demonstrably or almost certainly true. You write Ⓕ above any basic premise that is clearly or almost certainly false. For example, the statement "Abortion has been a hotly debated issue in the United States" gets a Ⓣ when it is used as a premise because, regardless of your own feelings on the abortion issue, you know that this topic certainly has caused much heated discussion in recent decades. On the other hand, the statement "No one in this country cares at all about the abortion issue" gets an Ⓕ for the same reason. See how this would look on the simple maps that follow. In order to present these statements as premises, conclusions have been created for the examples. However, for the mment, ignore the inferences and take note of how the Ⓣ and Ⓕ are placed.

You won't do evaluative mapping for long before you find that the categories *true* and *false* are simply too restrictive. You will find that you sometimes cannot say confidently that the premise is true or that the premise is false. Add the symbol Ⓠ to your toolbox of mapping devices. The Ⓠ can be used in two circumstances. First, you can use it when you simply don't know at all whether the premise is true or false. For example, you might not know whether "Small classes have a learning advantage over larger classes in reading and math in the early primary grades." If you are uncertain about the reliability of this premise, you can assign it a Ⓠ, at least until you have reason to change that assessment. The second use of the circled question mark is this. Even when you have a strong opinion of your own about a claim that is contentious and not easily verified, you can use this symbol to acknowledge that, even if it is true (or false), the persuasiveness of the argument relies on this easily challenged premise. To return to our previous issue, the statement "Abortion is always morally wrong" might get a Ⓠ even from someone who personally agrees (or disagrees) with the statement, to acknowledge how readily contended this nonempirical claim is. (Unpopular views that are demonstrably false can still get an Ⓕ and unpopular views that are demonstrably true can still get a Ⓣ.)

Most veteran mappers find it useful to add two more symbols: Ⓣ? and Ⓕ?. Ⓣ? is for statements that the mapper assesses as *probably* true. The earlier example about class size and learning might have been assessed as probably true on the basis of a mapper's strong intuitions, although that mapper had no actual evidence to support the claim. Ⓕ? is for statements that are assessed as *probably* false. Many mappers would assign this symbol to a statement like this one: "Professional basketball players are emotionally more mature than the general population." Even taken as a general statement, as it is almost certainly intended, rather than as a universal statement, this leaves most people skeptical—at least. Of course, some people will just give it a shrug and assign a Ⓠ. A few others will offer some defense of the claim. There will inevitably be disagreement on how to assess some statements. Still, without making a tentative assessment of the truth of the premises, a person can't decide whether to accept the overall argument and act on its conclusion.

PRACTICE WITH SHORT MAPS

To prepare yourself for making evaluative maps of long arguments, start with single-step (one arrow) arguments. After all, the longer arguments are just series of single-step arguments that are connected by transitional conclusions (and sometimes involve separate arguments for one conclusion).

Examine the following argument. Before reading past the map itself, decide how to assess the inference and the premises. Ev, who is so often critical and pessimistic, comments to a companion: "Why are you taking another college course? You failed the other one you took. Do you think it would be any different this time?" Taking the conclusion of Ev's reasoning to be the unstated—or not directly stated—"You will fail your second college course," the basic map for this single-inference argument looks like this:

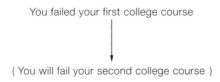

The conclusion is in parentheses because it was unstated—although quite clearly implied. Now, if you haven't already, decide whether to use a Ⓣ, Ⓣ?, Ⓠ, Ⓕ?, or Ⓕ for the premise, and decide what to write beside the arrow. Do not read the next paragraph until you have decided how to assess both the premise and the inference.

The inference is weak. In fact, it is very weak. You may write "Weak" or "Ind. Weak" to the right of the arrow that represents that inference. Although the premise is not completely irrelevant to the conclusion, it establishes nothing near a probability that the conclusion is true. The premise is probably true only because someone who directly addresses another in this way would not be likely to have contrived a falsehood about the person being addressed. A (T?), then, is as appropriate as anything here. Since we don't even know who is speaking and who is being addressed, we can't personally attest to its truth with a stronger assessment. A very cautious mapper might prefer a tidy (?) instead, simply because of that lack of personal knowledge. That, too, is acceptable.

Now consider the following argument: "Milan Kundera's book, *The Unbearable Lightness of Being*, is a sexually evocative book and this kind of material offends many people, so it should not be in the collections of public libraries." Examine the following basic map and decide how to complete it as an evaluative map before reading the paragraph that follows the map.

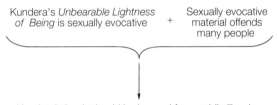

The premise on the left warrants a (T). Unless you have unusually strict criteria for applying the label "sexually evocative," this claim about Kundera's book is simply true. Of course, if a mapper doesn't know about the book, the symbol (?) would be assigned to the premise. The premise on the right is true (although the terms "sexually evocative" and "many" are not precise). The inference is quite weak. Consider other cases of books that include sometimes offensive material. Literary depictions of grisly deaths offend many people, but who would ban Homer's classics *Iliad* and *Odyssey*, or Dostoyevski's *Crime and Punishment*? Profanity offends many people, but lots of worthwhile and even very important books include this. Offensiveness of material is not itself enough to warrant exclusion from a society that values free expression and inquiry. A powerful statement of our deep concern about book censorship is made by author Ray Bradbury in *Fahrenheit 451*.

Some mappers will brand this inference "weak to no support" or "no support." What makes the inference weak is the quite challengeable assumption that "books that offend many people should be excluded/banned from public libraries." A mapper who includes this asumption as part of the map will produce the following:

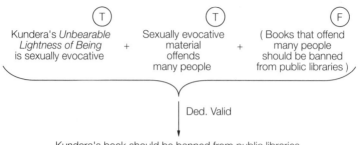

The rationale that was given for discounting the inference on the previous map is now relevant to our rejection of the new premise. Making the unstated premise explicit simply shifts the argument's weakness from form (inference) to content (evidence). Someone who feels more tentative about the unstated premise might give it an Ⓕ?, but the stronger Ⓕ would be acceptable as well. The truth or falsity of this premise is not established merely by empirical demonstration, and some variation of judgment may be expected. The inference is now deductively valid because *if* those three premises had been true, the conclusion would have to be true, too. Mappers who avoid technical terms could write "Nec." beside the arrow of inference to indicate that if the premises were true the conclusion would necessarily, not possibly, follow. Keep in mind that when you add unstated premises to the map there is often a risk of "reading in" too much. When mapping someone else's reasoning, you are just trying to show the arguer's *intended* reasoning.

Now, try mapping an argument of your own. Either write out a narrative argument and then map it, or just start with the map itself by writing the conclusion, then drawing arrows to it as you think of reasons for believing it. Use no transitional conclusions this time, even though much of your detailed evidence will be omitted from the map. If you have more than one premise, decide whether they should be joined by a plus and brackets. For premises that depend on each other in the making of a single point, provide the plus and brackets. If the points can be evaluated separately, use separate arrows. Now evaluate each inference. Imagine that the premises are true, and ask how likely the conclusion would then be. If those premises, imagined to be true, necessitate the truth of the conclusion, write "Ded. Valid" and indicate any special form that assures this, e.g., *modus tollens* (or write "Nec."). Otherwise, indicate the level of support (strong, moderate, weak) that the premises provide for the conclusion, or indicate why the evidence doesn't support the conclusion, e.g., "fallacy of attacking the person." After this, evaluate the premises. Assign a Ⓣ for reliable premises, Ⓣ? for ones that are probably reliable, ? for unknown or commonly challenged and hard-to-prove ones, Ⓕ? for probably unreliable premises, and Ⓕ for ones that simply should be rejected.

Now, look at your completed map. Are any of the inferences so weak that they should be deleted? If so, scratch out that arrow, erase it, or start over.

Are any of the premises more open to challenge than others that could be used? (When you replace it with a more cautious version, you also may have to reword the conclusion.) Change them. Can you now think of additional evidence to support your conclusion? Add it. Is your arrow-notation understating or overstating the strength of an inference? Adjust by changing your notation.

Just as the first draft of an essay can almost always be improved through reflection and rewriting, the first version of your map is more useful as an aid for continued evaluation of the reasoning, rather than as a final judgment of the worth of that reasoning.

Notice the difference between map-making for someone else's reasoning and for your own. As you map someone else's argument, you try to get at the originally intended reasoning; you don't try to improve on it. As you map your own, you rework the wording until you have the strongest case that you can make; revision is at the heart of it.

Finally, before moving on to consider maps that include transitional conclusions, let's try to map out the reasoning of U.S. Senator Hawkins from Florida in part of a speech on drug abuse delivered on the floor of the Senate. We can begin with this section:

The university encourages physical fitness and good health; it discourages smoking and alcohol abuse. It follows then that institutions of higher learning have an obligation to wage war on drugs.

A basic map of this portion of the speech looks like this.

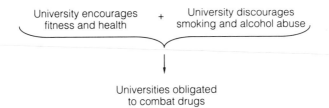

Unless you detect a clearly implied but unstated premise or conclusion, your map will look much like the preceding one. If you go on to make an evaluative map, it may look like this.

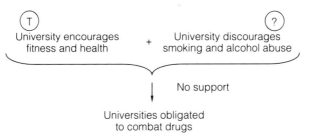

For this argument, the (T)/(F)/(?) premise signs may be assigned differently, depending on perspective. In the preceding map, a (T) has been assigned to the first premise because of the existence of interscholastic and intramural sports and various health programs; a (?) has been assigned to the second premise because discouragement of smoking and alcohol abuse is often token and unsystematic. Although these seem to be reasonable assignments, a focus on different aspects of the universities' approach to these problems might result in a different assessment. For this argument, however, that issue is not crucial because *even if both premises were true,* they would provide no real support for the conclusion.

Assume, for a moment, that both premises are true. Neither the universities' encouragement of fitness and health, nor their discouragement of smoking and alcohol abuse, nor these facts considered together, could possibly establish that universities have an obligation to combat drugs. Universities provide many services they are not obligated to provide, so the existence of the programs mentioned establishes no obligation of any sort. If it could be established that these fitness, health and smoking, and alcohol-abuse programs fulfilled actual university obligations, *then* an argument through analogy might be attempted. However, this has not been established. As the argument stands, the premises provide virtually no support for the conclusion.

Let's now return to Senator Hawkins's speech, adding the three sentences that she delivered immediately before the ones we have already considered.

Students are capable of individual and independent action. They are free to make decisions about their own lives. But they need guidance and leadership. The university encourages physical fitness and good health; it discourages smoking and alcohol abuse. It follows then that institutions of higher learning have an obligation to wage war on drugs.

This might result in the following evaluative map.

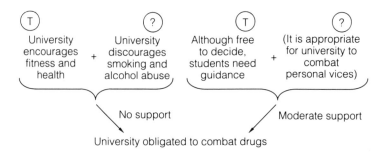

The three added sentences have been combined to read "Although free to decide, students need guidance." This is quite a compression of the three statements, but it seems to do no injustice to the intended meaning. Furthermore, to make mapping a useful and practical tool, we simply must combine and abbreviate. This three-in-one premise seems to function as a premise to support the conclusion we have already identified. Since the issue of the students' needing guidance is separate from the issue of which programs have actually been provided in the past, the additional premise is not linked to the two that we previously examined. A separate arrow joins this premise and the conclusion.

An unstated premise has been added to the map and joined with this new premise. The students' need for guidance would not lead us to believe that the *universities* are obligated to provide that guidance unless we accepted the unstated, but disputable, belief that it was appropriate for universities to provide such guidance. Actually, more than "guidance" must be allowed. We must accept that it is appropriate for universities to *combat* (whatever that may imply) personal vices. These two new premises join to provide at least a moderate degree of support for the claim that the universities are obligated to wage war on drugs. The premise that students need guidance has been assigned a (T) (though some people will disagree), and the unstated premise has been assigned a (?). *If* the two premises were true, the conclusion would demand consideration, but the truth of the unstated premise requires examination.

We can increase the degree of support that these recent premises provide for the conclusion if we interpret the argument differently. Let's try an unstated premise that is more strongly worded. Consider the following map.

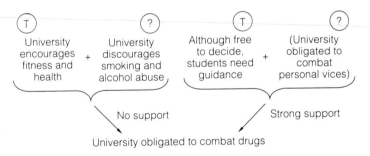

Here the unstated premise is considered to be "Universities are obligated to combat personal vices." While this premise definitely strengthens the degree of support provided for the conclusion, it is more contentious *and less clearly implied* by the senator's words than the other unstated premise we tried. This version of the argument is thus less accurate and less defensible than the last.

Despite the preference of the first interpretation of the senator's reasoning over the second, one more observation about the second map should be made. The two premises on the right side of the map might be said to produce more than an inductively strong argument. If, after all, every university is obligated to combat personal vices, then it is *necessarily* true that those universities are obligated to combat drug abuse. If we ignore distinctions between drug use and abuse, then, this part of the argument — this subargument — is deductively valid if we assume both that the drug activity to be combatted is a personal vice and that the claim "Universities are obligated to combat personal vice" implies that they are obligated to combat *all* personal vices.

MAP LONGER LINES OF REASONING

Whether you are doing basic mapping or evaluative mapping, those multiple-conclusion arguments can be mapped by considering each subargument as a separate building block. These can be considered separately, then fitted to the whole structure at the right place. If you can analyze single-step arguments, you should be able to analyze a series of these arguments, too. A long line of reasoning is nothing more than a series of subarguments.

In evaluative mapping, keep two things in mind. The first has already been discussed: Assess the inference without being influenced by your beliefs about the truth or falsity of the premises. Inference and evidence, form and content, are evaluated separately on these maps. The second thing to keep in mind is that each inference should be assessed without regard to the strength of any inference that precedes it (that is, any arrow that is above it) on the map.

The first mapping example for this section of the chapter is not much longer than the preceding map of Senator Hawkins's reasoning about universities and drug abuse. However, it does have at least one transitional conclusion. The excerpt is from George Will's January 14, 1991 *Newsweek* essay on war in the Persian Gulf. When Mr. Will wrote the essay, the 1991 war with Iraq had not yet begun and the U.S. Congress had not yet approved offensive military action against Iraq. While this issue of *Newsweek* was still on the newsstands, however, the Congressional approval that eliminated any prospect of President Bush's "initiating war on his own hook" was accomplished, and shortly after the following issue of the magazine arrived at those same newsstands, the war had begun.

Could Bush get away with the anti-constitutional act of initiating war on his own hook? Sure. Once the shooting starts, Congress has only two weapons and neither blunderbuss is practical: impeachment or defunding the war. So Bush is inhibited only by his oath of office (about preserving the Constitution) and prudential consideration.

Although evaluation of an excerpt from a longer line of reasoning invites misunderstanding, we can map the preceding passage just for practice. The evaluative map might look like this.

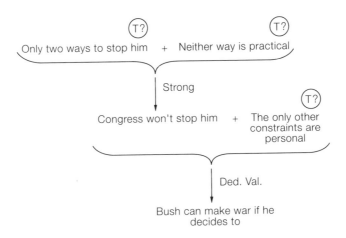

The upper inference on the map is inductively strong; if the premises were true, the conclusion probably would be true also. If the only two options open to Congress were notably impractical, they probably would not have been pursued. We don't even know if Congress would have chosen to oppose the president. (Although Congress doesn't always pursue avenues that consensus deems practical, it is perhaps more likely to do so on such a grave issue.) Now let's consider the lower inference on the map. If Congress wouldn't have stopped him, and there were no other external constraints, then he could do as he chose, subject to personal constraints that might include both moral and prudential concerns. Now, what about the premises? It's a good idea to evaluate the inferences before the evidence, so your decision about the strength of the inference is not influenced by your decision about the reliability of the premises. The ability to separate these two usually contributes to clear thinking. On this map, each premise has been assigned a (T?), although they all invite reevaluation; the issue is not simple and the wording is not precise.

Sometimes there is more than one way to map an argument. This is true of the George Will passage. Consider this reconstruction of that reasoning.

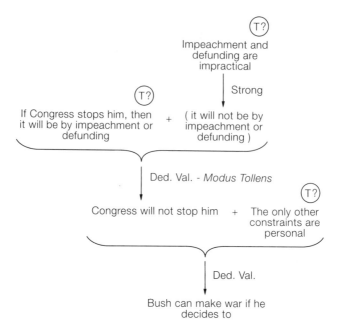

Maps are rough sketches of the actual argumentation. When you consolidate statements, articulate assumptions, or delete and reword phrases or entire statements, you alter some of the subtleties of the communication. Sometimes, as you see, it is even possible to construct alternate versions of the reasoning. Nevertheless, carefully drawn maps can help you analyze reasoning. Because of the possibility of misrepresenting and trivializing someone's reasoning, let's agree to apply the *principle of charity*: Don't intentionally misconstrue someone's reasoning and, when two readings of the intended meaning are possible, assume the more reasonable and defensible version.

Let's examine one more mappable line of reasoning. Barbara Ehrenreich's *Time* magazine essay, "Real Patriots Speak Their Minds," is like a lot of our everyday reading. Much of the detail can be omitted from an overview of the line of reasoning. Not only can the essay be mapped in slightly different ways, a practical mapping requires some paraphrasing. You will combine, reword, and omit as you sculpt a map that doesn't misrepresent the author, but still takes the main argument and "puts it in a nutshell."

A paraphrase of an argument is a shorter version of the argument that includes the essential evidence and conclusions. Effective mapping of arguments requires skill at paraphrasing because, very often, not all the statements in an argument should appear on the map; rewording, combination, and omission of statements are routinely required.

We can see some of this compacting in the mapping of Senator Hawkins's speech earlier in this chapter. For example, three sentences were reduced to one when our map showed the premise "Although free to decide, students need guidance," which served to represent this entire passage: "Students are capable of individual and independent action. They are free to make decisions about their own lives. But they need guidance and leadership." Notice that the entire map served as a paraphrase of both the content and the logical structure of the senator's argument. Once an argument is reduced to its "bare bones," it is typically easier to assess.

Like most published writing, Barbara Ehrenreich's essay will lose some of its tone and subtlety in a map. However, the map can enable you to (1) see the heart of her reasoning more clearly, and (2) analyze it more incisively. After reading the essay, you may choose to map it before examining the map provided, or you may choose to go immediately to the map in the text without making your own effort to reconstruct the argument.

Patriotism should bring us together but not so close that we begin to look like sheep. One could detect the bleatings of the herd in a recent televised exchange between columnist Robert Novak and Congressman Joe Kennedy. Frustrated by the Congressman's failure to agree with him on a range of issues, Novak suddenly snapped, "Where's your American-flag lapel pin?" Never mind that young Kennedy has chosen to serve his nation on a full-time basis, he wasn't, in the conservative columnist's eyes, patriotically correct.

There are other signs of a confusion in some quarters between patriotism and conformity. During the Gulf war, peace vigils were occasionally disrupted by frat-house zealots. According to a study done by a media watchdog group, Fairness and Accuracy in Reporting, television executives virtually excised antiwar voices from the air. Bumper stickers advised good citizens to SAVE A FLAG, BURN A PROTESTER. And the nastiness didn't end with the hostilities overseas. One of the official entertainers for the June victory parade in Washington was radio talk-show personality Blake Clark, whose theme is, "If you aren't homeless, if you aren't sick, if you have all your body parts, if you have a job, then just shut up."

Well, whoa there, Mr. Clark! No one should have to prove love of country by wearing an American-flag patch stitched tightly across the mouth. Let's recall what distinguishes our country from your run-of-the-mill nation-state. We Americans have no history of dynasties or dictators, no tradition of scraping and bowing, cringing or marching in step. This is a nation founded in revolution, birthed by rebels and dissidents. They had a lot to say on many subjects, like God and country, duty and freedom — and none of it was "shut up."

Consider Tom Paine, the immigrant artisan who became the ablest propagandist of the American Revolution. At first he could find no one in Philadelphia willing to print the pamphlet he called *Common Sense*. It was too fiery, he was told, too seditious, and at this point a more cautious man might have learned to seal his lips. But finally a fellow radical, notorious, among other things, for living openly "in sin," agreed to roll the presses. *Common Sense* was born, with its great news that Americans had it in their power to overthrow the "crowned ruffians," the "royal brute," and "begin the world over again."

Most of the revolutionaries were wealthier, more respectable types than Paine, including, shamefully, even slave owners like Tom Jefferson. But whatever their limitations, they were all proud sons of the Enlightenment. They believed fiercely in the power of individual reason as a guide to action, which is why so many of them defied majority opinion with their radical views on God. Any 1990s-style political handler could have advised them to go to church and mouth the prayers along with everyone else, but men like Paine, Ben Franklin and John Adams were deists, holding that God had created the universe and then departed from the scene. Jefferson won the presidency despite being baited as an atheist, and Ethan Allen authored a scathing attack on Christianity, titled *Reason, the Only Oracle of Man*.

To these, our first patriots, freedom of speech, even jarring, unpopular speech, was a right worth dying for. Paine upheld "the right of every man to his opinion, however different that opinion may be to mine." Franklin said, "Without freedom of thought there can be no such thing as . . . publick liberty." Jefferson believed "uniformity of opinion" was no more desirable than uniformity "of face and stature." Staid George Washington warned against "the impostures of pretended patriotism."

Jefferson's Declaration of Independence defines patriotism in an implicitly rebellious fashion. According to that precious document, we do not owe our allegiance to a government or its leaders — and certainly not to its army or its flag — but to each other and to our common right to liberty and the pursuit of happiness. "Whenever any Form of Government becomes destructive of these ends," the Declaration states, "it is the Right of the People to alter or abolish it . . ." Thus for Jefferson, dissent was not only a right but also a necessity: "I hold that a little rebellion now and then is a good thing . . ." God forbid, he added (meaning what he called "Nature's God"), that we should ever go 20 years without one.

And, fortunately, we've seldom had to go that long. Ten years after the Revolution, there was Shay's Rebellion, in which poor farmers challenged the new Republic's monied elite. In the 1820s and '30s, there was the Workingmen's Movement, pitted against the evils of "kingcraft, priestcraft and lawyercraft." That fed into the abolition movement, which in turn helped launch the women's suffrage movement in 1848. Near the turn of the century, there was the middle-class Progressive Movement for civic reform and a near insurrection by the new industrial working class. In our own time we've seen fresh rebellions on behalf of minority rights, women's rights, peace and disarmament, and gay rights.

In fact, dissidence ought to be regarded as one of our finest traditions and proudest exports to the world. The feminist movement began here and spread throughout the world. Our civil rights movement has inspired the downtrodden in dozens of nations, and gay rights was practically invented here. Jefferson, I daresay, would be proud.

Sure, it would be a quieter, tidier land if we all agreed on everything and if those who didn't would shut up. But in the voice of the dissident, the oddball and the minority, however wrongheaded from one's own point of view, we should learn to hear the echoes of men like Jefferson and Paine. They didn't goose-step to the tune of the reigning authority. They didn't shut up when more timid souls said it wasn't wise to speak. And suppose they had? Then the flag we'd be pinning to our lapels today would be the Union Jack.

"Real Patriots Speak Their Minds," essay by Barbara Ehrenreich, Time, *July 8, 1991.*

As you examine the following map, remember that variations on the map can be created by combining or separating premises, by including more detail, or by rewording some statements. Now, here is one correct way of looking at the skeleton of Ehrenreich's reasoning.

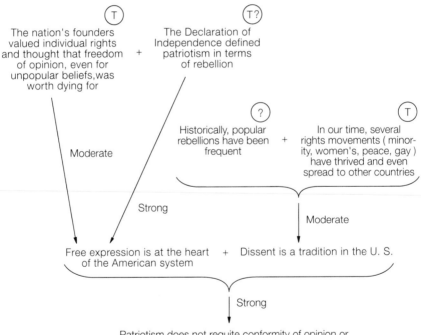

First, let's consider the basic mapping, apart from the evaluation of inferences and premises. The two transitional conclusions, "Free expression is at the heart of the American system" and "Dissent is a tradition in the U.S.," could easily be collapsed into one, with all three of the arrows that are at the top of the map pointing down to that composite transitional conclusion. Besides this, more detail and different wording might make an alternate map look a bit different.

Now, let's consider the evaluative side of the mapping. The inference represented by the upper left arrow warrants only a "moderate" since not all of the founders' values are retained as inherent in the political system they championed. In the inference represented by the arrow to the right of that first one, "strong" is an appropriate label (but not "deductively valid" because of the imprecise relation between "free expression" and "rebellion," and because founding documents do not always accurately describe the actual workings of a political system). In the inference represented by the arrow at the top right, we find moderate strength, because such a visible role for dissension may generally support the transitional conclusion that dissent is traditional in this country, but a mere history of conflict and dispute is characteristic also of other countries — ones that do not include, in our sense, dissent as a tradition. The phrase "dissent is a tradition" is vague, and might only warrant a "weak" for the inference that leads to it on this map, according to some mappers. The lower arrow is labeled "strong." If free expression and dissent are so central and vital to the system, uniformity of perspective would be something that might not even be desirable.

Two of the premises on the map have a T to indicate their reliability. They seem to be simply true — matters of fact. One has a T?. That patriotism is actually defined in terms of rebellion might be overstated, even though the patriots who signed the Declaration were obviously prideful of that right to rebel that they took to be ever so justified. Finally, one premise has a ?. The author of the essay has cited several examples of rebellions. Does this constitute reason for believing that rebellions have been "frequent" and truly popular? Difference of opinion, resting on some varied definitions of terms and dispute of facts, makes this a difficult premise to assess. The circled question mark is appropriate here.

■

PRACTICE ACTIVITIES

Set 9.1 *Turn to Practice Sets 8.2 in Chapter 8 and 6.1 in Chapter 6. For each of the arguments in these two practice sets, create an evaluative map that displays (1) your understanding of the intended reasoning, and (2) your evaluation of the inferences and basic premises.*

Set 9.2 *Create an evaluative map that displays (1) your understanding of the intended reasoning in the following conversational arguments, and (2) your evaluation of the inferences and basic premises.*

1. Stalin was a dictator and he was ruthless. Hitler was a dictator and he was ruthless. Castro is a dictator. So he must be a ruthless leader, too.

2. You say that women are always deeply religious. This generalization of yours is, not surprisingly, false. In fact, I can logically demonstrate that at least some women are atheists. First, all serious scholars are atheists. That's common knowledge. Second, some women are serious scholars. This clearly proves my point. And if you doubt that all serious scholars are atheists, think about the facts that all serious scholars are extremely analytical and that all extremely analytical people are atheists. Logic alone proves my point. There's no denying it!

3. A foreign language is an important subject of study for college students. Through studying foreign languages, students learn about diverse cultures. They also learn about conceptualization by seeing how parallel words in different languages are not completely interchangeable. No college student's schedule should omit a foreign language, even if it is not required by the school.

4. Belmont High would certainly be a good school if all the instructors were good ones. And we do know that Belmont is a good school. Thus, all of the instructors there must be good ones. Any good instructor, I might add, is concerned about her or his students. Therefore, all Belmont High instructors are concerned about their students.

5. Private investigators are all neurotic, and some of the people we classify as neurotic are actually dangerous to society. As you can see, then, at least some private investigators are actually dangerous to society. Furthermore, of these people who are a danger to society, many have had sexual problems as adolescents. What you see now is that the problem with at least some private investigators is rooted in their adolescent sexuality.

6. The practice of grading students' school assignments should be abolished. In the first place grading is unfair. Second, besides its being unfair, there are practical disadvantages in focusing on grades. Both students and teachers can be distracted from the actual learning process with excessive concern for measurement, recording, and justification of the quality of performances in the course. This distraction seriously impairs the educational process. Now, back to the point of the unfairness. Some students have much more time available to study than others. Often, the difference in grades reflects just this. Also, speaking of fairness, no one is really qualified to judge the work of another person, and this is exactly what grading amounts to.

Set 9.3 *Create an evaluative map that displays (1) your understanding of the intended reasoning in the following arguments that have been excerpted from magazine articles, and (2) your evaluation of the inferences and basic premises.*

1. From "Fact and Comment" by Malcolm S. Forbes, Jr., *Forbes* magazine, July 22, 1991:

   > Poland has hit upon a wonderfully simple idea to quickly privatize a significant portion of its state-owned companies: Put these assets in mutual funds and give their shares to all adults.
   >
   > This move will truly give ownership to the people, something communism promised but never fulfilled. More important, it will help ameliorate the hugely debilitating feeling among the people that, so far, the spin-off of state assets has benefited old-line communists, that the fruits of change have thus far gone to the wrong crowd.
   >
   > The Polish proposal poses immense practical problems, but the idea is politically brilliant — and necessary. Wouldn't it be a fabulous gesture for the U.S. to offer the technical assistance to make this idea a reality?

2. Also from Forbes's "Fact and Comment" in the July 22 issue of *Forbes*:

   > In the wake of a TV expose about alleged baby selling in Romania, U.S. officials have cracked down on issuing visas for Romanian babies adopted by U.S. parents. We're overreacting. There may be abuses, but that's no reason to victimize couples who have acted in good faith.
   >
   > Under the late dictator Ceauescu, Romania banned all birth control, with a result that over 100,000 children were dumped into hideous orphanages. When their plight became known here, numerous Americans responded by going to Romania to adopt some of these kids.
   >
   > Not surprisingly, some Romanian con artists tried to make a quick buck by, in effect, "arranging" adoptions for big fees. As a result, Romania has suspended adoptions, and the U.S. is suddenly becoming persnickety about issuing visas to dozens of parents in Romania who already have legally adopted babies. This sudden bureaucratic crackdown is misplaced. The victims are these children, who desperately need new homes with loving parents.
   >
   > Why can't President Bush have officials issue humanitarian paroles to prevent inhumane delays in getting these children to the U.S., particularly for those cases that have already met

Romania's adoption rules and for those parents who have already received approval from the Immigration and Naturalization Service to adopt these kids?

3. From "Government Is Strangling Transit" by John Semmens, *The Freeman*, July 1991:

> Publicly owned and operated transit has been a colossal failure. Billions of taxpayer dollars have been frittered away with little or nothing to show for it.
>
> In 1964, the year the Urban Mass Transportation Administration was created by Congress, eight billion trips were taken on urban transit carriers. Twenty-seven years later, public transit ridership is still eight billion trips. This total lack of progress hasn't been without cost. Since 1964 the federal government has squandered over $35 billion on public transit. State and local governments have tossed in another $30 billion.

For Further Reading

Thomas, Stephen Naylor. *Practical Reasoning in Natural Language.* Englewood Cliffs, NJ: Prentice-Hall, 1986.

A guide for mapping arguments.

Toulmin, Steven, Richard Rieke, and Allan Janik. *An Introduction to Reasoning.* New York: Macmillan, 1984.

A book with an alternate approach to mapping arguments.

P A R T

FOUR

Reason
in Action

■

C H A P T E R

TEN

Writing to Make a Point

Literate people can read about other people's thoughts and write about their own. When your thoughts on a topic are extensive or complicated, it usually helps to get them down on paper. Often, only after trying to put your ideas into words can you refine them. You can restate your ideas until you clarify them in your own mind. In this way, you write for your own benefit. Usually, of course, the reason for writing is different. Your thoughts are meant to be communicated to someone else. If you don't say what you mean in these cases, the reader will simply assume that you meant what you said—although, of course, you didn't.

KNOW WHY YOU WRITE

The printed word is all around us. Streets are lined with traffic signs and billboards. Businesses splash their names, services, and commercial enticements over the front of their buildings. Newspapers, books, pamphlets, flyers, notes, and memos are so common in our daily experience that, as we zip through them or ignore them, we take for granted the written language that makes possible this kind of communication.

You can also take for granted your own writing skills. Whether it's a note to a friend or family member, a school assignment, or a memo at work, you *know* that you know how to write it. Sometimes the result is that you don't think enough about how you could say it best. Certainly, the precision that results from crafting a line carefully is not always worth the effort. A quick note scrawled on paper may require no more reflection than you have given it. However, if you don't practice saying just what you mean and saying it well, the skill won't be there when you do need it.

Good writing is guided by the question: Why am I writing? Think about who your reader will be. For this reader, what kinds of sentence structures and vocabulary should you use? What kinds of imagery will be effective?

214

What assumptions can you make about the reader's prior knowledge and biases? Think about what you want that reader to feel and understand. Do you intend to communicate information, evoke certain emotions, or move the reader to act in a certain way? You may intend a combination of these reactions to your writing.

There are many different reasons for writing and many different forms of writing. Kurt Vonnegut's reason for writing the novel *Hocus Pocus* was different from Lee Iacocca's reason for writing a memo to the vice presidents of Chrysler Corporation. Vonnegut's intentions for his novel were also somewhat different from those of other novelists, and were even different from his own intentions in other novels. So the language and organizational structures are different in each case. The essayist Michael Kinsley's article for *Time* displays a different kind of writing than a technical manual for the operation of an industrial air compressor, and it's different from the kind of writing we find in other magazines. All this is obvious. Still, the point is important. Precision, vividness, and the general effectiveness of your writing can only be improved by keeping your audience and purposes in mind as you write.

High school and college students sometimes find it difficult to have a clear sense of audience and a compelling reason for writing as they work on school assignments. Because they think of themselves as writing for the teacher, they sometimes leave out important steps in their thinking, assuming the teacher knows all that. The result is writing that is sketchy rather than rich and detailed. Students sometimes lack enthusiasm for the project. After all, they think, I'm just writing an assignment rather than convincing a reader of something I really want to get across. These students might benefit from a change in their thinking about their audience. Usually it is helpful to think of the reader as an intelligent person who is not knowledgeable about the topic—someone with whom the writer is unacquainted. With this change of perspective, the academic writer is less likely to leave out detail that the teacher may know but want to have included in the writing. It also allows some writers to feel more of a sense of purpose. It adds a reason for writing. Of course, this also requires the writer to think about the main point or even the feelings to be conveyed.

There are many kinds of writing. In this book, the specific focus will be on articulating evidence and conclusions. This "argumentative" kind of writing is not only common in educational settings. It can be found, done well or poorly, in many settings in which a writer wants to make a point and support it with reasoning. Certain newspaper editorials, letters to the editor, magazine essays and articles, business reports and memos, and newsletter columns, for example, employ a basic premise-and-conclusion structure.

Your own reasoning skills have almost certainly been sharpened as you have explored and studied the ideas and examples in this book. You may also be able to improve your skill at writing your premises and conclusions in an easily read format. In this chapter, mapping skills, basic and evaluative, will serve as a foundation for developing and presenting a well-written discussion of any arguable position on an issue. The other skills examined in this book (for example: keeping an open mind, using fair and precise language, and the specific skills of argument assessment) are integrated with the mapping. The result is that you can simultaneously connect the themes of everyday reasoning that you have been studying and improve your writing.

RECOGNIZE BIAS

When the bias in your written work is evident and extreme, you can count on "convincing," with a rousing cheer, people who share your views. You can also count on offending others, or at least being dismissed by them as a less than credible advocate of those views. They will suspect that you are willing to twist the facts to fit your conclusions.

When you write to support a conclusion and hope to be taken seriously by unbiased and even skeptical readers, your writing should convey the tone of a reasonable and open-minded person. The importance of open-mindedness was explored in Chapters 1 and 2, and that theme has been developed throughout this book. You can convey this tone of reasonableness and open-mindedness by:

Watching your language. Don't hold back the evidence for your conclusion, but strive for a reserved spirit of expression. Avoid personal attacks on opponents and don't describe their views in unnecessarily demeaning ways. When describing your own view, resist temptations to use smug language that communicates an offensive self-righteousness. Be attentive to the powers of language that we examined in Chapter 3.

Avoiding extremism. Don't overstate the degree to which your evidence supports your conclusion. If you have proven that "Most college presidents are not very interested in the sports programs at their schools," don't overstate and claim that you have shown that "No college presidents are interested in the sports programs at their schools." You will turn your adequate support into inadequate support, because your evidence will not support this conclusion. We discussed this problem in Chapter 6. Similarly, you should not present your ideas as if weak evidence were strong evidence. We discussed the rules of good reasoning in Chapters 6, 7, and 8.

Acknowledging objections. Anticipate and articulate the most likely objection to your argument or to your conclusion. Take the objection seriously and acknowledge any strengths it has. There is almost always at least one minor point that each side agrees on. You achieve a more objective tone by letting the reader know that you are not blinded by emotion and you can understand the other viewpoint, even if you don't think it outweighs the opposing evidence. If you don't articulate the objection, the reader might think that you have failed to recognize this point of view, or that you would spurn counterevidence with a closed mind. Don't leave the impression that you are picking and choosing evidence in order to slant the issue unfairly. In Chapter 2, ways to identify good counterevidence were presented in the section, "See Another Side."

You sound as if you have thought through the issue better if you adopt the three practices mentioned above. In addition, you usually appear to be in better control of your ideas and to have surveyed the issue well if your ideas are presented in an orderly way, rather than haphazardly as they just happen to come to mind. Chapters 4 and 5 can remind you of how to organize your ideas so someone else can follow them.

MAP YOUR REASONING BEFORE YOU WRITE

When you are writing to support a thesis (a "stand"), you should have an idea of where you will end up before you start even a rough draft. Prethink your topic by trying to formulate your thesis — your ultimate conclusion — and write down several versions. Then scratch down related thoughts, main ideas, likely premises. Some people do this with a tape recorder to catch their thoughts as quickly as they can be put into words. The advantage of writing it down is that your eyes can skip from one note to another, seeing relations that might determine the structure of your thesis defense. Certainly you can go from tape recorder to notes, if you choose to combine the methods. Then follow these steps:

1. *Draw a rough map.* Write a rough version of the ultimate conclusion near the bottom of your page. Construct a basic map by selecting from your notes the ideas that will support this conclusion and that, in turn, will themselves be supportable. Enter these premises on your map, deciding where to make a plus sign and where to draw a separate arrow. Add any missing premises to your map.

2. *Reword the ultimate conclusion, then its premises.* The need for precise wording is as great in thesis defense writing as in any other kind of writing. Seldom is your thesis well-stated on your first attempt. Think about whether the wording for your ultimate conclusion conveys exactly what you intended. Are some of the words or phrases misleading? Are they specific enough? Rewrite that thesis statement. Then look at the premises (they may be basic or transitional premises) that lead directly to

that thesis, which is your ultimate conclusion. Do the premises support it well? Think about — or actually write out — what an evaluative map for your argument would look like. (As you think or write, simply superimpose this on the basic map you are already working with.) If the premises don't support the conclusion as it's written, a further change in wording might strengthen the inference. A slight change in wording will often change a weak inference into a stronger one.

3. *Create an outline.* Title your project if you can at this point. Use roman numerals (I, II, III, IV, V) to indicate each main section. These often correspond to each of the premises or sets of premises that have mapping arrows leading directly to the ultimate conclusion. Under the roman numerals, you may indent and identify subpoints with arabic letters (A, B, C). Further subpoints can be marked with consecutive numbers: 1, 2, 3. For thesis defense writing, you will generally begin with an opening paragraph (assign it roman numeral I in your outline) in which you state your thesis and perhaps offer the main avenues of support. This previews the structure of the whole project. If you mention, let's say, three main avenues of support in your opening paragraph, you can follow with three paragraphs or sets of paragraphs (roman numerals I, II, III, etc.) to develop these lines of support. Present them in the same order in which you previewed them. End with a closing paragraph in which you restate your thesis. You may also quickly review the main avenue of support you employed. This mirrors the opening paragraph and restates the heart of your argument. Since it's often useful to anticipate and respond to a likely objection to your views, consider fitting this into your outline. Although placement of this objection and reply will vary from one writing project to another, try placing it right before the closing paragraph. It is not always necessary to refer to this section in your opening preview or your closing review of main points.

4. *Write.* Readers of your written work do not have the advantage of using your map or outline to figure out how each of your observations is related to the others. The premise-and-conclusion relations that are obvious to you as the creator of this line of reasoning may not be obvious to your reader. So use conclusion indicators, premise indicators, and any other rhetorical tools you have as you try to make clear to the reader the structure of the map you drew during the planning stage of your writing.

Except for the outlining and writing, these steps have been discussed in previous chapters. Let's refer back to Chapter 5. In the section of that chapter titled "Map Your Own Reasoning," a map was pieced together, not from any previous written or spoken passage, but as if the writer were mapping the ideas as they came to mind. Although that was a very small map representing a very short argument, let's create an outline from the map and a letter or article from the outline.

Roman numeral I designates the opening paragraph, in which the conclusion is stated and each main inference is previewed. Roman numerals II, III, and IV designate the three main inferences or lines of support as they are presented in the body of the letter or article. An objection to the conclusion is acknowledged and answered next. This is marked with a V in the outline. Roman numeral VI designates the closing paragraph.

I. Opening paragraph
   A. Thesis statement
   B. Main support introduced

II. Teaching award

III. Popularity of professor

IV. Student performance on national test

V. Objection and reply
   A. Obj: Researchers often don't make the best teachers
   B. Reply:
      1. That is a generalization and she is an exception
      2. Her research makes her a better teacher

VI. Closing paragraph
   A. Restatement of main support
   B. Restatement of thesis

Sometimes it's more useful to use complete sentences in your outline rather than brief phrases or key words. Usually there will be lots of subheadings under the roman numerals, reflecting additional mapped premises for these main points (which then would be transitional conclusions). In many cases, you may find that omitting the outline and writing straight from the map is easier. That depends on both you and the argument. Still, even when you do outline to plan the order in which you will present the various premises and conclusions, you should keep an eye on the map from which you developed the outline. The map will show which premises lead to which conclusions in a direct way that is difficult to match in an outline.

Although the argument just outlined is so brief and has little detail, let's see how this set of ideas might be written. The brevity will enable you to see basic elements and structure more clearly.

> Professor Chu is an excellent teacher. This appraisal is supported by her peer assessment, her popularity with students, and the performance of her students in national testing.
>
> The professor's professional peers have recognized her excellence. At her previous college, they honored the professor by conferring on her an award for excellence in teaching.
>
> She is also extremely popular with her students. Many of them go out of their way to enroll in every single course she teaches. This, of course, is very rare and is only true of the most exceptionally talented teachers in the whole school.
>
> Professor Chu's students not only like her, they perform well. Over the past eight years, her students have taken nationally standardized tests in her field, and have an average score at the ninety-first percentile.
>
> Dr. Chu is a noted researcher in her field. For this reason, some people may be skeptical about her dedication to teaching. University researchers are often criticized for considering teaching as a chore that takes time from their real love, which is research. Frequently this reputation is justified. Anyone who knows the versatile Professor Chu, however, recognizes that she is a stellar exception. In fact, her engagement in research projects enriches her classes because she consistently finds interesting ways to introduce even the more specialized projects into her teaching plans. Furthermore, she is a caring teacher who is regularly available to students outside the classroom.
>
> Since her expertise and dedication are affirmed by peer assessment, popularity with students, and student performance on national testing, we can confidently conclude that Dr. Chu excels as a teacher.

MAP OTHERS' REASONING BEFORE YOU CRITIQUE

The mapping method of preparing for your thesis defense writing is carried out a bit differently when your purpose is to assess someone else's reasoning (usually it's something in print) rather than simply to present your own thoughts on the issue. Now you need to organize the other person's comments and make an assessment, then organize your own critical comments. This results in a five-step plan:

1. *Draw an evaluative map of the other person's reasoning.* A basic map of someone's reasoning graphically describes your understanding of the point to be proven and how it was supported with evidence. In other words, it shows what the person claimed and how the person reasoned (assuming that the line of reasoning was clear enough and you mapped well). An evaluative map goes beyond this, showing your assessment of the argument's strengths and weaknesses. Mapping is good groundwork for deciding how you will critique the reasoning.

2. *Decide on a thesis.* What position do you want to take (and support) in regard to that reasoning you just mapped? You should be able to offer a general assessment in the form of a thesis statement. That will help your reader more than a mere list of strengths and weaknesses. Your thesis statement could describe the *kinds* of strengths and weaknesses the argument has. Then you would go on to support these observations with specific examples. On the other hand, your thesis statement could identify one or two major and specific problems, which you would then go on to detail. Examples: "Although the president's premises, if true, would warrant concern about the conclusions he offers, there is reason to believe that one of those premises is false and two are very questionable." "Mr. Mehta is correct in his judgments about the character of the people of Ukraine, but makes a false assumption in his prediction of their response to the looming national crisis." "The author of *Health Care Today* bases her conclusions about the future of HMOs on information that is dated and incomplete."

3. *Map your own argument.* Draw a basic map of your own intended support for the thesis statement you developed. Either write in or think through the evaluative elements for your map, i.e., the premise and inference assessments. Change your thesis statement if necessary.

4. *Create an outline.* This is an outline of *your* argument, not the one you are evaluating. It should have opening and closing paragraphs, as described before. If there is a credible objection to your critique, insert in the outline a place for your acknowledgment of it and your reply.

5. *Write.* Avoid sarcasm, smugness, and overstatement in your critique. It will have more persuasive power with a tone of objectivity.

Now look back to Chapter 9. The U.S. senator's comments on the university's role in opposing drug abuse were mapped. In fact, two evaluative maps were drawn because the strength of part of the argument depends on how we word the unstated premise. Let's use this as an example. We will decide on a thesis, map our counterargument, create an outline, and write a brief critique of Senator Hawkins's reasoning. (In briefer writing projects like this one, the outlining step is sometimes omitted.) Take time now to reread the senator's comments, examine the maps, and review the text's discussion of them (pages 199 — 202).

The senator's comments may be critiqued in more than one way. Still, as an example, let's use this thesis statement: "Senator Hawkins has failed to establish her conclusion that universities are obligated to combat drug abuse." When we write our critique itself, we can agree to the desirability of this kind of university commitment, while we disagree with the claim of an actual obligation. We can also, if we see it that way, agree that such an obligation exists, but argue that the author of that original view failed to establish the obligation. In this case, of course, we can either go on to present a stronger argument of our own, or leave it at a critique of the senator's remarks. Our choice here depends on the purpose of our critique: Who are we addressing and why?

Perhaps we would then produce the following map to guide our writing.

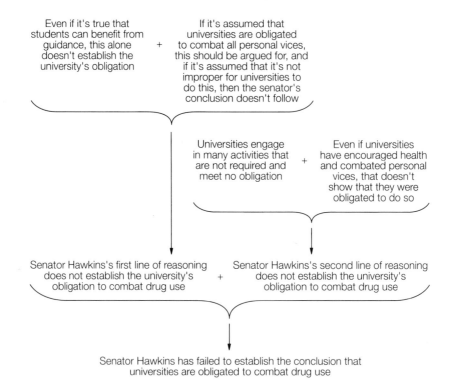

You will probably notice that the two transitional conclusions seem to contribute little to the strength of the reasoning. Look at the pair of premises that leads to the first transitional conclusion on the left side of the map and the pair that leads to the one on the right side of the map. Neither pair *alone*

establishes that the senator has not proven her point, since in each case the other pair might have been sufficient to prove the point. Thus, we cannot assign to each pair of premises a separate arrow leading to the ultimate conclusion. (There may be additional ways to map the senator's reasoning fairly.)

Now let's produce an outline from which we can write our critique. An objection and reply will be placed before the closing paragraph.

   I. Opening paragraph
     A. Thesis statement
     B. Objection and reply
     C. Main support

  II. Students' benefit from guidance doesn't establish obligation.

 III. Examples of what universities currently encourage and discourage doesn't establish obligation.

 IV. Objection and reply
     A. Obj: There are many good reasons for universities to combat drug abuse.
     B. Reply: This is true. The senator could have presented a strong argument with a more moderate conclusion.

  V. Closing paragraph
     A. Restatement of main support and objection and reply
     B. Restatement of conclusion

This time you have seen a complete-sentence outline, except for the opening and closing paragraphs, which also can be presented in sentence form. (For example, instead of writing "thesis" on the outline, you would write out the thesis statement.)

Now you write from the outline.

Senator Hawkins, in a speech to the U.S. Senate on drug abuse, failed to establish her conclusion that universities have an obligation to combat drug abuse. Although there is a strong case to be made for university participation in the war on drug abuse, Senator Hawkins tried to establish too much — an obligation to participate — and damages her argument by overstating the conclusion that can be supported with the premises she offered. Neither the insistence that students would benefit from guidance nor the citing of past university support for personal health issues is sufficient to establish such an obligation.

Senator Hawkins first argued that autonomous university students still need guidance and leadership. Certainly this abstract claim is true not only of university students but also of the general population. The argument falls far short of establishing an obligation for any particular educational, business, or government institution. Perhaps the senator's unstated assumption was that universities are obligated to combat all personal vices. If so, she should have argued for this position, since its truth is not obvious and uncontentious. Perhaps the senator's unstated assumption was merely that it is not improper for universities to combat personal vices. Although this position is more easily defended, it is too weak to establish the claim that any obligation binds those schools. The conclusion simply does not follow.

In a related line of reasoning, Senator Hawkins observed that universities already encourage fitness and health, and that they discourage smoking and alcohol abuse. Generally, this is correct. It's true that universities encourage fitness and health in many ways. Although their efforts to discourage smoking and alcohol abuse may be viewed as token or feeble, some such efforts have been made on most campuses. Still, even if their advocacy of personal health were methodical and rigorous, that would establish neither that they were obligated to have done this, nor that they are obligated to combat drug abuse.

An objection to this line of criticism might be made. After all, the challenger will protest, isn't it a good idea for universities to try to discourage drug abuse? Indeed, no case has been made here against the value or even the desirability of such efforts. Criticism has been limited to the claim that the argument establishes an obligation. Such an obligation may exist, but that has not been demonstrated — it has only been claimed — by the senator from Florida. The senator's reasoning might have merited praise rather than dissent if the conclusion drawn had been expressed more carefully.

Senator Hawkins's reflections on the desirability of guidance concerning drug issues and on the universities' history of encouraging health and discouraging personal vices, then, fail to establish that the universities have an obligation to lead in our efforts to combat this social problem. If that conclusion is a well-founded one, it will take different arguments to establish it, and if the senator's evidence is to stand alone, the conclusion it supports will be a more modest one.

EDIT YOUR OWN WRITING

The best writers—whether they are novelists, essayists, poets, analysts, academics, technical writers, or people who draft business memos—have to rewrite their first drafts in order to craft their best work. You will not articulate your best ideas with precision if your first draft is your last draft. It doesn't matter how smart you are. First ideas may be inspired, but they are hardly refined. The novelist John Gardner has reminded writers that "getting down one's exact meaning helps one discover what one means."* Your work must be edited if it is to represent you well, and you are your most important editor.

To thoroughly proofread and edit your work, you must check for (1) clear transitions between points, (2) grammatically correct wording that flows well as you read, and (3) correct spelling and keying (on your typewriter or computer keyboard). After a short discussion of these three topics, some of the basic markings used by professional proofreaders and editors will be introduced.

First, make sure the parts of your essay (or other writing project) are clearly distinguishable in the written draft. The map and outline are graphic methods for showing the relation of these parts (e.g., the thesis and the premises) to each other. Remember that the reader will not have these graphic aids. You will have to use transitional expressions to illuminate the structure of your argument. Premise indicators and conclusion indicators are useful for this purpose. Also be sensitive to the subtleties of other transitional expressions, such as "on the other hand," "nevertheless," "moreover," and "however." These can be used even for minor shifts of direction within the presentation of a single idea.

A second thing to check for is language usage: grammar, sentence construction, and clarity. Although much can be said on these topics, only a few reminders will be given here. Be sure your subject and the pronouns that refer to it agree, in the sense that they must both be singular or plural. If you write, "Any thoughtful student has their own way of viewing college," you have matched a singular subject (*student*) with a plural pronoun (*their*). Avoid the remedy of using the masculine pronoun (*his*, in this case). Consider rewording the sentence. Here, you could correct the problem simply by using a plural subject and keeping the plural possessive pronoun: "All

*John Gardner, On Becoming a Novelist (*New York: Harper & Row, 1983), p. 19.

thoughtful students have their own way of viewing college." For thesis defense or "argumentative" writing you should use complete sentences. This sentence is not complete: "Which was the best thing he could have done in the circumstances." This sentence is complete: "The president vetoed the bill, which was the best thing he could have done in the circumstances." Don't let sentence fragments stand, except when it is done in a deliberative and effective way.

Third, do not let misspellings and typos detract from whatever persuasive force you may have developed through careful reworkings of your argument. Even if you proofread your writing specifically for spelling errors, you may fail to notice some of them simply because you know the phrases and can hardly help reading for meaning as well as hunting for spelling errors. Some people recommend reading your writing backwards. You start with the last word on the last page and look at all the words in the order that is opposite of how they were meant to be read. Now you won't skim over errors while you are caught up in the meaning of sentences. You will more easily notice a misspelled word. However, neither this technique nor a computer spellchecker will alert you to the use of the wrong homonym. For example, *their* is sometimes incorrectly used in place of *there* or *they're*. *Affect* is used in place of *effect*, and *except* is used in place of *accept*. Even if you spell very well, your proofreading should be thorough, since almost everyone makes occasional keying errors — the infamous typos.

When you edit your own writing, you may choose to use standard proofreaders' marks instead of a notation system that you have devised yourself. The following table shows how to use some of the basic marks.

Proofreaders' Marks		
Mark in Margin	**Explanation**	**Mark in Text**
ℰ	Delete and close up	he assﬆumed that
tr	Transpose	raeson
#	Insert a space	followsfrom
⌣	Close up	hones ty
₱	New paragraph	to try.₱Unless he
no ₱	No paragraph	to try.↰ Unless he can
caps	Use capital	Geneva college
lc	Use lowercase	to the North

To strike out words or sentences, draw a horizontal line straight through them. If you change your mind, draw a horizontal series of dots underneath the words to be put back into the text (sometimes you want to replace only some of the words you struck out) and write *stet* in the margin. To add a comma or a period, just mark it in where it belongs and circle it so you don't miss it. (Proofreaders often put a carat in the text where the punctuation mark goes and show in the margin which mark is to be inserted.)

PRACTICE ACTIVITIES

Set 10.1

1. Choose a controversial topic about which you don't believe yourself to be unfairly biased. Write a single page discussion of the issue keeping in mind the advice in Chapter 10's *Recognize bias* section. As you argue a thesis, try to use fair and precise language, avoid extremism, and consider objections in a spirit of open-mindedness. Ask someone else to read your essay and assess your success.

2. Write a single page discussion of a controversial topic as in the previous activity, but choose a topic on which you have strong opinions. Again, ask someone else to read your essay to assess your success at using fair and precise language, avoiding extremism, and considering objections in a spirit of open-mindedness.

Set 10.2

1. As described in Chapter 10's section *Map your own reasoning*, map an argument and then outline and write an argumentative (but fair) essay.

2. Choose two arguments from Practice Activities Set 9.2 in Chapter 9. Write a critique of these arguments following the steps described in Chapter 10's section *Map others' reasoning before you critique*.

3. Choose one argument from Practice Activities Set 9.3 in Chapter 9. Write a critique of this argument following the steps described in Chapter 10's section *Map others' reasoning before you critique*.

For Further Reading

Gardner, John. *On Becoming a Novelist.* New York: Harper & Row, 1983.

A well-written book that provides insight into good writing, although the focus is on writing fiction.

Meiland, Jack W. *College Thinking: How to Get the Best out of College.* New York: Mentor, 1981.

An introduction to colleges, with an excellent and detailed section on writing an argumentative paper.

Turabian, Kate L. *A Manual for Writers of Term Papers.* Fifth edition. Chicago: University of Chicago, 1987.

A classic manual on mechanics and style of presentation in academic writing, written for students.

Salomone, William, and Stephen McDonald. *Inside Writing: A Writer's Workbook.* Belmont, CA: Wadsworth, 1991.

A practical guide to writing with many suggestions on how to edit your writing.

■

C H A P T E R

ELEVEN

Working with Hypotheses and Statistics

Science has come to be a part of our everyday lives. We take for granted, with the push of a button or the turn of a key, a dozen or more convenient mechanisms each day. We also read and hear continually about technological innovation in genetic engineering, health care, space travel, automotive production, disease treatment—the list is long. While so many of the products of the scientific age are right in our homes and offices, the principles of scientific reasoning that result in the constant technological change may seem quite distant and alien.

Actually, some kinds of reasoning that are characteristic of the sciences do become regularly involved in our everyday thinking. Two of these are hypothesis formation and evaluation, and reasoning with statistics. The formation and evaluation of hypotheses is a familiar process for us all but the scientist's attention to the systematic analysis of hypotheses provides a skill that is worth learning. Reasoning with statistics, as physical and social scientists do through their own professional investigations, has become important for all of us. News reports, magazines, and books present us with statistical claims and with conclusions drawn from those claims. Recognizing good and bad patterns of statistical reasoning is preferable to unreflective acceptance, skeptical disbelief, or the shoulder shrug of those who always suspend their judgment.

HYPOTHESIZE INTELLIGENTLY

For the scientist, a **hypothesis** is an explanatory claim that is assumed to be true for the purpose of testing it to determine if it is, in fact, correct. The hypothesis is proposed as an explanation to account for an observed fact or set of facts, or as a prediction based on inference from prior observation. Observations and experiments are then arranged in an effort to confirm or disprove the hypothesis. We also say informally, however, that any person who offers one of two or more possible explanations to account for an observed fact or set of facts is offering a hypothesis. Sometimes, little or no effort goes into the testing of that hypothesis. The general ways to choose and evaluate an everyday hypothesis are similar to the scientist's ways, though in everyday life we often pursue our actual investigations differently.

Hypothesis guides inquiry in the sciences and in our own backyards and living rooms. We come up with explanations and expectations that can be evaluated by simply observing our world or by constructing experiments to test our hypotheses.

Alexander Graham Bell hypothesized in 1865 that speech could be transmitted by electric waves. He pursued the hypothesis through experimentation in 1875 and transmitted the first telephone message in 1876. (Usually, we need to determine the reliability of our hypotheses more quickly than that.) This is an example of scientific hypothesis that is predictive and is based on theory and on other knowledge. Sometimes we also encounter pseudoscientific claims. Pseudoscience, or "seeming-science," rests on theories, assumptions, and methods that are falsely considered to be rigorously scientific. Astrology is an example. A person who claims that the reason you were fired from your job today is that your horoscope read, "Beware of career obstacles" and that the stars were against you is offering a hypothesis. We encounter hypotheses not only in scientific and pseudoscientific contexts, but in the very ordinary speculations and discussions that we experience daily. Essentially, Dad's speculation that the recent poor health of the house plants is due to the dry heat of the furnace is a hypothesis.

None of these hypotheses—the scientific one, the pseudoscientific one, and the everyday one—is exempt from rigorous evaluation, though the testing process in each case is rather different. After some discussion about the formation of hypotheses, we will explore four considerations for hypothesis evaluation.

Forming Hypotheses

A scientist may spend much time and study formulating a hypothesis that will guide a string of investigations and experiments over a period of several years. On the other hand, a hypothesis may occur to the scientist almost instantaneously. Still, the investigation of the hypothesis is likely to take some time.

For the rest of us, also, one hypothesis may be pieced together over years and another may be chanced upon with sudden insight. For example, you might take years to come to a well-considered conclusion about why children learn some tasks so much more readily from other children than from adults, but you might see "in a flash," without a prior hint, a likely explanation for the poor air circulation in your house.

Of course, getting an insight "in a flash" is not an instance of magic or miracle. Intuition is based on an accumulation of information that is suddenly recognized as part of a pattern. Virtually all hypotheses are based on something; they are not absolutely blind guesses. Scientific hypotheses and most of the best general hypotheses are based on observation of the world, and they are confirmable or falsifiable through additional observations. Sometimes hypotheses are based on theory: a theory that is accepted implies or suggests the hypothesis. Of course, the theory is probably based on observations. Guglielmo Marconi, who shared the 1909 Nobel Prize in physics for his wireless telegraph, did not simply chance upon the telegraph or hypothesize on no foundation. Earlier work on electromagnetic waves had prompted his hypothesis that signals could be transmitted without wires. Sometimes hypotheses are created on the basis of authority alone. An orthodox religious belief, for example, can prompt a hypothesis that purports to show a relation between the data and the authority. Ultimately, then, hypotheses are not without basis, though they are sometimes without a *good* basis.

Reasonable hypotheses are, first of all, compatible with all of the known data; they "fit the facts" without ignoring some observable facts or overemphasizing others. The International Flat Earth Research Society publishes the *Flat Earth News* and insists that we live on a flat plane rather than a globe. This society maintains its hypothesis by downplaying innumerable scientific observations and contriving seemingly incredible arguments for its position.

The observations on which a hypothesis is built may be made incidentally in the course of daily events, or they may be gathered purposefully. The most rigorous observation gathering in science takes place through controlled experimentation.

Reasonable hypotheses that are consistent with the data to be explained should be examined, but there is no need to consider only one hypothesis at a time. It is good to form several hypotheses, as long as they are all reasonable and not too unlikely. With those several hypotheses in mind, you can continue to observe, remain tentative in your judgment, and evaluate the hypotheses until it is time to act on the most promising one. The open mind is the one most likely to get at the truth.

Evaluating Hypotheses

It is easier to discredit a hypothesis than to confirm one. If enough counter-evidence becomes available, the hypothesis must be rejected. However, many hypotheses are well established but still subject to being disproven through further evidence. They are at best the conclusions of inductively strong arguments that cite the supporting evidence as premises.

Good sense and honest reasoning require that we be especially wary of hypotheses we would want to be true and especially charitable toward hypotheses we are disposed against. Points of logical vulnerability take their toll, even from relatively levelheaded people. There are four considerations to keep in mind when evaluating a hypothesis, whether it concerns a technical scientific matter, a social issue, or a household topic.

Amount of Confirming Evidence Certainly a hypothesis becomes more reliable with additional evidence. The ancient Greek poet Homer told grand tales of Greece and Troy that historically have come down to us in the volumes *Odyssey* and *Iliad*. Some people have hypothesized that the cultural power of these epics stems from their being based on real events and places. At first this was mere supposition, a hypothesis supported by some argumentation but no physical evidence. Then Heinrich Schliemann, who had been fascinated with Homer's tales as a boy, dedicated his life to proving that the stories were based on actual fact. In 1873 he unearthed walls, a city gate, and various artifacts that seemed to be from Troy itself. This evidence strengthened his hypothesis. After this success, he went to Greece in 1876 and discovered the Royal Grave Circle and other sites and objects from ancient times. His excavations were guided largely by his knowledge of Homer. Now his hypothesis was further strengthened. As the amount of confirming evidence increased, the credibility of his hypothesis increased. As the credibility of his hypothesis increased, the opposing hypothesis that the stories were wholly mythical was put into question. Notice that the burden of proof was on Schliemann: While the inductive strength of his conclusions increased with each discovery, the opposing hypothesis was supported primarily by a *lack* of physical evidence. Finally, it should be noted that some of Schliemann's findings were criticized as being inaccurately dated. Whether this lessens the strength of his hypothesis depends on an evaluation of those criticisms.

Consider a different kind of example. You planted a vegetable garden but harvested no vegetables. You cared for it well but nothing grew besides a few sickly sprouts that died quickly. You hypothesize that the soil in your yard is unsuitable for a vegetable garden and conclude that no garden will thrive here. Your hypothesis is weak, since not much evidence supports it. "You mean you just tried a garden once, and you're giving up?" someone challenges you. Certainly you would have a stronger hypothesis if you had planted and cared for a vegetable garden for the past several years and hadn't produced any eatable vegetables. Again, as the amount of confirming evidence increases, the credibility of the hypothesis increases. However, even with twenty years of crop failure as evidence (persistent, aren't you?), your hypothesis will gain no more than a moderate degree of strength. This leads to the next topic.

Variety of Confirming Evidence   Was the continually failing vegetable garden always planted in the same location? Might you have had better results at the other end of the yard? Are you a poor gardener, with even your best efforts seemingly doomed to failure in any garden? You failed for twenty years. The amount of evidence is relevant but a variety of evidence would strengthen the hypothesis. If you had planted the garden in different locations in the yard, and other people — perhaps other family members or the previous owner — had also failed in their attempts to grow vegetables in your yard, then the hypothesis would be much stronger. A soil analysis would add yet better evidence for your conclusion. Although you would have no practical need for all this evidence, you should maintain your hypothesis only rather tentatively without some variety of evidence. (Such variety is not possible for some hypotheses.) The desirability of having a variety of confirming evidence introduces the next topic.

Testability   "If this hypothesis is true, what else can I expect to find?" This question sets up valuable tests for a hypothesis. If a necessary consequence of the hypothesis turns out to be false, the hypothesis itself is false.*

After the preceding question is considered and relevant kinds of evidence are acknowledged, the evidence must be found. This sometimes sparks the idea for an experiment. In the previous example about gardening, you might actually invite your neighbor to garden in your yard for a season, just to see how well he does. You hypothesized that no garden would thrive there because of the soil. What else, besides your own failures, would be true if the problem were the soil? A change in gardeners would not result in a decent garden. If the neighbor produces a good garden, your hypothesis about the soil is wrong.

A good hypothesis, then, has predictive strength. We should be able to deduce specific consequences to be expected under certain conditions. If these consequences are absent, three possibilities must be considered: these are not really necessary consequences, the experiment or observation was flawed, or the hypothesis should be rejected. In the simple gardening example, it's clear that the hypothesis should be rejected.

If your hypothesis were "schizophrenia is generated by genetic rather than environmental factors," the observation and experimentation would, of course, be much more complicated. (The false dilemma beckons here.) The social scientist's training would be invaluable in constructing appropriate investigations for this kind of topic.

Some hypotheses are not just more difficult to test, they are *impossible* to test. Among these, some are untestable because of practical limitations. Others, however, are untestable in principle. Such "irrefutable hypotheses" do not defy refutation because they are good hypotheses but because they

---

The reasoning in this sentence reflects the form of a modus tollens *argument: If the hypothesis is true, then the necessary consequence is true. The "necessary consequence" is false. Therefore, the hypothesis is false.*

are defended as if they were compatible with any possible state of affairs in the world. "All college professors who teach colleges in Marxism are communist spies." Such a brash hypothesis invites challenge: Many of these professors behave very patriotically and defend the American way of life as well as the United States Constitution. "Yes," comes the response, "but this is just to make them appear to be loyal." It may be that nothing at all would count as evidence against this hypothesis for the biased witch-hunter. What could count against such a hypothesis?

Some of these irrefutable hypotheses are really "self-sealers" in the sense that their very wording rules out counterevidence. A person loses her job and is consoled with the remark, "That's just the way it was meant to be. There's nothing you can do about such things." More generally, the claim might be, "Whatever occurs happens that way because it was meant to be that way." What does this mean? It's certainly a vague claim, but it seems to mean that nothing could have happened differently and that there is some mystical intention, if not purpose, in every event. What can count as evidence against this hypothesis? *Nothing* can count as evidence against this hypothesis. If the woman lost her job, "that's the way it was meant to be." If she kept her job after almost losing it, then *that's* "the way it was meant to be." The hypothesis is compatible with any possible situation that could ever occur in the world. Then what does it tell us about the world? It tells us nothing. It's true that no evidence can count against it, but it's also true that no evidence can count for it. The hypothesis is vacuous. The price for its being irrefutable is that it is also unsupportable.

Simplicity   **Rival hypotheses** are incompatible explanations that are offered for the same data. PMS, premenstrual syndrome, was thought to be due to an imbalance between estrogen and progesterone in the body. More recently, two new hypotheses have been advanced. One suggests that opiates occurring naturally in the body diminish before menstruation and that PMS is a kind of narcotic withdrawal. Another hypothesis offers thyroid disorder as the crucial link to PMS. More research is required before the medical community accepts a single hypothesis.

Often, none of the rival hypotheses are obviously false. In fact, each of the rival hypotheses may be quite consistent with the data that are being explained. How, then, can a person decide between such rival hypotheses? Primarily, the way is to wait and watch for more evidence or to create experimental situations that will produce more evidence. If the conflict still cannot be decided, and there is a need to choose one hypothesis over the other, the principle of simplicity may come into play.

The principle of simplicity suggests that we endorse the simpler of any rival hypotheses. This principle was at work when Nicolaus Copernicus' hypothesis that the earth and planets revolve around the sun superseded the Ptolemaic hypothesis, according to which the moon, sun, and planets revolve around the earth. From the perspective of the sixteenth century, each hypothesis accounted for the data that described the observable movements of the heavenly bodies. The Ptolemaic hypothesis, however, had become complicated through modifications that were designed to preserve its predictive strength in the wake of more and more precise observations. The circular orbital paths this system described eventually failed to predict the correct location of a body, so epicycles — small circular detours — were added at a single point on those orbital paths. Then, when even with this modification the system was inaccurate, little epicycles were added to those original epicycles. The hypothesis became unreasonably complicated. Copernicus' hypothesis was more efficient. It was simpler in its basic conception and displaced the other hypothesis.

Earlier, this "irrefutable hypothesis" was discussed: "All college professors who teach courses on Marxism are communist spies." Counterevidence would include the observations that many of these professors are not involved in anything worth spying for, that some offer harsh criticism of present communist societies, that some have died for their country, and that some are fervent Christians or politically conservative. As qualifiers are added in defense of the original hypothesis, as farfetched explanations of each act are given, the hypothesis becomes more complicated *and less believable.* The principle of simplicity and common sense thrust us toward a simpler hypothesis: These professors teach these courses out of an interest or expertise in Marxism, without necessarily being Marxist or communists themselves.

KNOW HOW TO QUESTION STATISTICS

"Statistics don't lie." "Statistics speak for themselves." "The fellow had statistics to back up his point and I didn't have any. What could I say?" "You can't dispute statistics." "The numbers were right there in black and white."

Underlying these common expressions ae the assumptions that all statistical claims are based on properly executed studies and that statistics cannot be misused and never mislead. Each of these assumptions is false.

Numbers present a mystifying world to many people. An engineer's complex formulas on paper are intimately and impressively related to the final product of a massive bridge that can bear hundreds of tons or to a successful space flight. Life in our modern scientific world easily generates awe and respect for the "power" of numbers.

Most of us do not deal with higher mathematics. We are not asked to work with them or to draw conclusions on the basis of some provided figures. However, we are invited to draw conclusions based on statistics, and sometimes the mystique of the numbers, their sources and implications, will overwhelm a person.

Here is an example of a statistical claim: "In 1978, 80 percent of Americans indicated that they would vote for a woman for president if she were qualified and nominated by the voter's preferred party." To assess this claim completely, we would want to know who did the research (it was the Gallup Poll in this case) and how it was done. We do not always have the leisure and resources or the interest to follow through with this line of investigation, but we should be aware of some relevant questions. Further, a complete assessment of the claim requires consideration of conclusions that such a claim would establish. The two general questions to ask, then, are "Is the claim justified?" and "What does it prove?"

Although statistics can be applied to other areas, this book will focus on the social and behavioral sciences, which study human behaviors and beliefs. Much of the statistical information the average person receives through the media is of this sort.

This chapter offers suggestions about the kinds of questions a person should ask when evaluating statistical evidence and conclusions. It is meant to stimulate the creative process of evaluating such material so the reader will not only remember the questions considered here but also continually come up with pertinent questions of his or her own.

We will consider eight questions under three headings. This is the structure of the chapter:

Compiling Statistics

Is the researcher qualified?

Is the sample reliable?

Presenting Statistics

What if the data were organized differently?

Does the chart invite misunderstanding?

Drawing Conclusions from Statistics

Have other studies produced different results?

Is the fallacy of questionable cause committed?

Is the comparison reasonable?

Does correlation establish causation?

Compiling Statistics

Very often we don't know how statistical information was compiled. This warrants more concern in some cases than in others. At times, we do have some idea of how the information was compiled. In either circumstance, we should be aware of the kinds of questions that bear on the credibility of any study.

BLOOM COUNTY

© 1987. Reprinted with permission. Washington Post Writers Group.

Is the Researcher Qualified? To be qualified to direct a statistical study, the researcher must be competent with the method of research being used. This enables him or her to identify the variables and to anticipate oversights. The person's "track record" of previous research can serve as a *general* guide to reliability. In other words, a researcher's previous work is a useful practical indicator of the quality of current work. Still, it is not a foolproof indicator, and information on the quality of previous work is not always easily obtained.

Even competent researchers can have a personal interest in producing one kind of result instead of another. They may resist, consciously or unconsciously, a result that would oppose findings already published under their name. This can affect the overall design of the study, the selection and presentation of data, and the drawing of conclusions. Political, moral, and religious commitments may also contribute to flawed investigation.

Assuring phrases such as "in research done by an independent research laboratory" or "in studies at a leading university" may be offered to imply objectivity, but they provide no guarantee. In the first case, some "independent" laboratories are small and may not be professionally staffed to do the specific work for which they contract. Some labs must rely on the specific character of their results to ensure continued business. In the second case, although the reader may conclude from the phrase "at a leading university" that the studies were performed by university personnel or other qualified people, this is not literally claimed and is sometimes not true. Occasionally, with such a general reference ("a leading university"), no study at all has been conducted. One producer of a miracle weight-loss powder deleted such a phrase from newspaper advertisements when challenged to name the medical school at which studies confirming the claims had supposedly been done.

Is the Sample Reliable? In a survey of people, those whom we actually observe or question comprise the *sample*. In studies that are not surveys of people, the sample may be comprised of objects, processes, or events. The results are then generalized to make a prediction about a larger group, a *population*. Generally speaking, very small samples produce less reliable generalizations to the complete population than do larger samples. As information users who get most of our statistics from the mass media, we often don't know the sample size for a particular study. The sample size can be important because very small samples allow a greater margin for error. To avoid a hasty charge that the sample is too small, however, we should know that a sample of even a few thousand Americans can form a reliable basis for the prediction of the outcome of a U.S. presidential election and can be expected to be within two percentage points of the actual vote.*

Since a minimally acceptable sample size is not easily determined by people who are not statisticians, let's watch for *obvious* deficiencies in sample size and become sensitive to the everyday form of the "small sample" error. People sometimes make broad generalizations on the basis of very limited observations. A parent may remark, for example, that he had never believed that infant boys and girls were very different, but that he now "knows better." In support of his conclusion, he may offer nothing but his own experience with his two children—a boy and a girl. Without the introduction of specific numbers, the parent's claim is only indirectly statistical. Still, he is projecting his observations to the population of all children. His sample is clearly too small. With only two observations—one of each sex—he should realize that he can justifiably project to neither a universal nor a general conclusion. Similarly, a sampling of fifteen New Yorkers, however carefully chosen, is not likely to provide a reliable basis for a statistical claim concerning New Yorkers generally.

The *composition* of the sample is important. If all, or an untypical proportion, of the people in the survey sample are from groups that are especially interested in the topic being investigated, or if they have personal characteristics that might affect their responses, then the sample is not representative. Suppose that, after conducting a survey at the front door of the local Baptist church, you were to conclude that most Americans believe in God.

*Ian Robertson, Sociology (New York: Worth, 1981), p. 37.

Your sample would be unrepresentative because we would, of course, expect that a higher percentage of those who attend church, in contrast to those who don't, are believers. Although 98 percent of the people who responded — the *respondents* — professed a belief in God, you would have no reliable basis for predicting that 98 percent of Americans would give similar reports.

Sampling through telephone inquiries — a frequently used method — can produce the same kind of problem because it excludes those who do not own a phone. Since we can expect that a significant proportion of those who do not own phones have severely limited incomes, the sample will be unrepresentative if the question calls for answers that may reflect financial status (for example, "Do you believe that welfare payments should be increased?"). If the sampling is unrepresentative, then the results will be unreliable. Telephone sampling can also produce an unrepresentative sample by oversampling or undersampling people of certain occupations, and thus certain economic ranges or political perspectives. In the hours during which the sampling is conducted, some categories of people may be more or less likely than others to be at a home phone.

Small research firms often conduct marketing research for local clients. In an attempt to obtain a wide-ranging sample, the firm may ask questions of people who are entering or leaving a grocery market. When you are evaluating this sort of research, you should ask the following questions, among others. In what part of town is the market? Is the majority of shoppers female or male? Do many elderly people generally shop less frequently than younger people? As you can see, an unintentionally unrepresentative sample can be produced. On some topics, categories of people can be significant, distorting the results of the study.

Some academic psychologists have sought paid volunteers for studies by advertising on the college or university campus. Generally the respondents are students. This can easily introduce imbalance on the basis of age, and the monetary reward introduces another imbalance. Again, depending on the topic of research, the results may be distorted when generalized to the public. Masters and Johnson are famous for their research on the physiology of sexual response. Following initial study of female and male prostitutes, Masters recruited paid volunteers from a university and a medical school. This was certainly not a representative sample. The researchers' assumption, correct or not, was that the kind of sexual functioning they were studying — not merely through questions but through laboratory observation — did not vary significantly between individuals.

Certainly questionnaires that are printed in a magazine will, when returned, reflect an unrepresentative sampling if the results are generalized to the national population. A questionnaire printed in *Cosmopolitan* or *Playboy*, for example, would not reveal the sexual attitudes of the American woman or man unless it were by coincidence. Consider the omitted attitudes of people who woud not be willing to buy or browse through such a magazine in the first place.

Presenting Statistics

The implications of statistical information can vary with the formulation or the format of its presentation. Here, an inquiring mind is essential if a person is to be aware of alternate manners of presentation that seem to change the significance of the data.

The first of the following questions is a general one concerning alternate presentations. The second question focuses specifically on graphic displays of statistical information.

What If the Data Were Organized Differently? Kimble Auto Sales advertises its 100 percent increase in sales over last year, boasting the greatest increase of any dealership in Lancaster County. The consumer is invited to conclude that something phenomenal is occurring at Kimble: Such an explosive burst of business must reflect both good management and exceptional deals on cars. Actually, Kimble Auto Sales has always been—and still is—a minor enterprise among dealerships in Lancaster County. While the major dealerships sell thousands of cars each year, Kimble is a vacant-lot operation that "moves" approximately one hundred cars per year. Last year was a particularly weak year in which only sixty-one cars were sold. This year, the sales are back up to, and slightly over, the average: 120 cars were sold.

If the increase had been expressed by stating the *number of cars* sold during the prior and present years, or if it were known that the previous year had been such a bad sales year, the advertisement would not have been impressive. Although the claim of 100 percent increase in sales is not false, it will nevertheless be misleading to many people.

Data for statistics can usually be organized in different ways, with different apparent implications. In the preceding example, the data presumably have been intentionally manipulated to mislead. Sometimes, even with the intention to organize the information fairly, the problem is difficult to avoid.

The state-normed test scores for the third graders in the South Bay Unified School District have arrived at the district office and have been made available to the press. Should the local headlines proclaim that the students have scored "8 percent higher than last year's South Bay third graders"? This is true and seems to be good news for the school district. In contrast, however, the headline might lament that the scores still fall below those of the neighboring districts. This is also true. In fact, the scores also fall below the statewide average. Perhaps this is what the newspaper's readers need to know. On the other hand, considering all the schools in the state that are of a comparable economic status, the district's third graders scored well. They were in the top 35 percent—almost the top third. Whatever headline is chosen for the news article, notice that all of this information except perhaps the "neighboring district" comparison should be presented to convey a full understanding and avoid false impressions. Perhaps additional perspectives should be included.

A similar array of claims may be revealed by applying such a variety of perspectives to business or government. In the case of business, the health of a company might be expressed in terms of total receipts, number of transactions or units processed, profit before or after taxes, or return on investment. For any of these contexts, a comparison might be made with previous years, other companies, or projections. Such a comparison might be in terms of raw numbers or percentages. Statistical claims that are considered in isolation from the body of data that generates them, or from other statistical perspectives, may mislead — not because they are false, but because they represent only part of the situation being described.

Finally, consider the ambiguous term *average* which is used quite often in statistical claims. We are informed about the average annual income for a family in Boston, the average pay for a symphony musician, the average number of weeks a U.S. senator spends actively campaigning during a reelection year, the average age of an American astronaut, and the average number of marriages for a Hollywood star. The word *average* may convey any of three concepts:

1. *Median*: the item that is midway between the extremes, with an equal number of items occurring above and below.

2. *Mean*: the arithmetical midpoint, determined by computation.

3. *Mode*: the item that occurs most often.

Suppose that in our office the manager is paid $47,000 anually. His assistant is paid $42,000, and the bookkeeper makes $35,000. There are six others in the office. One is paid $29,000, another is paid $20,000, and four others are paid $18,500 each. The median is $20,000, since four people in the office make more money than this and four make less. The mean is determined by adding all the salaries (this comes to a $247,000 payroll), then dividing by the number of people in the office (nine). This yields a figure of $27,444. Notably, no one on the office staff makes this amount, and only one person has a salary that is even near this figure. The mode is $18,500, since this is the salary amount that occurs most frequently on the payroll.

The "average" salary in the office, then, can be truthfully claimed to be $20,000, $27,444, or $18,500. This ambiguity allows misunderstandings and even intentional slanting of the data.

Does the Chart Invite Misunderstanding? When statistical findings are compared in a graphic presentation, the format can affect the apparent signficance of the information being presented. Examine these two graphs showing the size of the graduation class of Truman High School.

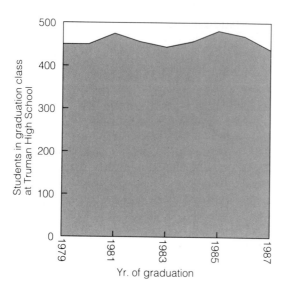

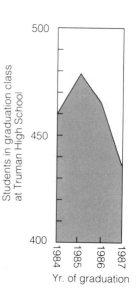

When we view the first graph, the size of the graduation class at Truman appears to be somewhat stable, despite fluctuations. The net loss of students from 1979 to 1987 has been only thirteen. When we view the second graph, however, we get the sense of a sharp and steady decrease. Parents in this school district, upon seeing the second graph, might wonder if a momentous shift has occurred. Actually, there is no contradiction between the graphs. Three related factors account for the difference in the apparent significance of the information on the graphs.

1. Line graphs have a horizontal axis and a vertical axis, each of which has scaled intervals indicating units of measure. The line that traces the data is altered when the size of the intervals on either side is changed. Although the data presented are the same in each of two graphs with different interval sizes, a person's impressions about the significance of this information might be different. Notice the greater distance between the markings for 400 and 500 students on the vertical axis.

2. The vertical axis on the second graph does not begin at zero. The descent of the data line is thus exaggerated.

3. The extent of data represented, meaning the years on the horizontal axis, is so much less on the second graph that no sense of the continuity of fluctuations is communicated. Even with the altered scale on the vertical axis that showed larger intervals and only a partial range, time's perspec-

tive would soften the sense that there is a disturbing drop in the number of graduates.

Although each of these three factors contributes to the second graph's capacity to mislead, not all of them are equally objectionable. A graph-wise person will not be bothered or misled by the "suppression of the zero," the elimination of the blank portion of the graph. This saves page space and allows an increased scale for the graph. The size of the intervals is not itself an issue, except that extreme changes in *both* axis intervals (one increasing while the other decreases) can radically alter the data-line pattern, inviting different interpretations of the significance of the data. In the preceding example, the factor that effects the contrast most is the range of years for which information is displayed. In the second graph, we simply get no sense of the regular ups and downs of the class size. This makes the already exaggerated descent seem noteworthy.

Bar graphs are generally simpler than line graphs in that there is usually only one scaled axis — either the vertical or the horizontal axis. Still, any of the three factors affecting the line-graph format can affect the bar-graph format as well.

This is a simple bar graph.

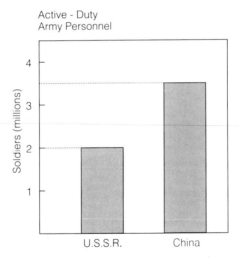

It clearly indicates that the U.S.S.R. had two million people on active duty in the army when China had three and a half million. The bars give a visual impression of these proportions.

In an abuse of the bar graph, images are used instead of bars, with these images varying not only in length but in width as well. The preceding graph might have been designed like this.

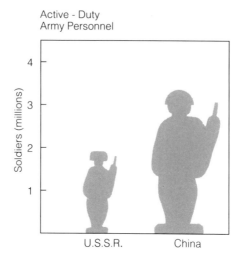

Active - Duty
Army Personnel

In the traditional bar graph, the two bars indicated the correct *proportion* to show the size relation between the two nations' armies. The image version of that graph displays an incorrect proportion. The total area representing the Chinese forces is now more than twice as large as the area representing the forces of the U.S.S.R. If you consider only the measurement from the bottom to the top of each image, the information is correct; if, however, the entire size of the image influences your assessment, the information is distorted.

Drawing Conclusions from Statistics

Even statistical claims that are well founded can provide a basis for faulty reasoning. When you draw conclusions on the basis of statistics, some of the following questions may be relevant.

Have Other Studies Produced Different Results? When the familiar phrase "in a recent study . . ." prefaces a confident statement of findings, one sometimes fruitful line of inquiry focuses on alternative studies. It would be worthwhile to know whether other investigation has either preceded or followed this particular study. If there have been no other reputable studies, then we should remember that the findings will be more credible when *replicated* (confirmed by others through similar studies). If, on the other hand, there have been other good studies, then it is important to know whether the results of those studies confirm or conflict with the results of the one currently being discussed. If there is a conflict, we should remain neutral on the issue or only tentatively accept the results of the study under current consideration. It is possible that "in a recent [perhaps poorly done] study," the findings run counter to much (or even all!) other research.

Is the Fallacy of Questionable Cause Committed? Statistics *do not* "speak for themselves." Failing to see different possible explanations for the available data will frequently yield false conclusions.

"Twenty-three percent more women are seeking out-of-home employment now than in 1960. Women must be less content with the role of housewife than they used to be." The second sentence is offered as an explanation of the first. It is also a conclusion drawn from the statistical claim that is stated first. One might accept the pair of statements without question, but in so doing one would be committing a version of the fallacy known as questionable cause. If one assumes the accuracy of the first sentence by verifying or failing to question the source of the statistic, the second sentence reveals the apparently obvious *cause* of the increase in women who are seeking out-of-home employment.

Aren't there, however, other possible explanations for the increase? Keep in mind the possibility that there may be several contributing causes. Perhaps, with economic change, more two-parent families feel the need for both parents to work "just to make ends meet." Perhaps social disapproval of leaving young children in day-care situations has lessened. Certainly we have more single-parent families, most of which are headed by women. Furthermore, the population has grown; we have more men *and* women. (Notice that the reference was not to 23 percent of all women but to a 23 percent increase in the number of women.) This can be a contributing cause as well. Certainly there may be, as people say, "some truth," or even much truth, to the original claim that women are less content with the role of housewife than they used to be. Still, considering the other possibilities, this dissatisfaction may not be the sole cause for more women seeking out-of-home employment. For that matter, the preceding list of possibilities implies that *even if women were generally as discontent with that role in 1960*, the number of women who are seeking out-of-home employment could have increased.

The first explanation for why the data stand as they do is not always correct. The explanation that occurs to you may not reflect the only contributing cause. Furthermore, your points of logical vulnerability invite you to find an easy answer that confirms a prejudice. It is good to develop a habit of considering alternative explanations.

Is the Comparison Reasonable? Perhaps you've heard the charge that someone is "comparing apples and oranges." The suggestion here is that a comparison is inappropriate because things of different — and, for the particular context, incomparable — kinds are being compared. This error can occur in the comparison of statistics as well as in other comparisons.

The means for computing our national unemployment figures are changed occasionally. Clearly, if we begin to include, or exclude, as "unemployed people" those students who are out of school for the summer, adults who are employed in household tasks and not seeking out-of-home employment, or marginally self-employed people, the national figures from before and after the change cannot be legitimately compared without prior adjustment or without reverting to the original definition. The same is true of changes in the computation of the Consumer Price Index (CPI) and other variable indexes.

When standardized test scores decrease in a school district, parents scowl and administrators squirm, but variables other than students' talent and education are occasionally involved. The recent version of the test may be more difficult than the last or have a different emphasis, making comparisons misleading. People have decried the decline in College Board (SAT) scores over recent decades, but attention should also be given to the fact that a larger proportion of high-school classes, which is to say not just the very best students, have been taking the test in many states.

As much as we would like to avail ourselves of quick comparisons, there's no use in comparing apples and oranges.

The statistical findings in studies on unemployment, inflation, psychological topics, opinion polls, or whatever are subject to some inaccuracy. The *margin for error* is the greatest plausible difference between the official figure and the actual rate. We should know the margin for error when we are comparing figures.

If a study of unemployment can be accurate to only two percentage points (2 percent), a published claim that unemployment is at 8 percent reflects the possibility that unemployment is actually as low as 6 percent or as high as 10 percent. Thus, if we observe that the rate was 8 percent last year and 9 percent this year, the margin for error (2 percent in this case) is greater than the difference between the compared figures, and unemployment *might* actually have decreased. In fact, it could have been as high as 10 percent for the first year and as low as 7 percent for the second.

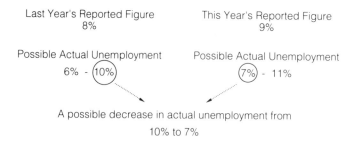

Last Year's Reported Figure
8%

This Year's Reported Figure
9%

Possible Actual Unemployment
6% - 10%

Possible Actual Unemployment
7% - 11%

A possible decrease in actual unemployment from
10% to 7%

Actually, the overall national unemployment figures are quite accurate. The margin for error is roughly two tenths of one percent (0.2 percent). For statistics that focus on a region (for example, Baltimore) or group (for example, blacks) or regional group (for example, blacks in Baltimore), the margin for error increases as the size of the sample and the estimate based on it decrease. In fact, for blacks in Baltimore, the margin for error is 16.3 to 23.4 percent.* For the relevant information for unemployment figures, contact your local Bureau of Labor Statistics office.

Clearly, we must be especially careful of our conclusions when the difference between compared figures is small and when the sampling and estimate sizes are small. In these cases the diligent thinker will want to know the margin for error. This applies not only to unemployment figures, of course, but to statistical comparisons generally.

Does Correlation Establish Causation? Two things are correlated (co-related) when changes in one reflect changes in the other. Correlations are sometimes observed in statistical data collection and stated in statistical terms.

A hypothetical example will illustrate how a correlation can be established. Suspecting a connection between cigarette smoking and stomach discomfort, the researcher sets up six groups of people. Group A includes people who do not smoke at all. Group B includes only people who smoke less than a pack of cigarettes each week. The other groups are as follows: Group C, one to two packs each week; Group D, up to a pack each day; Group E, one to two packs each day; Group F, more than two packs each day. The researcher finds that in Group A there is a very low *incidence* (number of occurrences) of stomach discomfort. She finds a higher incidence in Group B, and Groups C, D, E, and F display a continued pattern of increase. Should she conclude that there is a *causal connection* between smoking and stomach discomfort? Does one (smoking, in this case) cause the other (the stomach discomfort, in this case)? Perhaps she should be tentative about such a conclusion. Although this may be the most obvious way to explain the correlation, another possibility (besides uncanny coincidence) does exist. Perhaps a *third* factor, yet unnoted, is the cause of both of these effects. If, for example, smoking was a common outlet for nervous tension and stomach discomfort was a symptom produced by the metabolism of a chronically nervous sort of person, then the smoking and the stomach discomfort might not be causally connected.

An inattentive researcher may too readily judge that a causal connection does in fact exist in such a case. While it is true that correlation does not prove causation, however, the failure to identify a "third factor" does not permit the discounting of intriguing correlations. The possibility or probability of a causal connection between the correlated items is compatible with continued vigilance for a third factor.

*Geographic Profile of Employment and Unemployment, 1984, U.S. Department of Labor, Bureau of Labor Statistics, May 1985 (Bulletin 2234).

■

A Less-Than-Serious Example of Correlation Without Causation

Let's say that we are investigating the cause of Logician's Disease, which inclines its poor victims to mistake affirming the consequent for *modus ponens* and to mistake denying the antecedent for *modus tollens*. In other words, the victims see invalid conditional arguments as if they were valid. (There are stronger and milder cases of this disease, as you may know.) The frequency of occurrence and the severity of this disease are found to correlate inversely with years of schooling. (Additional years of schooling correlate with decreases in the frequency and severity of the disease.) We naturally conclude that Logician's Disease is caused by Education Deficiency. Later we discover that a third factor, "Apathetic Genes," is the direct cause of both Logician's Disease and Education Deficiency. The latter two were not causally related at all.

The expression *linked to* obscures the distinction between correlation and causation. We frequently read in the newspaper or hear on radio or television news programs that a certain food or other substance has been "linked to" a serious disease. Often, while the expression was justified by a discovered *correlation*, the person who is reading or hearing the report understands the expression to mean "caused by."

Many completely insignificant correlations can be constructed. Should you worry if you hear a report that "82 percent of all persons who committed violent crimes last year had eaten yogurt within a month prior to the crime"? You should *not*, of course, worry about such a report. Still, besides wondering about how the data had been collected, you should know how to demonstrate that this statistic is insignificant. The revealing question is this: "How often, on the average, do people eat yogurt?" If the frequency among violent criminals and the general public is the same, the statistic is insignificant. No significant statistical connection has been established between the consumption of yogurt and violent crimes.

By changing this silly example a bit, we can create a more credible argument. "Eighty-two percent of all preadolescent children who committed violent crimes last year had watched an average of six hours of television a day for the year preceding the crime." The inferred conclusion is, of course, that the television watching was the cause, or at least *a* cause, of the violence. What question now must be asked? "How much television, on the average, do preadolescent children watch?" If the percentage is similar, the implied argument has no strength at all. Here the general population of preadolescents functions as a *control group* to place into its proper perspective the specific claim about the children who had committed violent crimes. The control group in such a study is actually, to be precise, the sample of preadolescents that was used to generate the statistical claim about the larger population of *all* preadolescents.

■

PRACTICE ACTIVITIES

Set 11.1 *Create two or more hypotheses to explain each set of facts.*

less traffic *not as much work they do* 1. At the naval base at Jacksonville, Florida, the officers' restrooms are usually cleaner than the enlisted personnel's restrooms.

2. Males generally are better at math than females are.

3. Females generally score higher on the language skills section of college entrance exams than males.

4. The public hears and reads more about professional athletes' disturbing behavior and comments now, in contrast to thirty years ago.

5. If we compare people who have been child abusers with people who haven't, the former group has a larger proportion of people who were themselves abused as children.

6. Children with middle-class backgrounds get better grades in the public schools than do children with economically poorer backgrounds.

7. On November 7, 1986, the pilot and the two crew members on Japan Air Lines cargo flight 1628 spotted lights moving alongside them. As they descended from 35,000 feet to 31,000 feet, the lights moved with them. At one point, the pilot says, he viewed a huge flying craft unlike anything he had seen. When the plane landed, FAA officials found the men to be "professional, rational, well-trained people." Events of this sort have occurred before.

More popular 8. There are more psychology courses than philosophy courses in American universities.

9. Morning editions of newspapers are more successful than afternoon editions.

10. Success in school correlated more closely with the number of magazines the household subscribed to than with family income, the parents' education, or any other factor surveyed.

Set 11.2

1. Create a hypothesis. First, describe the facts to be explained. Then state your hypothesis. Finally, evaluate the hypothesis according to amount of confirming evidence, variety of confirming evidence, and testability. Is there any counterevidence against your hypothesis? Do this as many times as are necessary to become familiar with these criteria.

2. Create two good rival hypotheses to explain something in an area with which you are very familiar. Evaluate your rival hypotheses according to the criteria mentioned in the preceding question. Also, evaluate the relative simplicity of each competing hypothesis if both hypotheses are so well supported that a choice is difficult. Otherwise, state which hypothesis is stronger and justify your selection. Remember that two hypotheses might complement rather than rival each other. Each might identify one contributing cause.

Set 11.3 *In each of the following examples of reasoning with statistics, an error is made or invited. Some types of errors have been covered in the preceding section. Others call for some reflective "common sense." Identify and explain the error.*

1. Contrary to some claims, Americans are *not* losing their faith in God. In response to questionnaires sent to twenty thousand church members of different denominations, 70 percent reported that their religious beliefs — including faith in God — were as strong or stronger than ten years ago.

2. Despite all the women's rights issues in the news, the American people are really quite content with the current role of women in our society. In response to a recent questionnaire printed in the magazine *Field and Stream*, 73 percent of the people indicated that they were content with the current role of women in society, seeing no need for major changes at this time.

3. People who are in good shape physically can bear 43 percent more mental stress than those who get no regular exercise.

4. Twenty-two percent of American families have incomes below the poverty level. That's because they're not interested in working as hard as the rest of us.

5. Two hundred complete skeletons of dinosaurs are yet to be discovered and unearthed on this continent.

6. Forty-two percent of the population has psychic powers of which they are unaware.

[handwritten margin note: informal: questionable cause]

7. Less than 2 percent of all symphony orchestras are led by female conductors. Apparently music conducting is just something for which women don't have much talent.

[handwritten margin note: questionable cause]

8. Twenty percent more television sets were sold last year than in 1970. This is obviously a reflection of America's increasing taste for violence.

[handwritten margin note: may not be a majority]

9. People in this nation are fed up with the welfare program. This was revealed in the results of a survey directed at readers of the *Wall Street Journal*. A majority of them—52 percent, to be exact—thought that all such programs should be scrapped completely.

10. Two excerpts from "Face-Lift for a Famous Test," *Time*, September 29, 1986:

> As the [Minnesota Multiphasic Personality Inventory] has come to be seen as a beloved landmark of American psychology, it has also come under frequent attack as dated and culture bound. Since empirical work on the test was done among pre-war, white, rural Minnesotans in their mid-30s, it does not account for newer values and is often a particularly unreliable test for blacks, women and adolescents.

> The revision committee is now testing two experimental booklets, one for adults, one for adolescents. Some 15,000 Americans and Canadians, randomly selected from phone books and replies to magazine ads in eight states and the City of Toronto, have taken the new forms of the test. Unlike the original sample—now regarded as "both small and parochial," according to Committee Member James Butcher of the University of Minnesota—the new group is carefully balanced by region, ethnic group, age, education, and gender.

Set 11.4 *A critique of each of the following examples of reasoning with statistics will yield a crucial question to be asked. For each of these examples, what is the question that provides insight into the implications of the statistics?*

1. From the *San Diego Union*, February 20, 1989:

> Most teenagers do not read the surgeon general's health warning in cigarette advertisements, according to a study by the Medical College of Georgia in Augusta.
>
> Equipment that tracked teenagers' eyes while reading showed that almost half of them don't even look at the warning.

Scientists concluded that the surgeon general's warning is not readable in its current form.

2. It's definitely true. More people prefer our local Royal cola over Coke and Pepsi. In a recent test conducted at the county fair, more people chose Royal over either of the two big-name colas.

3. A picture of Lee Iacocca of Chrysler Corporation is on the first page of a seven-page advertisement in the October 6, 1986, issue of *Time*. At the top of that first page, the following is printed:

Last year you made Chrysler the fastest-growing* car and truck company in America.

The next seven pages are for anybody foolish enough to think we're resting on our laurels.

In tiny print at the lower-left corner of the page, we find this:

*Based on market share increase, 1984 vs. 1985 model year.

4. In "Reagan Aide: Pot Can Make You Gay," *Newsweek*, October 27, 1986, it is reported that White House drug adviser Carlton E. Turner says that when he visits drug-treatment centers for patients under 18, he finds that roughly 40 percent of them have also engaged in homosexual activity. "It seems to be something that follows along from their marijuana use," says Turner, who is convinced that the drugs come first, the homosexuality second.

5. From a letter to the editor of the *San Diego Union*, November 17, 1985:

Your editorial (Nov. 21) asks the question, "Should minority students or any students receive preferential treatment in order to play football, or be in the marching band?" You then answer the question by stating, "Of course not."

I can concur with the idea that the main purpose of school has been to encourage academic performance as a preparation for life, but I believe that some exceptions need to be made for those students who cannot meet the scholastic requirements that are a prerequisite for extracurricular activities.

Research shows that the young person engaged in extracurricular activities remains in school. The model prisoners are those engaged in the athletic and artistic programs in our correctional institutions.

6. In September 1986 *Success!* magazine published "Marriage, Inc.," an article on spouses who have gone into business to-

gether as "mom and pop entrepreneurs — literally." Here is an excerpt from that article:

> The couple's rising fortunes are due, in large part, to women's increased training and expertise. Women today make up almost 40 percent of office workers and more than 50 percent of those in the professions. As a result of women's broadened business experience, husband and wife teams now represent one of the country's largest reserves of entrepreneurial energy. The Small Business Administration reports that the number of joint proprietorships — one of the legal forms that couples starting a business often use — has grown by 20 percent per year since 1980. That's almost four times as fast as other business proprietorships.

7. Again, from "Marriage, Inc.":

> Today mom has a C.P.A., pop has an M.B.A., and they're turning their store into a franchise. In 1974 only 1 percent of U.S. families, just 600,000, had an income above $50,000. Currently 16 percent, or almost 10 million families, earn that much. These new entrepreneurs — power partners, if you will — are finding that when it comes to doing business, two heads are often better than one.

8. From "Are We Safe at Any Speed?" in *Newsweek On Health,* Winter 1986:

> The logic of the "double nickel" is as plain as can be: speed kills. The year the [55 mile-an-hour] limit was imposed, the highway death toll fell abruptly from 55,000 fatalities in 1973 to 46,000 in 1974. But what is mysterious is that since then, even though speeds actually driven have been rising, the national death rate has continued to fall. Last year there were only 2.48 deaths for every 100 million miles driven, down from 2.58 in 1984, and 4.24 in 1973. Especially on the interstates, which were engineered for speeds up to 75 mph, the death rate continued to fall as speeds rose.

9. From a letter to the editor of *The New York Times,* January 10, 1986:

> Fred Hechinger (column, Science Times, Dec. 31) says that despite many calls for reform, "There has been no serious departure from the way the American school has been organized for more than 100 years." Why such resistance to change?
>
> One answer may be that the testing system is the tail that wags the dog; we may need to trade in the old tests for new

ones. Teachers are constantly training children to pass tests that certify them for passing into next higher levels. These tests require manipulating word and number symbols or regurgitating knowledge such as the difference between a paramecium and a euglena. The tests demand that the old system remain intact.

What old system? The system that classifies knowledge into such subjects as English, history, biology, and math—the system that pins students to desks and forces them to swallow masses of material of little interest to them. Forty percent drop out of high school before graduating. Isn't there a strong message in that statistic?

10. From *Special Report on Tax Reform,* a letter Congressman Ron Packard sent to voters in his district:

> This summer, I asked you and your neighbors . . . to evaluate [the President's] proposed tax reforms. The response to our survey was strong—10,000 families participated districtwide. The consensus was equally strong—overall, *76% supported the . . . tax reforms as our best course.*

For Further Reading

Huck, Schuyler W., and Howard M. Sandler. *Rival Hypotheses.* New York: Harper & Row, 1979.
   A compilation of alternate interpretations of data-based conclusions.

Huff, Darrell. *How to Lie with Statistics.* New York: W. W. Norton, 1954.
   A light-hearted introduction to the assessment of statistical claims.

Katzer, Jeffrey, Kenneth H. Cook, and Wayne W. Crouch. *Evaluating Information.* Reading, MA: Addison-Wesley, 1982.
   A guide for users of social science research statistics.

McCain, Garvin, and Erwin M. Segal. *The Game of Science.* Pacific Grove, CA: Brooks/Cole, 1988.
   An enjoyable discussion of scientific inquiry.

Moore, David S. *Statistics: Concepts and Controversies.* San Francisco: W. H. Freeman, 1985.
   A well-written introduction to statistical analysis.

Quine, W. V., and J. S. Ullian. *The Web of Belief.* New York: Randon House, 1978.
   A philosophical discussion of rational belief and scientific thought.

Radner, Daisie, and Michael Radner. *Science and Unreason.* Belmont, CA: Wadsworth, 1982.

A readable, example-filled discussion of pseudoscience.

Vernoy, Mark, and Judith Vernoy. *Behavioral Statistics in Action.* Belmont, CA: Wadsworth, 1992.

A readable introduction to statistical analysis in the behavioral sciences.

C H A P T E R

TWELVE

Making Difficult Decisions

E very day we make decisions that affect our own lives and others.' Sometimes the decisions have a great impact; sometimes the impact is less dramatic. Sometimes the "small" decisions turn out to produce significant consequences. Following both our heads and our hearts, we often make excellent decisions. Still, there are times when the need to grapple with a difficult decision is more than we care to bear. There can be so many factors to consider and so little knowledge of how to weigh them that we shirk the task and make a decision without efficient reflection.

Decisions cannot really be avoided. When you fail to act, certain consequences follow in place of those that would have followed if you had acted. In a sense, then, you have *chosen* to allow events to occur without your intervention. A responsible person must accept reasonable risks and act to bring about the best results that the available alternatives offer.

USE GRAPHIC AIDS IN DECISION MAKING

Although even the least complicated decisions are sometimes difficult to make, complex decisions that involve many elements, all of which must be kept in mind, present a special challenge. It is difficult to keep track of all the relevant considerations, even after we have identified them.

After we have considered a decision from many angles and mulled over many pros and cons, we might not recall some of those thoughts at the moment of the final decision. Bad decisions have been made on the basis of those particular considerations that happened to have been on the person's mind in the moments or hours immediately preceding the decision, while some strong reason for deciding differently has been lost in the shuffle of ideas. It's simply too taxing to keep track of all those ideas. It seems to be beyond the capacity of most of us. The solution to this problem is to *write down* these thoughts as they occur and to order them in some way.

Identify the Alternatives

Beware of the false dilemma! We sometimes are cautioned to look at *both* sides of an issue. It's easy to overlook *third* and *fourth* sides. We encounter the same kind of problem in decision making. We can fail to identify some alternatives simply by presuming that no more than the two obvious alternatives exist. In short, we sometimes don't even consider the possibility of other answers. In asking, "Should I bring grandma home to live with me or should I have her moved into a nursing home?" a person might neglect other possibilities. (Perhaps another relative might be willing, or even glad, to have grandma as a long-term house guest. Perhaps some settings other than nursing homes would meet grandma's needs.) We should at least think through possible alternatives. If there are several, it is helpful to list them on paper.

Consider the Consequences

One common method that people use to enumerate the consequences of a decision calls for drawing a line down the middle of a sheet of paper, dividing the page into left and right columns. *Pro* is written at the top of one column; *Con* is written at the top of the other. (This method clearly invites the false dilemma.) Then the desirable and undesirable consequences for each column are listed.

Pro	Con

The main benefit of this method is that it enables the decider to keep many consequences in mind while making an assessment. The next chart presented here is a variation of that simple two-column listing of consequences. This chart invites the listing of multiple alternatives and their consequences. To use this chart, first list your alternatives — your possible courses of action. If you think that you might have overlooked any, describe your situation to another person and ask if there seem to be other possible ways to deal with the situation. Then list the significant consequences of each alternative, regardless of whether the consequence is desirable or undesirable and regardless of whether it is a certain or a possible consequence. Again, you may want to enlist another person to help you think this through.

Alternatives	Consequences	Probability	Desirability	Kind of Gain/Loss

Assess the Probability and Desirability

The probability of a consequence is certainly relevant to the consideration of a course of action. Probable results generally concern us more than unlikely results. Still, if an unlikely consequence is very desirable (or undesirable), it may justifiably sway the decision more than some probable or certain consequences. Clearly, *both* the probability and the desirability must be considered and each must be considered in light of the other.

Evaluate the probability of a consequence before concerning yourself greatly with its desirability. This helps to avoid an irrational concern with a very desirable or undesirable but farfetched consequence.

For the chart, use symbols to indicate the probability (as far as you can determine it) of each consequence. You should feel free to devise your own set of symbols, but here is a suggestion.

C	Certain
AC	Almost certain
Prob	Probable
Poss	Possible (a reasonable possibility, but less than probable)
NL	Not likely

If, after entering the symbols for a few consequences, you feel a need to distinguish between two that have been assigned the same symbol, you can use a plus or a minus. For example, Prob + is considered more likely to result than Prob. Further variations might be necessary.

Assign a numerical value to indicate the desirability of each consequence. Plan to assign a maximum of 5 for the most desirable and −5 for the least desirable. Remain flexible, however, and extend or change the numerical scale if that will clarify the options. When a single consequence has both good and bad sides, use the line below to add the opposing value.

Determine the Kind of Gain or Loss

Think about the standpoint from which each desirable consequence is desirable. Is there a personal benefit for you? If so, is this a financial gain, an improvement of reputation or character, or an opportunity for new experience, skill, or knowledge? Does it fulfill an obligation? If so, is it a legal or a moral obligation? Does fairness or sympathy call for this result? After deciding on this, write a word or phrase that will remind you of this when you scan the chart. For example, write *money* or *reputation*, or *career*, or *common decency* on the chart to indicate the kind of benefit that is to be gained.

Similarly, think about the standpoint from which each undesirable consequence is undesirable. Is there a personal harm or inconvenience? If so, is this a financial loss, jeopardy of career, or loss of reputation? Does it involve breaking a promise, or another sort of moral wrong? As before, write a word or phrase on the chart to remind you of this when you scan the chart. For example, write *physical comfort*, or *education*, or *others' feelings*.

Scan the Chart

In some decision-making systems, you are told to compute the right decision by using a formula, sometimes a numerical one. Although such a system has the advantage of avoiding mental and moral strain and putting the decider's mind to rest, it does so precisely because of its artificiality. No system can consistently produce the best decisions. Common sense and moral sensitivity are excellent tools in human judgment. If these can be aided by a means of tracking and remembering the consequences of each available alternative, there is seldom reason to yield important decisions to a contrived decision-making plan.

Just examine the alternatives. Think about the probability and desirability of the consequences of each possible choice. Strict adding, subtracting, or multiplying will not weigh the consequences better than you can generally weigh them informally. Think about the kind of gain or loss. Moral rights and wrongs do not automatically outweigh safety considerations, personal hurt, or even all cases of private gain. There is no simple ordering of such things. The issue cannot be decided without the integrated consideration of each of the columns on your chart.

None of us is absolved from making personal decisions and bearing the responsibility for these decisions. The chart is merely a list of items to keep in mind when weighing the alternatives.

SOLVE PROBLEMS WITH A SYSTEM

We typically make decisions in order to direct specific actions. We may decide whether to renew a magazine subscription, whether to join a certain political party, whether to accept that new job offer, or whether to report a crime. Larger, less well-defined circumstances call for the creative processes of problem solving. Here, rather than starting with a focus on specific alternatives, we begin by surveying a general situation that calls for a kind of remediation that the problem solver has not yet identified. In such cases, it is often difficult even to know where to begin.

The distinction between decision making and problem solving is not always clear. Still, we will consider problem solving to be a creative process, even in the organization of data. This organization gives us a way of approaching the issue.

Sometimes we solve problems intuitively or by haphazard approaches. Sometimes, however, a systematic approach to the problem is invaluable, and it need not be less creative for being systematic. Six steps will be presented in this guide to problem solving:

1. Statement	**4.** Incubation
2. Quick start	**5.** Dialectic
3. Analysis	**6.** Implementation

Each step is important:
Step 1 calls for a clear formulation of the problem.
Steps 2 and 3 include direct problem-solving techniques.
Steps 4 and 5 allow for review of the process.
The final plan is carried out in step 6.

Statement

People sometimes try to solve a problem without ever clarifying the nature of the problem. This can result in a confused search for solutions because the problem solver may inefficiently shift attention from one version or aspect of the problem to another without realizing that there has been any failure to stay on track. If more than one person is involved in the problem solving, the possibility of conceiving the problem differently or shifting focus is increased. Essentially, the problem is being *defined* at this point. Precision is important. Time and care taken at this point can minimize tangents and straw men later.

When there is more than one problem solver, a restatement technique is useful for achieving precision. After one person states the problem, another restates it, simply trying to put the first person's point into different words. The first person corrects any misunderstanding. Then they discuss which of the two versions is most appropriate. It may be that the *misstated* version — the second person's misunderstanding of the first person — is the better definition of the problem. The problem solvers restate the problem as often as necessary. However, if this step becomes tedious, it is advisable to go on to the second step, quick start, and to return later. Note that the completion of step 1 can occur incidentally during step 2.

In order to get a clear statement of the problem, a distinction between *means* and *ends* should be kept in mind. An end is a purpose or a desirable end-result. A means is a way to achieve that purpose or end-result. As far as possible the problem should be stated in terms of ends rather than means. Consider, for example, the predicament of the owner of a public parking lot in the business area of a city. Although his lot is generally full, he makes little profit. He decides that he needs to restripe his lot so that more cars can be parked in the same space. He sees his problem as a need to determine where to paint the stripes to create more spaces. Restriping the lot, however, is a means to his actual end. What he *really* needs is to make more money from his property. By focusing on a means rather than an end, he unnecessarily limits his perspective. Although he has probably already considered raising his rates, other income-increasing moves may elude him. By focusing on a restriping pattern, he will be less likely to consider (a) hiring parkers to park the cars for the customers (they can arrange the cars tightly on an unstriped lot), (b) putting up a several-story parking structure (financing this may require separate problem solving), (c) selling the property and investing the money differently, or (d) converting the property to a different use.

Quick Start

After the problem has been stated with precision, or when further effort at definition would be counterproductive, it is time to jump right in to the assessment and solution of the problem. Step 3 will dictate a methodical approach to this, but often it's worth letting enthusiasm and intuition run free to discover shortcuts. For the quick start, either brainstorming or categorical analysis can be used as a means to set forth (a) aspects of the problem that must be considered, and (b) solutions to the problem.

Brainstorming is a process designed for multiple problem solvers who are cooperating on one task. A moderator writes down on a list, preferably where all can see, each suggestion that a member of the problem-solving group mentions. The problem solvers offer any suggestions that come to mind, even though they may be unusual or not well thought out. There is no limit to the number of suggestions that one person, or the whole group, may generate. *No discussion of, or comment on, any suggestion is permitted while the list is being compiled.* After compilation, the moderator may help the group consolidate or eliminate items on the list. Any such action comes only after discussion and only by unanimous vote. The problem-solving group must be small—ideally two to ten members—and the list should be reduced to as few items as possible.

The group must understand which kind of suggestion is being sought: problem aspects to be considered or solutions to the problem. Clarification on the statement of the problem can also be the focus of the search, but this often occurs as a by-product of the other two kinds of brainstorming sessions. If only one person is attacking the problem, the basic brainstorming approach may still be useful, though much of the power of the approach comes from the cooperative effort of minds with different knacks and insights.

Categorical analysis, which professional problem solvers call morphological analysis, is another approach that can be used either to identify the problem's various aspects (this is its main strength) or to investigate solutions. It is a suitable approach for problem solving by individuals or by groups.

If we want to identify the various aspects of a problem, we simply list the most general aspects. Under each aspect we then list specific facets of that aspect. For example, a factory manager who is grappling with low morale might list working conditions, supervisory personnel, pay, and job security. Under working conditions she might list cleanliness, temperature, schedule, noise, and crowding.

If we want to identify solutions, we list the various kinds of solutions or causes for the problem. We then list specific possibilities within each category. For example, a student who is surprised to be getting low grades in a course might list course content, instructor, class setting, and study habits. Under study habits he might specifically list note taking, text reading, review, time spent, and distractions when studying.

Brainstorming and categorical analysis are quick starts in the sense that these "scouting" processes, while meant to prepare the problem solvers for step 3, sometimes actually accomplish much of the business of the analysis step by calling on intuitions and creating an overview of the entire problem situation.

Analysis

If the problem appears to have been solved during step 2, the problem solver can skip step 3 and go directly to 4. If not, it is time to consider the problem in the light of current and desired outcomes.

Compare Current and Desired Outcomes Keeping in mind the distinction (from step 1) between means and ends, the problem solver restates the desired outcome(s). The question here is this: What is the *desired* end-result in this activity or process that is seen as problematic? Then the problem solver states the outcome that is currently being produced. If several desired outcomes are identified, they are classified in order of importance.

Determine the Means to Get from Current Outcome to Desired Outcome   Clear thinking and creativity are indispensable. It may help to break the problem down into parts. For example, if the needs of many people are involved, the needs of each can first be considered separately, then need-conflicts can be recognized and a solution worked around these. At this stage, assumptions must be examined and the solution of previous similar problems must be explored.

Assess Alternatives   If more than one plan for getting from current to desired outcomes has been devised, these are assessed and compared for overall desirability. At this point the decision-making chart is useful, since some of the same factors are considered — at least consequences, probability, and desirability. Note that the far-right column on the chart can be used or ignored, depending on the problem. The preferred solution is then identified by considering both the achievement of desired outcomes (remember that they have been ranked) and unintended negative features such as difficulty or inconvenience.

Incubation

A period of incubation, in which the problem solver "sleeps on it," follows the hard work of analysis. During this period of rest, the problem solver sometimes reflects on the problem but does not work with great effort unless the urge is compelling. Incubation ends either when ideas begin to flow freely, unravelling parts of the problem, or when the problem solver's schedule has dictated that incubation should end. The period of incubation is normally kept to a week or less. Otherwise, points of the preceding analysis fade in memory. Unfortunately, the incubation step in problem solving is often left out because of the pressing requirements of time. Nevertheless, this is a valuable step that has often been a key to effective problem solving.

Dialectic

Presumably, a solution is at least tentatively decided on in step 3, analysis. If not, the incubation step should cycle back to analysis for another examination.

When a sense of the proper direction toward a solution has been determined, it's time to enter into dialectic with other people or to pass by this step and begin implementation. Dialectic is simply the process of reviewing a solution by exposing it to the informal analysis of people who have not taken part in its formulation. A brief account of the problem and the solution is presented to another person, who is then invited to anticipate flaws in the solution. Worthwhile suggestions are written down for further consideration. The problem solvers follow up any suggestions that undercut the entire selected solution by asking for the critic's own intuitions about the best course of action. Crucial to the success of the dialectic is the general character of the interaction. The atmosphere must be relaxed, with the critic feeling that any suggestion, however hard to accept, is welcome.

Taking time for dialectic can obviously be helpful for both individual problem solvers and groups. It is usually more important for the individual problem solver, however, because a person often needs someone else to identify those almost inevitable mental lapses or idiosyncratic perspectives. The problem-solving group has already had a form of dialectic in its earlier idea sharing.

Implementation

The final plan is implemented, or carried out, only with the serious commitment of everyone involved in implementation. Like programs within larger social systems, problem-solving plans are "only as good as the people involved." A plan has its best chance of being effective when it is implemented with intelligence and sensitivity. One person or group can mechanically "go through the motions" the plan prescribes and fail or succeed only marginally; another can make the same plan shine by retaining the determined spirit of a good problem solver. In the implementation of the plan, personal interactions are designed to maximize cooperation, and good timing is always observed. Finally, the person or persons who are implementing the plan keep an eye on changing circumstances and adjust the plan whenever a reassessment demands it.

When these six steps in problem solving are followed in actual application, points of logical vulnerability may become involved. Functional fixation, a resistance to conceive something apart from its usual function, may impede the process as well. Both of these hazards are well worth anticipating.

■

PRACTICE ACTIVITIES

Set 12.1 *Use the decision-making chart to consider a decision in the following cases.*

1. Choose a situation in your life that calls for a decision. Fill in the blanks on the chart. Consider your alternatives and their consequences.

2. Ask a friend or relative to let you use the chart to help her or him think through a problem that requires a decision. With that person's help, fill in the blanks on the chart, and then give that person the chart.

3. Revise the chart itself in light of difficulties you have had in using it. Make copies of your revised chart for personal use. Share the revision with others who are using this book.

Set 12.2 *Use the decision-making chart to consider a decision in the following cases. Add details to the example to fill out the chart.*

1. Maria takes a bus to school each day. The fare is fifty cents. She gets a ride home for free with her neighbor, who leaves for school too late for her in the morning, but waits an extra hour at school each day to drive her home. Lately, the neighbor has been making casual comments about the inconvenience of staying the extra hour. Maria can't easily afford the dollar it would cost for a round trip each day. Her brother has offered to give her his old car, but she hates to take it because she knows that he needs the money he would get if he sold it instead of giving it to her. She is also aware that, despite the good mechanical condition of the car, maintenance and repair costs, together with fuel costs, might exceed the bus fare. If she gets a job to make more money, her studies will suffer. She wants help in deciding what to do.

2. The beautiful twenty-acre site just north of the shopping mall had been identified as the location for a city park. The city has no parks in the area now, and children between ages five and seventeen play on the roads and sidewalks. The park development plans may be abandoned because of the cost of constructing and maintaining the park. If the city were to develop the park, its support of the library and the annual parade might be cut drastically. There's a fifty-fifty chance that insufficient funds would remain for building a new elementary school in another part of town where the current school is overcrowded. Now a housing developer has offered to buy the land from the city at a handsome price that would virtually ensure that the needed school would be built and that additional funds would be left over. You are on the city council. Your votes on the park proposal and the housing proposal are important.

3. Study the newspaper and newsmagazine coverage of a topic of national interest that calls for a legislative or executive decision. Follow the television newscasts and discuss the issue with acquaintances. Then make an expanded chart and plot out the consequences of the most promising alternatives.

Set 12.3 *Complete the following problem-solving tasks.*

1. As a lone problem solver, consider a personal problem of your own through application of the six steps in problem solving: statement, quick start, analysis, incubation, dialectic, and, if appropriate, implementation.

2. As a lone problem solver, consider a personal problem of someone you know well, using the first four steps in problem solving: statement, quick start, analysis, and incubation. If you feel that it is appropriate, discuss your thoughts with that person.

3. If you know another person, or other persons, who know these six steps or who would be pleased to try them after reading this section of the book, choose a topic and solve a problem with that person. Problems of home, work, or school are possibilities for discussion.

4. Study (alone or with others) the news coverage of a topic of social or political importance. Use library research skills to find additional information. Identify a problematic aspect of that topic and apply the first five steps in problem solving: statement, quick start, analysis, incubation, and dialectic. You may choose to contribute to the likelihood of implementation through a letter to a legislator or by another means, depending on the problem and the nature of your solution.

For Further Reading

Rubinstein, Moshe F. *Concepts in Problem Solving.* Englewood Cliffs, NJ: Prentice-Hall, 1980.

An innovative approach to explaining problem solving and decision making. The context for each explanation is the book-long conversation between young Alex and his uncle, Professor Gordian.

Sanderson, Michael. *Successful Problem Management.* New York: John Wiley & Sons, 1979.

A good introduction to problem solving.

Answer Key
FOR PRACTICE
ACTIVITIES

Some of the Practice Activities in *Open Minds and Everyday Reasoning* cannot be answered in this section because they require creative activity that may issue in a variety of correct responses. Even so, some of those activities are illustrated here through examples of correct responses. Only the first several items in each set are keyed here. They are intended for use by students who are eager to see if they are on the right track with their responses.

Practice Activities

Set 2.1

The following are examples of how each item might be rewritten. Certainly they are not the only correct responses. Your wording may be different.

4.a. I am concerned with the fact that smokers pay exorbitant cigarette taxes and yet we face increasing limitations on where we may smoke. Since we possess high technology that allows us to send shuttles into space, it must be possible to create ventilation systems for buildings and airplanes so that neither smokers nor nonsmokers will be penalized.

  b. When excise taxes are earmarked, the revenue raised by the tax is used to support a particular program or public project. Earmarking (of tobacco products) is just another method used to make excise tax increases more palatable. Anti-smokers claim that the earmarked excise tax is really charitable—a few pennies donated by everyone. Only it's not from everyone and it's not donated. Smokers alone are the ones who must pay.

  c. Publicly owned and operated transit has not been successful. Billions of taxpayer dollars have been spent with little or nothing to show for it.

Set 2.2

These creative tasks can issue in a variety of correct responses.

1. Relevant kinds of evidence:

  The career success of graduates of Harvard and other schools that might deserve the distinction.

  The success of changing occupations for graduates of Harvard and other schools.

The breadth of course offerings for Harvard and other schools.

The kinds of assignments that are made in courses.

The other teaching methods that are used regularly.

The performance of graduates of Harvard and other schools on appropriate standardized tests.

The list could be extended. To determine what evidence is available within each of these categories, research is almost certainly required.

2. Relevant kinds of evidence:

Repair records for Chrysler models.

Crash test results.

Owner satisfaction ratings.

Return buyers: How many previous Chrysler owners have purchased another Chrysler?

Comparison of Chrysler models with other American-built cars.

To understand "best" in America relative to the world market, compare with foreign makes.

There are several consumer publications available that provide the information you seek.

3. Relevant kinds of evidence:

Historical evidence that reveals the kinds of actions taken by both Republican and Democratic presidents during a variety of international crises.

Foreign policy espoused by both Republican and Democratic leaders.

Set 2.3

1. People who are inclined to agree with this view might feel *prideful* of their own capitalistic system and *angry* at the dictatorships we often associate with communism. People who are inclined to disagree with this view might feel *resentful* of a capitalistic system that they think rewards a shallow cleverness and manipulation of others for personal gain in an amoral (or immoral) competitive struggle.

Various specific arguments may be produced in support of each side after you attempt to feel these emotions. You may have named different emotions and the evidence that this enables you to produce will vary from person to person.

Set 3.1

The following are examples of how each statement might be rewritten.

1. The wedding was especially touching because of the personal messages that the bride and groom delivered and because of the personal warmth of the minister.

It was a memorable wedding because the bride and groom are both in their eighties but seemed like two young kids as they stood holding hands and beaming at each other in front of the minister.

2. He's a dramatic storyteller, pausing at just the right points and using facial expressions to accentuate the suspense.

He's an engaging storyteller, capable of bringing characters in a story to life by changing voices and cavorting about, much to the delight of children and adults alike.

3. She's mentally alert but she's physically weak because of the lack of exercise.

   She has a form of anemia which affects the bone marrow and leaves her susceptible to infection and bruising; she also suffers from frequent nosebleeds.

4. This newspaper is consistently biased on many social and political issues.

   This newspaper is notorious for its lack of timeliness and the inaccuracy of its news reports once they actually get reported.

5. I liked the bartender's composure and his articulate response after that customer threw her drink in his face.

   I laughed when the bartender, after a customer threw her drink in his face, poured himself a drink, took a sip, and then poured the rest into her purse.

Set 3.3

2.a. Generalization. This claim is clearly intended to apply to many, but not all, scholars.

  b. In reference to "products of a committee," this is a universal statement. *All* such products, it was claimed, are shoddy in these ways.

   There is a generalization in the same statement. Not all sections of every such document are said to be "banal, bland, and leadenly written." The documents are "for the most part" like this. The author is generalizing about the content of all products of a committee.

  c. Generalization. This is how Japan's economy looks to "many investors," but not necessarily to all investors.

  d. Although this statement could be understood as either a universal statement or a generalization, it is only defensible as a generalization.

Set 3.4

1.a. Broad. The definition includes bullies, some of whom are children, and many common, nonpolitical criminals.

  b. Narrow. The definition excludes television journalists and people who write articles for newspapers.

  c. Broad. The definition includes many other emotions, including jealousy.

  d. Narrow. The definition excludes officials who have no White House assignment.

  e. Broad. The definition includes members of the U.S. House of Representatives.

Set 4.1

1. Setting up a straw man.

   Senator Bonds is putting words in the mouths of those who are proposing the new tax. A reasonable assumption is that beer tax proponents are not claiming that beer drinkers are somehow more responsible for the deficit and therefore should pay more tax. The senator, in a facetious manner, is misrepresenting the position of the other side.

2. Shifting ground.

   Rubens insists he claimed only that in "big-time national politics" corruption had touched every politician. Of course, this is not what he actually said. If this is what he originally meant, then he expressed his view incorrectly. If he is now changing his mind, he should acknowledge this.

3. Pursuing a tangent.

   The team manager gets off track by pursuing a "stars of the past" tangent instead of discussing David's batting stance. Their time is limited, and the digression may cost them a hit.

4. Setting up a straw man.

   Lisa has misrepresented Steve's claim. He did not say that "the Greeks were the smartest people in history." His actual claim that they had "made great strides in scientific thinking" does not commit him to the position that Lisa is criticizing.

Set 4.2

1.a. Non-argument. These are simply informative statements.

   b. Argument. The passage contains a conclusion (*Our world is a fragile one.*) and reasons for the conclusion.

   c. Non-argument. There is no conclusion for which evidence is presented.

   d. Argument. The conclusion is "Words are not the real thing, the item in life itself."

   e. Argument. Two premises and a conclusion are contained in this single sentence. The conclusion that any stone is worthy of worship is supported by the claims that all stones are divine and that everything divine is worthy of worship.

   f. Non-argument. Notice that there is no attempt to persuade you that he moved to Detroit. Rather, a reason is given to *explain* his motivation for moving there.

2.b. Unstated: *Iraq invaded Kuwait* and *an invasion involves subjugation of a government and its citizens* and *a subjugated citizenry endures hardship and atrocity at the hands of a malevolent conqueror* and *Saddam Hussein, the leader of Iraq, is a malevolent conqueror.* Also, *several countries have sent troops into Saudi Arabia in preparation for conflict with the Iraqi military* and *those troops who are in Saudi Arabia are separated from home and family and are enduring less than ideal conditions* and *the families and friends of those troops are concerned and upset.*

   These unstated premises, along with the stated premises, support the claim that one man has made life truly miserable for tens of thousands of people.

   People invest money in the stock market with the hope that stocks will go up so that they will make money and *when stocks go down, billions of dollars can be lost by investors* and *stocks have gone down during the past four trading sessions.*

   These unstated premises support the claim that billions of dollars have been lost in the stock market in the past four trading sessions, which in turn supports the ultimate conclusion that one man has made life truly miserable for tens of thousands of people.

   d. Unstated: *Abstractions are not the real thing.*

   e. Unstated: Nothing.

Set 4.3

1. That house is too expensive for you.
2. No one can predict political events with consistent reliability.
3. The Toronto Blue Jays are likely to win the division again.
4. There's no way I could pass that math course (even if I did register for it).

5. I will have to move out.

6. There are at least some intelligent people who aren't dishonest.

7. Mr. Allison must be in charge today.

Set 5.1

1.

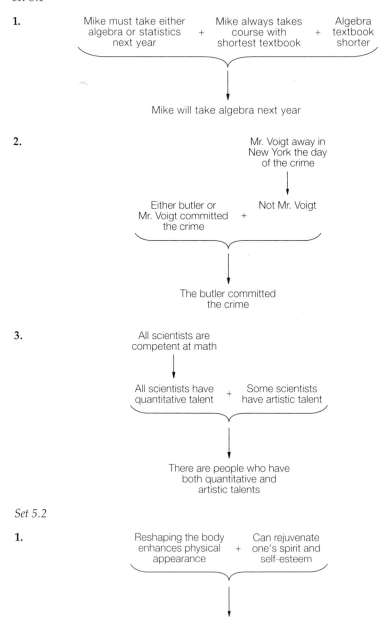

Mike must take either algebra or statistics next year + Mike always takes course with shortest textbook + Algebra textbook shorter

Mike will take algebra next year

2.

Mr. Voigt away in New York the day of the crime

Not Mr. Voigt

Either butler or Mr. Voigt committed the crime + Not Mr. Voigt

The butler committed the crime

3.

All scientists are competent at math

All scientists have quantitative talent + Some scientists have artistic talent

There are people who have both quantitative and artistic talents

Set 5.2

1.

Reshaping the body enhances physical appearance + Can rejuvenate one's spirit and self-esteem

Performed by a qualified surgeon, cosmetic surgery can work wonders

2.

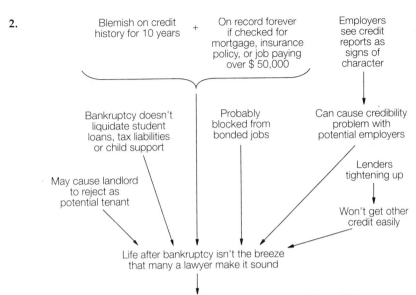

Blemish on credit history for 10 years + On record forever if checked for mortgage, insurance policy, or job paying over $ 50,000   Employers see credit reports as signs of character

Bankruptcy doesn't liquidate student loans, tax liabilities or child support   Probably blocked from bonded jobs   Can cause credibility problem with potential employers

May cause landlord to reject as potential tenant

Lenders tightening up

Won't get other credit easily

Life after bankruptcy isn't the breeze that many a lawyer make it sound

Bankruptcy is a rotten choice for anyone who can possibly avoid it

Set 6.1

1. Invalid. The evidence does not establish that *all* Italians are intelligent.

   Unsound. If it is invalid, it fails the first test for soundness.

   Inductively weak. Although the evidence is relevant, it is not enough to support the conclusion strongly.

2. Invalid. Although it is likely that Harcourt committed the murder, he might not have. In television dramas we are often shown that the strongest of circumstantial evidence might point in the wrong direction.

   Unsound. If it is invalid, it must be unsound.

   Inductively moderate. There is enough relevant evidence to establish a probability that the conclusion is true if the premises are true.

3. Invalid. To establish the conclusion with certainty, the word *most* would have to be *all*.

   Unsound. Again, soundness presupposes validity.

   Inductively moderate. The evidence establishes probability that such courses would be offered.

4. Valid. If the premises were true, the conclusion would have to be true.

   Unsound. The first premise is false. Don't you agree?

Set 6.2

1. R: Yes; E: No.

   The evidence is relevant because an intelligent and principled editor would contribute to the journalistic quality of a newspaper. However, this evidence is not enough to support the conclusion. One good editor does not a top-notch newspaper make.

2. R: Yes; E: Yes.

There is certainly enough relevant evidence here to establish a likelihood that the conclusion is true (if the premises are true). A college president with a doctorate and teaching experience at more than one university would very probably have a good grasp of the issues in higher education.

Set 7.1

1. Attacking the person.

Instead of attacking the reasoning of those who are against the death penalty, the author attacks those groups or individuals themselves by implying that they would not be willing to support their position financially. In other words, the position of being against the death penalty is rejected because anti-death penalty proponents would not be willing to "put their money where their mouths are." This is irrelevant to the issue at hand.

2. False dilemma.

This statement implies that the two extremes are the only available alternatives. Other possible alternatives that are worthy of consideration are omitted. The only choices given are either a war in which Americans must die (thereby requiring a memorial wall) or a complete withdrawal of aid.

3. Two wrongs make a right.

#1 The premise used to support the claim that Pete Rose does not deserve to go to jail for tax evasion is that some corporations have done the same, thereby making it morally permissible for Pete to have done it.

#2 Again, the implication is that Pete Rose is being punished for doing something that others have done and therefore does not deserve his punishment.

4. Questionable cause.

In this example, a cause (fear of failure) has been attributed to student motivation without regard for the possibility that other factors may account for such motivation. What about desire to learn? Obviously, fear of failure as a "cause" for student motivation is "questionable."

5. Questionable cause.

What is questionable is the cause of death purported by Panamanians. Without sufficient evidence, and in the face of an alternative conclusion in the form of a suicide ruling, some have concluded that Noriega's wife pushed his mistress out the window. The fact that she was the last to see the victim alone is insufficient evidence for the claim.

Set 7.2

1. Look-alike for fallacy of argument from ignorance.

The claim is **not** made that passive smoking does not cause heart disease due to lack of proof that it does. In other words, the position that passive smoking causes heart disease has not been rejected. Rather, it has been concluded that there has been no proven link between the two, not that there is no link.

2. Look-alike for fallacy of division.

In this example, the following claim is made: The white man (collectively) is the devil. The qualifying statement that this is true "without any exception" implies that this is a claim that also applies to each and every white man. Therefore, two claims are being made. Neither claim is used to support the other. In other words, it is not being claimed that because A is a white man and is the devil that all white men are also the devil. Nor is it claimed that because the "collective" white man is the devil, then A must also be the devil because he is white. In fact, no evidence at all is offered to support either contentious claim.

3. Look-alike for fallacy of argument from ignorance.

The columnist is skeptical of the suggestion that Justice Bird has exhibited prejudice in interpreting the Constitution. He does not claim that his own view is true and that lack of proof establishes it as true. This is what it would take to commit the fallacy. He would have to write, "That is not true because it has not been proven to me."

4. Look-alike for contrary-to-fact hypothesis.

If, indeed, Arlene had gone into financial planning, she would not be in a profession in which she would be subject to charges of medical malpractice.

5. Look-alike for fallacy of attacking the person.

The claim that, with his teaching, Augustine "weighed down Christianity with his pessimism" might simply be regarded as a relevant claim — true or false — about the history of Christian doctrine. Even if Guitton's charge is taken to be unnecessarily sharp in tone, it's hard to argue that there are separable statements, one of which is a factual claim offered as a conclusion and the other of which is an irrelevant personal attack offered as a premise.

Set 7.3

1. Questionable cause.

The Thai village men commit the fallacy of questionable cause by attributing the unexplained deaths to the actions of a ghost. Other possible causes cited by health experts are apparently not given much, if any, consideration. The villagers have taken action against what they believe to be the cause of their troubles in the form of a large phallic symbol.

2. Argument from ignorance.

A conclusion that Tower's confirmation would not be a detriment is reached on the grounds that no evidence to the contrary has been offered.

3. Attacking the person.

The daughter rejects her mother's advice with only a reference to the mother's now unfashionable girls'-school background. Instead, she could have expressed relevant concerns about the advice itself.

4. Look-alike for fallacy of argument from ignorance.

The simple claim that "no link to the shuttle explosion had been established" does not imply that the debris and the explosion are unconnected. It allows for the possibility that a link may yet be established or that, even if no link is found, there is nonetheless a connection.

5. Begging the question.

"He meant to," "he intended to," and "it was his purpose" are synonymous expressions. Since they are interchangeable in this context, each premise has simply restated the conclusion.

Set 8.1

1. The point of the analogy is that just as a husband may be wrong for ignoring the needs of his own family, so also a woman would be wrong in serving others so much that she neglects to develop her personal potential. In both cases, one's duty to one's own (family or self) is sacrificed unjustifiably.

   How good is the analogy? This depends in part on whether the woman's duty to develop her *personal* potential is as strong as the husband's duty to the *others* in his family. Some people will still argue that duties to others are nobler than duties to self, at least up to a certain point. (Has the woman in the example reached that point?) At the least, the analogy suggests that often service to one's own self is a high priority duty, and that women should not give to the exclusion of getting.

2. People can become so fearful of excessive penalties that they completely avoid the situations that make even remotely possible the imposition of these penalties on them. If parking violators were executed, people would think twice before using — or even owning — cars. Similarly, if the judgment that you or your business had violated the rights of a woman or minority could lead to unreasonably severe penalties, you might try to eradicate all differing treatments of men and women — or minorities and others — even when those differing treatments were not so obviously unfair. (Example: requiring men to wear ties but not women.)

   Is the analogy with the parking violation a good one? It may be true that severe penalties for civil rights violations would lead to some overreaction. The parking violation example illustrates the psychology of this kind of reaction. However, if the implied conclusion is that we should not impose severe penalties for civil rights violations, the argument is weakened.

   Justice hardly demands the death penalty for parking violations. Social justice may demand severe penalties for civil rights violations even if one consequence is that some people overreact.

3. This analogy is more seriously flawed than the previous two. The author of this analogy suggests that parents of children who are involved in many out-of-home activities are like orchestra conductors who are directing an orchestra of musicians who, besides having never met each other, are playing different music, all of which is written out using different systems of notation.

   It's true that coordination between the activities and their directors is sometimes helpful. It's also true that many specialty areas use different concepts and technical terms. However, the suggestion of the orchestra comparison is that the disharmony is so great that the entire effort is futile and foolish. This greatly overstates the parent's problem.

   Very often, no coordination between the directors of these activities is necessary. Besides, the parents can understand most of the specialists' conversation, since they share a common natural language (e.g., English) and the specialist can reword technical issues for the public. Finally, children are not so likely to be thoroughly ruined by such a lack of coordination between soccer coaches and piano teachers as a concert would be ruined by players who perform different pieces of music at the same time, and all in a notation inscrutable to the conductor. The analogy is a poor one.

4. This analogy does not work. Even if we agree "for the sake of argument" that the relationship of the Army to a soldier is like that of a parent to a child, the right to

health care beyond the term of service would be analogous only if parents were normally considered to be responsible for the health care of their nondependent adult offspring. This is not the case.

5. This is a poor analogy. It's true that competitive games, unless played "just for fun," require a performance comparison—a score. The object of such games is to outscore an opponent. Education need not be measured in terms of outdoing others. The nineteenth-century rural school, which had no means of comparison with other schools, still had a reason for being. If the students learned to read, write, and think, they were successful. Similarly, I can learn a foreign language without measurement of my skills against those of another learner.

Set 8.2

1. Valid. Universal-to-particular syllogism.
2. Invalid. Counterfeit of universal-to-particular syllogism.
3. Invalid. Counterfeit of universal-to-particular syllogism.
4. Invalid. Affirming the consequent.
5. Valid. *Modus tollens* (because it denies the consequent).

Set 8.3

1. First conditional argument:

Whenever (if) Dad takes the medicine, he will feel dizzy.

Dad feels dizzy.

∴ He took the medicine.

Invalid. Affirming the consequent.

Second conditional argument:

If he took the medicine this morning, then he won't be alert enough to go to the game.

He took the medicine. (This is the conclusion from the previous argument.)

∴ He won't be alert enough to go to the game.

Valid. (*Modus ponens* because it affirms the antecedent.) There is another *modus ponens* at the end of Chris's last comment. The conditional premise is unstated in this incidental argument.

Set 8.4

1. Some R are PC.

Some R are ALAP (advocates of liberal abortion policies).

∴ Some PC are ALAP.

One possible logical analogy is this:

Some dogs are German shepherds.

Some dogs are Chihuahuas.

∴ Some German shepherds are Chihuahuas.

2. All S are CEP.

Some CEP are PAT (people with artistic talents).

∴ Some S are PAT.

As always, there are many possible logical analogies for the invalid argument. Here is one:

All scientists are college-educated people.

Some college-educated people are nonscientists.

∴ Some scientists are nonscientists.

3. Some T are S.

Some S are H.

∴ Some T are H.

A logical analogy for this invalid argument might be:

Some Catholic priests are tall people.

Some tall people are atheists.

∴ Some Catholic priests are atheists.

Set 9.1

1.

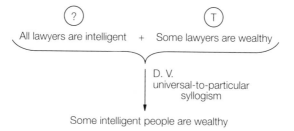

2.

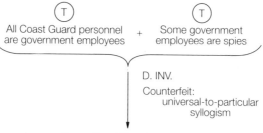

3.

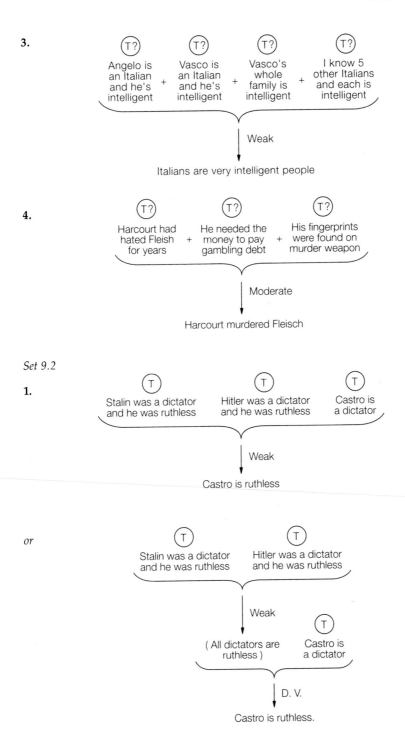

T? Angelo is an Italian and he's intelligent + T? Vasco is an Italian and he's intelligent + T? Vasco's whole family is intelligent + T? I know 5 other Italians and each is intelligent

Weak

Italians are very intelligent people

4.

T? Harcourt had hated Fleish for years + T? He needed the money to pay gambling debt + T? His fingerprints were found on murder weapon

Moderate

Harcourt murdered Fleisch

Set 9.2

1.

T Stalin was a dictator and he was ruthless   T Hitler was a dictator and he was ruthless   T Castro is a dictator

Weak

Castro is ruthless

or

T Stalin was a dictator and he was ruthless   T Hitler was a dictator and he was ruthless

Weak

(All dictators are ruthless)   T Castro is a dictator

D. V.

Castro is ruthless.

Note: You can also map as separate premises:
Stalin / Hitler was a dictator and *He was ruthless.*

Set 9.3

1.

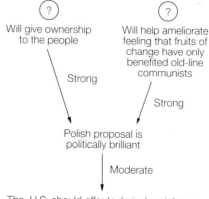

Set 11.3

1. Twenty thousand questionnaires may have been sent out, but how many were returned and who was most likely to return them? We might wonder about both the size and the representative character of the sample. Furthermore, the sample is assuredly unrepresentative on other grounds. Although the questionnaire was sent to people of many different denominations, it sounds as if none were sent to non-churchmembers.

2. We might wonder about the kinds of persons who would be likely to take the trouble to return the questionnaire. Even more important is the fact that the questionnaire was printed in a magazine with a predominantly male readership. The statistics were projected to "the American people." The sample will be unrepresentative. (The males who read the magazine may even tend to be in certain socio-economic groups.)

3. The statistic could not be determined. Mental stress is not easily measurable. If measurable, the degree of precision implied by the 43 percent figure is not possible. Moreover, the concept "in good shape" would have to be more specific and precise to conduct any study of this sort.

Set 11.4

1. What other factors might account for the fact that almost half the teenagers did not look at the warning? Other explanations are possible other than that which was concluded.

2. If the Royal cola is local, this study could not be projected to a much larger population. The taste may not be what is measured here.

Bibliography

Adler, Mortimer J. *How to Speak, How to Listen.* New York: Macmillan, 1983.

Barash, David P. *The Arms Race and Nuclear War.* Belmont, CA: Wadsworth, 1987.

Barry, Vincent E. *Invitation to Critical Thinking.* New York: Holt, Rinehart and Winston, 1984.

Beardsley, Monroe C. *Thinking Straight.* Englewood Cliffs, NJ: Prentice-Hall, 1975.

Belamy, Edward, *Looking Backward.* Putney, VT: Hendricks House, 1946.

Bramson, Robert M. *Coping with Difficult People.* New York: Dell, 1988.

Cederblom, Jerry, and David W. Paulson. *Critical Reasoning.* Belmont, CA: Wadsworth, 1986.

Copi, Irving M. *Introduction to Logic.* New York: Macmillan, 1986.

Creighton, James L. *Don't Go Away Mad: How to Make Peace with Your Partner.* New York: Doubleday, 1990.

Damer, T. Edward. *Attacking Faulty Reasoning.* Belmont, CA: Wadsworth, 1987.

Engel, S. Morris. *With Good Reason: An Introduction to Informal Fallacies.* New York: St. Martin's Press, 1986.

Evans, Jonathan St. B. T. *Thinking and Reasoning: Psychological Approaches.* London: Routledge & Kegan Paul, 1983.

Fogelin, Robert J. *Understanding Arguments.* San Diego: Harcourt Brace Jovanovich, 1987.

Govier, Trudy. *A Practical Study of Argument.* Belmont, CA: Wadsworth, 1988.

Hamblin, C. L. *Fallacies.* Suffolk, England: Methuen & Co., 1970.

Huck, Schuyler W., and Howard M. Sandler. *Rival Hypotheses: Alternative Interpretations of Data Based Conclusions.* New York: Harper & Row, 1979.

Huff, Darrell. *How to Lie with Statistics.* New York: W. W. Norton & Co., 1954.

Hurley, Patrick J. *A Concise Introduction to Logic.* Belmont, CA: Wadsworth, 1991.

Johnson, R. H., and J. A. Blair. *Logical Self-Defense.* Toronto: McGraw-Hill Ryerson Limited, 1983.

Kahane, Howard. *Logic and Contemporary Rhetoric: The Use of Reason in Everyday Life.* Belmont, CA: Wadsworth, 1992.

Katz, William. *Your Library: A Reference Guide.* New York: Holt, Rinehart and Winston, 1984.

Katzer, Jeffrey, Kenneth H. Cook, and Wayne W. Crouch. *Evaluating Information: A Guide for Users of Social Science Research.* Reading, MA: Addison-Wesley, 1982.

Kaufman, Roger. *Identifying and Solving Problems.* San Diego: University Associates, 1976.

Kepner, Charles H., and Benjamin B. Tregoe. *The Rational Manager.* Princeton: Kepner-Tregoe, 1976.

Key, V. O., Jr. *A Primer of Statistics for Political Scientists.* New York: Thomas Y. Crowell, 1966.

Kimble, Gregory R. *How to Use (and Misuse) Statistics.* Englewood Cliffs, NJ: Prentice-Hall, 1978.

Mayfield, Marlys. *Thinking for Yourself: Developing Critical Thinking Skills Through Writing.* Belmont, CA: Wadsworth, 1991.

McBurney, Donald H. *Experimental Psychology.* Belmont, CA: Wadsworth, 1983.

McCain, Garwin, and Erwin M. Segal. *The Game of Science.* Monterey, CA: Brooks/Cole, 1977.

Moore, Brooke Noel, and Richard Parker. *Critical Thinking: Evaluating Claims and Arguments in Everyday Life.* Palo Alto, CA: Mayfield, 1992.

Moore, David S. *Statistics: Concepts and Controversies.* New York: W. H. Freeman and Co., 1985.

Moore, W. Edgar, Hugh McCann, and Janet McCann. *Creative and Critical Thinking.* Boston: Houghton Mifflin, 1984.

Murphy, Kevin J. *Effective Listening: Your Key to Career Success.* New York: Bantam Books, 1987.

Quine, W. V., and J. S. Ullian. *The Web of Belief.* New York: Random House, 1978.

Radner, Daisie, and Michael Radner. *Science and Unreason.* Belmont, CA: Wadsworth, 1982.

Ray, William, and Richard Ravizza. *Methods Toward a Science of Behavior and Experiment.* Belmont, CA: Wadsworth, 1985.

Richards, Tudor. *Problem Solving Through Creative Analysis.* New York: John Wiley & Sons, 1974.

Robertshaw, Joseph E., Stephen J. Mecca, and Mark N. Rerick. *Problem Solving: A Systems Approach.* New York: Petrocelli Books, 1978.

Rubinstein, Moshe F., and Kenneth Pfeiffer. *Concepts in Problem Solving.* Englewood Cliffs, NJ: Prentice-Hall, 1980.

St. Aubyn, Giles. *The Art of Argument.* Buchanan, NY: Emerson Books, 1962.

Sanderson, Michael. *Successful Problem Management.* New York: John Wiley & Sons, 1979.

Skyrms, Brian. *Choice and Chance: An Introduction to Inductive Logic.* Belmont, CA: Wadsworth, 1986.

Tannen, Deborah. *That's Not What I Meant!: How Conversational Style Makes or Breaks Relationships.* New York: Ballantine Books, 1986.

Tanur, Judith M., et al. *Statistics: A Guide to Political and Social Issues.* San Francisco: Holden-Day, 1977.

Thomas, Stephen Naylor. *Practical Reasoning in Natural Language.* Englewood Cliffs, NJ: Prentice-Hall, 1986.

Toulmin, Steven Edelston. *The Use of Argument.* London: Cambridge University Press, 1958.

Toulmin, Steven, Richard Rieke, and Allan Janik. *An Introduction to Reasoning.* New York: Macmillan, 1984.

Vernoy, Mark and Judith Vernoy. *Behavioral Statistics in Action.* Belmont, CA: Wadsworth, 1992.

Wallis, W. Allen, and Harry V. Roberts, *The Nature of Statistics.* New York: Collier Books, 1962.

Whimbey, Arthur, and Jack Lochhead. *Problem Solving and Comprehension: A Short Course in Analytical Reasoning.* Philadelphia: The Franklin Institute Press, 1980.

Williams, Frederick. *Reasoning with Statistics.* New York: Holt, Rinehart and Winston, 1979.

Zeisel, Hans. *Say It with Figures.* New York: Harper & Row, 1968.

Index